W9-BUD-415

EMERSON COLLEGE LIBRARY

The Native Peoples
of North America

The Native Peoples of North America

A HISTORY   VOLUME I

Bruce E. Johansen

NATIVE AMERICA: YESTERDAY AND TODAY
Bruce E. Johansen, Series Editor

PRAEGER

Westport, Connecticut
London

E
76.6
.J65
2005
v. 1

Library of Congress Cataloging-in-Publication Data

Johansen, Bruce E. (Bruce Elliott), 1950–
    The native peoples of North America : a history / Bruce E. Johansen.
        p. cm.—(Native America: Yesterday and Today, ISSN 1552-8022)
    Includes bibliographical references and index.
    ISBN 0-275-98159-2 (set : alk. paper)—ISBN 0-275-98720-5 (vol. 1 : alk.
paper)—ISBN 0-275-98721-3 (vol. 2 : alk. paper) 1. Indians of North
America—Study and teaching. 2. Indians of North America—History. 3. Indians
of North America—Social life and customs. I. Title. II. Native America
(Praeger Publishers)

    E76.6.J65 2005
    970.004'97—dc22   2004028732

British Library Cataloguing in Publication Data is available.

Copyright © 2005 by Bruce E. Johansen

All rights reserved. No portion of this book may be
reproduced, by any process or technique, without the
express written consent of the publisher.

Library of Congress Catalog Card Number: 2004028732
ISBN: 0-275-98159-2 (set)
        0-275-98720-5 (vol. I)
        0-275-98721-3 (vol. II)
ISSN: 1552-8022

First published in 2005

Praeger Publishers, 88 Post Road West, Westport, CT 06881
An imprint of Greenwood Publishing Group, Inc.
www.praeger.com

Printed in the United States of America

The paper used in this book complies with the
Permanent Paper Standard issued by the National
Information Standards Organization (Z39.48-1984).

10 9 8 7 6 5 4 3 2 1

Every reasonable effort has been made to trace the owners of copyrighted
materials in this book, but in some instances this has proven impossible. The
author and publisher will be glad to receive information leading to more
complete acknowledgments in subsequent printings of the book and in the
meantime extend their apologies for any omissions.

Contents

Preface

This book is a revival of a rather old tradition—an attempt to survey Native American history in North America. This tradition has been represented admirably in the past by, among others, Brandon (1961), Collier (1947), McNickle (1949), Driver (1969), and Maxwell (1978). The idea of a single historical treatment is being revived by other authors as well, including Robert W. Venables's *American Indian History: Five Centuries of Conflict and Coexistence* (2003) and Steve Talbot's *Contemporary Indian Nations of North America: An Indigenist Perspective* (Talbot, 2004).

A need for such a work exists for the many students at university level who take introductory classes in Native American studies. My own institution, a state university of middling size in the Midwest, offers six to eight sections of this class each semester, with thirty-five to fifty students in each section. The field is interdisciplinary, so content depends on the academic origins of instructors: One may hail from religion, but others are from history, literature, sociology, law, and other fields. Given the lack of general texts, students often are told to read a broad survey of books, such as those by Oswalt (2002), Wilson (1998), Stannard (1992), Garbarino and Sasso (1994), Kehoe (1992), Nabokov (1991), and Wright (1992).

My scope is historical, mainly across the continental United States, with occasional forays into Mexico and Mesoamerica. The cultures are so fascinating that I feel no book of this type could be complete without a description of them. I also occasionally take up subject matter in Canada, mainly concerning contemporary affairs, such as the plight of Pikangikum, one of the most desolate native settlements in North America, as well as Canadian Native peoples' efforts to win compensation for abuses suffered in residential schools.

My wife, Pat Keiffer, asked me once if this book would be "complete." No, I answered, not in the sense that it will encompass all that is known about

Native American history. Such a publication would be too heavy to lift. As with any survey of a much larger body of knowledge, this book is selective and is reflective of work I have done and people with whom I have worked during the past 30 years.

Each attempt to survey this body of knowledge has been different in time and temper. I have sought to bring my account up to date, again being selective. Readers will find an emphasis, for example, on new developments in archeology, which is a surprisingly fluid and lively field. For example, new information has emerged regarding the antiquity of the Olmecs' (and, later, Maya's and Aztecs') writing systems. New information on the Incas' writing system and that of the Iroquois is included as well.

New evidence also is offered here that drought as well as intensifying warfare played important roles in the demise of high civilization among the Maya. New information also has been described in primary literature regarding the antiquity of human occupancy in the Americas going back 30,000 years or more, mainly in present-day Chile and at other sites in South America. The new finds generally impeach assumptions that all Native Americans migrated to the Americas over the Bering Strait, or that Clovis-style cultures were the earliest peoples in the Americas. New archeological findings (notably regarding the nearly complete skeleton of 9,300-year-old Kennewick Man) bring into question simplistic assumptions about how human beings came to the Americas. Recent studies also have produced new information regarding the founding date of the Haudenosaunee (Iroquois) confederacy that places this important event at about 1100 C.E., three to four centuries earlier than most academics previously had supposed.

I describe current controversies in Indian country, among them sports mascots, language revival, gambling, repatriation, land claims, and environmental issues, such as the effects of uranium mining on the Navajos. Many contemporary political issues have evolved from earlier events, such as the campaign to revoke Congressional Medals of Honor awarded at Wounded Knee after the massacre there late in 1890. This book also provides in-depth surveys of Native American contributions to general society: political ideas, medicines, foods, women's rights, and so on. This area has been one of my specialties for more than thirty years.

This work also offers analysis of U.S. Census data for 2000, which indicate that Native Americans, once regarded as the "vanishing race," are now the fastest-growing ethnic group in the United States. Some of this is actual increase, and some is the fact that the census now allows people to list more than one ethnic background. Because the census is self-defining, part of the increase may also be "wannabes."

The fact that hundreds of thousands of non-Indians would like to be listed as such at the dawn of the third millennium might have astonished just about anyone living a century earlier. They also might have been astonished to know that many college students today take courses in Native American history—hardly a vanishing race, hardly a vanishing culture, and by no means a vanishing history. Join us on a journey that is wondrous but by no means without profound pain.

In compiling these volumes, I should acknowledge my colleague Barbara Alice Mann for extracts from her work on the Goschochking (Ohio) genocide of 1782 and the Haudenosaunee origin story. I also acknowledge Donald A. Grinde Jr.; a few sections of what follows are adapted from our *Encyclopedia of Native American Biography* as well as from parts of a prospective textbook manuscript that we developed during the early 1990s but never published, notably parts that he contributed on John Collier's tenure as Indian commissioner, as well as some materials on repatriation. In addition, I need again to thank all the people who keep me going, including wife Pat Keiffer; University of Nebraska at Omaha Communication School Directors Deb Smith-Howell and Jeremy Lipschultz; editor Heather Staines; and the librarians of University of Nebraska at Omaha, who have gotten to know me very well.

FURTHER READING

Brandon, William. *The American Heritage Book of Indians*. New York: Dell, 1961.

Collier, John. *Indians of the Americas*. New York: New American Library, 1947.

Driver, Harold E. *Indians of North America*. 2d Ed. Chicago: University of Chicago Press, 1969.

Garbarino, Marvyn S., and Robert F. Sasso. *Native American Heritage*. 3d ed. Long Grove, IL: Waveland Press, 1994.

Kehoe, Alice Beck. *North American Indians: A Comprehensive Account*. 2d ed. Englewood Cliffs, NJ: Prentice-Hall, 1992.

Maxwell, James A., ed. *America's Fascinating Indian Heritage*. Pleasantville, NY: Reader's Digest, 1978.

McNickle, D'Arcy. *They Came Here First: The Epic of the American Indian*. Philadelphia: J. B. Lippincott, 1949.

Nabokov, Peter, ed. *Native American Testimony*. New York: Viking, 1991.

Oswalt, Wendell H. *This Land Was Theirs: A Study of North American Indians*. 7th ed. Boston: McGraw-Hill, 2002.

Stannard, David E. *American Holocaust: The Conquest of the New World*. New York: Oxford University Press, 1992.

Talbot, Steve. *Contemporary Indian Nations of North America: An Indigenist Perspective*. New York: Prentice-Hall, 2004.

Venables, Robert W. *American Indian History: Five Centuries of Conflict and Coexistence*. Santa Fe, NM: Clear Light Publishers, 2003.

Wilson, James. *The Earth Shall Weep: A History of Native America*. Boston: Atlantic Monthly Press, 1998.

Wright, Ronald. *Stolen Continents: The Americas through Indian Eyes Since 1492*. Boston: Houghton-Mifflin, 1992.

Introduction

My sketch of Native American history in North America has been gathered here into two volumes. The first begins with Native origins and ends with European colonization and its explosive movement westward during the first years of the nineteenth century. The second volume continues the narrative from the nineteenth century through Native peoples' present-day economic and cultural revival.

This account begins with human origins in the Americas—an account, like many to be considered here, which is subject to conjecture. The hundreds of Native peoples who lived in North America before sustained contact with Europeans and other immigrants have their own explanations of how and when they originated. An example is provided by the origin account of the Haudenosaunee (Iroquois) story, by Barbara Alice Mann, of Turtle Island's origins, Skywoman's descent, and the adventures of her two sons.

This volume next considers origin accounts advanced by Western scientists, principally archeologists. Fifty years ago, Native Americans generally were believed by such academicians to have arrived in the Americas across the Bering Strait within ten thousand years of the present, a neat migration pattern that was said to have filled various parts of the continent with a trail of Clovis spear points. Since then, origin dates have receded; thirty thousand years is becoming respectable now, with speculation reaching further back in time. The Bering Strait is still one possible route but probably not the only one. The first chapter of this book details an irony that has been receiving increasing attention: If the primary migration route was the far north, why are some of the oldest native remains being found in South America, notably present-day Chile? Another complicating factor has been the recent discovery of Kennewick Man, a nearly complete skeleton dated to more than nine thousand years of age, with features closely resembling no present-day ethnic group.

Development of human societies in North America are followed in this account to the point at which sizable urban areas such as Cahokia (near contemporary St. Louis, MO) served complex trading networks. Some insight is then provided into Native systems of agricultural production and family life that may have greeted the first Europeans, the Vikings, who probably explored small parts of North America about a thousand years ago.

A major issue of conjecture in scholarly circles has revolved around the number of people living in North America before sustained contact with Europeans began following the voyages of Columbus. This subject has sparked intense debate because various population estimates for North and South America differ by at least a factor of ten, from perhaps 12 million to about 120 million. The higher estimates provided by demographic historian Henry F. Dobyns have prompted some of the most intense debate.

Chapter 2 describes the fascinating histories of early Mesoamerican peoples, beginning with the Olmecs, continuing with residents of Mexico's Central Valley, culminating with the Aztecs and the Maya. Special attention is paid to recent discoveries of complex written communication among the Olmecs that probably provided a basis for similar writing systems used by the Maya and Aztecs. Emphasis is provided for recent findings advancing archeologists' understanding of the Mayan language and its revelation of frictions swathed in bloody conflict resulting in widespread war between city-states that probably ended the Maya's classic civilization. Before their decline, the Maya produced considerable written history, a precise calendar reaching to 3114 B.C.E., and a wealth of astronomical observations, some of which even today are among the most accurate in the world. Chapter 2 concludes with the Spanish conquest of Mesoamerica; the Spaniards marveled at the Aztec capital of Tenochtitlan (on the site of today's Mexico City) before their diseases and gold lust destroyed it.

The Spanish soon extended their influence north, west, and east as well, from Florida to California, the primary focus of the narrative at the beginning of chapter 3. This chapter details the expansion of the Spanish Empire and the toll it took on Native peoples, notably the cruelty chronicled by the Catholic priest Bartolome de las Casas, the leading advocate of inquiries into the cruel underside of the Spanish conquest. Las Casas himself chronicled the Spanish brutality against the Native peoples in excruciating detail, as he campaigned to end at least some of it.

Chapter 3 continues the historical narrative of European immigration with the first substantial English colonization on the eastern seaboard of North America, first at Jamestown, in Virginia (1607), then at Plymouth Rock, Massachusetts, in 1620. From a Native point of view, the story is told with some irony as Squanto, who had been to both England and Spain before the Pilgrims set foot in America, greeted them in English. Particular attention is paid to the associations of Roger Williams (dissident Puritan founder of Rhode Island) with Native peoples of the area because these events provide a rare window on intercultural life at the time. Williams was a witness to events, such as the Pequot

War and King Phillip's War, which markedly diminished Native populations and estate in the land that came to be called New England. Williams also was one of few European Americans known as a friend of the native leader Metacom, who was drawn and quartered at the end of the war named after his English name (King Phillip).

Chapter 4 begins with a description of the Iroquois Confederacy's influential role in the seventeenth century, detailing the confederacy's influence in shaping immigrant Europeans' notions of democracy during the next century. The founding of the confederacy is described in detail, with relatively new information regarding its founding date, which is now believed to be about 1142 C.E., about four centuries earlier than most dates advanced heretofore by scholars. (The 1142 C.E. date, advanced by Barbara A. Mann and Jerry Fields is, however, close to some estimates maintained by several Iroquois traditionalists.) This chapter ends with consideration of the Iroquois role in treaty diplomacy and the fur trade, as well as the advent of Handsome Lake's code, a religion that combined traditional and European American religious elements.

By shortly after 1800, European American migration was exploding westward across North America, propelled by the deteriorating economic situation in Europe (especially for the lower-middle classes of the British Isles, a motor of emigration). By midcentury, completion of cross-continental railroad links sped westward movement considerably. Only sixty years separate intensive European American settlement in the Southeast (with the Removal Act of 1830 and the Trail of Tears eight years later) from the Wounded Knee massacre in 1890. The intensity of conflict in the Ohio Valley often has been downplayed in survey histories. The Ohio area was key to the rush westward as several Native alliances tried and eventually failed to stem the advance, beginning with Pontiac, continuing with Little Turtle and Tecumseh, ending with Black Hawk. This period included not only vicious genocidal attacks, such as one at Goschocking, described in chapter 5 by Barbara A. Mann, but also the largest single battlefield defeat of the U.S. Army at the hands of Native Americans during 1791.

In the Southeast, the Cherokees and other "civilized" Native nations prospered for a time in their homelands by building European-style farms and villages until removal forced them westward on the many trails of tears. This narrative includes human history's only single-handed construction of a written language (Sequoyah, in Cherokee), as well as high drama regarding removal in front of John Marshall's U.S. Supreme Court. Marshall found for the Cherokees, but President Andrew Jackson ignored the Court, an impeachable offense under the Constitution. Why wasn't Jackson impeached? Removal had become a states rights issue; enforcement of the Constitution could have provoked the Civil War during the 1830s instead of the 1860s. In this case, states rights politics trumped the Constitution.

The first volume of this set ends in the middle of the nineteenth century, as a young, muscular United States of America, empowering itself with the national creation myth of "manifest destiny," exploded across North America, east to west, pushing surviving Native Americans westward as well, in one of human history's swiftest demographic movements. Within a generation of the Civilized Tribes' trails of tears, the United States had severed nearly half of Mexico, discovered gold in California, sent Native peoples packing from the site of Seattle, and sent its Navy to Japan to deliver a forceful knock on its door, demanding trade relationships. The speed of U.S. expansion is illustrated by the fact that the Navy's visit to Tokyo occurred during the same decade (the 1850s) that the government negotiated treaties in the Pacific Northwest, not even a generation after the Cherokees' removal. Volume II opens in the Northwest, surveying a high civilization very much unlike those of Native peoples further east.

CHAPTER 1

Early Indigenous North America

AN OVERVIEW

Exploration of indigenous North America's prehistory can be an unexpectedly rocky journey, full of questions raised to challenge assumptions often based on scant evidence. It also can be a journey into a world of wonders, of watching, as best we know on limited evidence, how hundreds of Native cultures evolved over many thousands of years. If human beings were present in the Western Hemisphere for at least 30,000 years before Columbus arrived, as now seems likely, they had been forming and re-forming societies for sixty times the length of time since "old" and "new" worlds began shaping each other in a substantial way with the arrival of Columbus. The most intriguing aspect of this journey is that many of us—even "experts" of various scholarly stripes—are still discovering America. Our knowledge, especially regarding how people lived before the coming of Europeans and other transoceanic immigrants, is still so scanty and subject to so much debate that we should be prepared to be surprised, and sometimes awed, by the peoples and cultures that flourished here.

For the most part, we have very little knowledge that has been related by Native peoples themselves describing how their ancestors lived before roughly 1500 C.E. Some had forms of writing, and they kept some records, but many of these records were misunderstood for what they were and were destroyed by European immigrants. Along with shreds of evidence provided by archaeology, often we have only verbal snapshots left us by immigrants whose main purpose was not preservation and description, but plunder and destruction. Even the best-trained modern experts sometimes have missed clues to the far past of indigenous America because of ethnocentric biases.

The texture of prehistory in the Old World is much more detailed, largely because the peoples who provided them to us still live in substantial numbers. In America, in contrast, we often have but fragments of oral history handed down by obliterated generations who have had to struggle to maintain their traditional ways of life. Native languages—entire "libraries" of native experience—are being lost with the rapidity of rare plant species. For every detail unearthed by scholars, more of America's earliest oral history is dying. Histories of great value have been lost when the people who maintained them through time dwindled to a few, then none. We frequently have tantalizing evidence of civilizations with nearly no voices from the past to explain how people lived, thought, fought, and died.

RECENT SURPRISES IN THE AMAZON VALLEY

Modern archeology regularly provides surprises. For example, researchers working in the Amazon River basin during 2003 discovered a fifteen-square-mile region at the headwaters of the Upper Xingu River that contained at least nineteen villages of 2,500 to 55,000 people each; these villages were spaced at regular intervals of between one and two miles, connected by wide roads, and surrounded by evidence of intense agriculture. This discovery upended long-held assumptions that the rain forest was a pristine wilderness before its first visits by Europeans, as well as assumptions that the environment of the area could not support sophisticated civilizations. For many years, archeologists had argued with considerable conviction that the soil of the Amazon Valley was too poor to support large populations. The ancient residents intensively cultivated cassava, which grows well in poor soil.

These researchers, including some descendants of pre-Columbian Native peoples who lived in the area, found evidence of densely settled, well-organized communities with roads, moats, and bridges. Some of the area's precisely de-signed roads were more than fifty yards wide. The people of the area cleared large areas of the rain forest to plant orchards; they preserved other areas as sources of wood, medicinal plants, and animals.

Michael J. Heckenberger, first author of an article in *Science* (2003), said that the ancestors of the Kuikuro people in the Amazon basin had a "complex and sophisticated" civilization with a population of many thousands before 1492. "These people were not the small mobile bands or simple dispersed popula-tions" that some earlier studies had suggested, he said (according to Recer, 2003). "They were not organized in cities," Heckenberger said. "There was a different pattern of small settlements, but they were all tightly integrated" (Recer, 2003). The extent of the road network is unknown at this time. "Here we present clear evidence of large, regional social formations (circa 1250 to 1650 c.e.) and their substantive influence on the landscape," wrote Heck-enberger and colleagues (2003, 1,710). "This is an incredibly important indi-cator of a complex society," said Susanna Hecht, a geographer at Stanford University's Center for Advanced Study in the Behavioral Sciences; "the extent of population density and landscape domestication is extraordinary" (Stokstad, 2003, 1,645).

According to a 2003 Associated Press account by Paul Recer, Heckenberger said that "the Amazon people moved huge amounts of dirt to build roads and plazas. At one place, there is evidence that they even built a bridge spanning a major river. The people also altered the natural forest, planting and maintaining orchards and agricultural fields, and the effects of this stewardship can still be seen today." Diseases such as smallpox and measles, brought to the New World by European explorers, probably killed most of the population along the Amazon, he said. By the time scientists began studying the indigenous people, the population was sparse and far-flung. As a result, some researchers assumed that the same pattern had been common prior to European exploration. Heckenberger's assertions have been questioned, however, by Betty J. Meggers of the Smithsonian Institution's National Museum of Natural History, who asserted in *Science* (Meggers et al., 2003, 2,067) that this study says little about population density in the Amazon Valley because the site is peripheral to the rain forest.

AMERICAN ORIGINS

Any serious student of Native North America will come to appreciate a diversity of peoples and cultures equal to any area of comparable size in the Old World. In 1492, Native Americans in North and South America spoke an estimated two thousand mutually unintelligible languages: roughly 250 in North America, 350 in present-day Mexico and Central America, and an astonishing 1,400 in South America. This is a greater degree of language diversity than existed in all of the Old World (Sherzer, 1992, 251). We have, however, little tangible evidence of what many of these different peoples may have talked about. Although bones and pottery can be unearthed and carbon dated, ideas are as perishable and mutable as memory in a time when few things were written and fewer writings preserved.

People in every culture on earth maintain accounts that explain how its people and their ways of life came to be. As with the Christian Garden of Eden's Adam and Eve, the Native American peoples of the Americas explained their own origins in their own ways. A condensed version of the Haudenosaunee (Iroquois) origin story follows. This account and many others may be compared with long-held assumptions of Western scholarly inquiry in which nearly all investigators believe that the first people of the Americas arrived from somewhere else. The most common point of origin is still believed to have been northeastern Asia, probably parts of Siberia. As arrival dates have been pushed back, however, the case for a simple, single migration across one land bridge has weakened. As the date when the first Americans are believed to have arrived recedes, the case for several migrations over land (as well as sea voyage arrivals from other continents, such as Africa to present-day Brazil) would seem to become more likely. Origins on the American land itself, maintained by many native peoples, also have a place in today's literature.

◠

The Haudenosaunee Creation

Barbara Alice Mann

The original ancestors of the Iroquois were the Sky People, denizens of *Karionake*, "The Place in the Sky," commonly called Sky World, a physical place that floated among the stars "on the farther side of the visible sky" ("Mohawk Creation," 32; Hewitt, 1903, 141). Sky World was well populated, with a social order that greatly resembled later Iroquoian society. The people lived in close-knit, matrilineal clans. The Sky People were greatly gifted with *uki-okton* power. In a Mohawk Keeping, it is said that the Sky People "had greatly developed what scientists call E.S.P." ("Mohawk Creation," 1989, 32), a talent later valued by their earthly descendants, especially for tapping into dream knowledge. The geography of Sky World also resembled that of Iroquoia, with trees, crops, and longhouses. All of the flora and fauna later present in physical form on earth had spiritual counterparts (Elder Siblings) preexisting in Sky World. These animal spirit Elders took part in Sky councils and performed creative tasks (Barbeau, 1915, 41–44; Hewitt, 1928, 465).

In the center of Sky World grew a wonderful tree that, running the length of Sky World, held it together from top to bottom. Some say it was a wild cherry tree, and others call it a crabapple tree; still others call it a pilar. The Tuscarora call it a dogwood tree. An Onondaga version named the tree *Ono''djä*, or "Tooth," presumably indicating the yellow dogtooth violet. The tree itself was sacred, supplying food that the Sky People might gather. It sprouted from the sides and fell to the ground to be collected, just for the thinking.

Several traditions speak of the conception, birth, childhood, and youth of the girl who was to become Sky Woman, also called *Awenhai* (Fertile Earth), *Ataensic* (Mature Flowers), *Otsitsa* (Corn), and eventually, *Iagentci* (Ancient One, or Grandmother). Sky Woman's mother dallied with a man she did not actually love, enticing him daily by "disentangling" his hair. ("Combing out the hair" was a metaphor for interpreting dreams, part of making them true. It was a spiritual talent.) This unfortunate man, the father of Sky Woman, died before she was born and was "buried" high in the tree of Sky World. His was the first death ever to occur in Sky World, a spirit sign. Sky Woman grew up quickly (another sign of spirit power), in constant mourning for the father she never knew, prompting her grandmother to show her where her father had been buried (Hewitt, 1903, 141–149, 256–265). In another version, the deceased was not a sperm father, but the girl's maternal uncle (Hewitt, 1928, 470). This cultural tidbit seems authentically old because the mother's matrilineal brother, not an out-clan biological father, was traditionally the male authority figure of a longhouse and often was called "Father."

Sky Woman's husband is usually called the Ancient. She was soon with child through the sharing of breath with her husband (Hewitt, 1903, 167).

Skywoman on Turtle's back. (Courtesy of John Kahionhes Fadden.)

In one Seneca version, Sky Woman gave birth to her child in Sky World, but this seems anomalous (ibid., 223). In nearly every other collected version, she was pregnant when she arrived on earth, delivering her daughter there. The Ancient was the presiding officer of Sky World, who lodged in the shade of Tooth.

Dreams were very important to the Sky People. It was necessary not only to understand them, but also to reenact them, thus continually creating reality. One day, the Ancient had a troubling dream, which made him ill. In a Seneca version, he had dreamed that a great "cloud sea" swam around under Tooth, the ocean of a restless and unlit world. Its spirit was calling out to the Sky People for aid in overcoming its extreme loneliness (Converse, 1908, 33).

All of the Elders of the later plants and animals, as well as the heavenly bodies and elements associated with earth, came to peer over the edge at the water world. Deer, Spotted Fawn, Bear, Beaver, the Moving Wind, Daylight, Night, Thick Night, the Sun, Spring Water, Corn, Beans, Squash, Sunflower, Fire Dragon, Meteor, Rattle, Otter, Wolf, Duck, Fresh Water, Medicine, Aurora Borealis, and of course, the Great Turtle, visited the window onto earth (Hewitt, 1903, 173–175). Some add that the Blue Sky, the Air, the Thunderers, the Tree, the Bush, the Grass, the Moon, the Star, and the Sun looked as well (Hewitt, 1928, 473). The hole at the base of Tooth became a regular Sky World tourist destination.

Skywoman Falls to Earth

Having uprooted the tree, the Ancient was thus able to fulfill the second part of his dream, that his wife was to fall through the hole in Sky World, down to the water world below. Occasionally, it is said that she fell because of her own curiosity, having leaned too far over the edge for a better look at earth (Parker, 1913, 6). Some Wyandot Keepings depict the illness as Sky Woman's, not the Ancient's, stating that, to cure her, an aged shaman uprooted the tree, laying Sky Woman as near as possible to its medicinal roots—too near, as it turned out because the soil was unstable, and the sick girl was sucked down into the hole and rolled into the void (Barbeau, 1915, 37).

In yet another variant, this one Mohawk, her husband was considerate, not cruel, and gathered the living bark of Tooth for tea to calm the cravings of his pregnant wife. It was his kind deed that caused the Sky tree to collapse, opening the window onto earth below and occasioning her slip ("Mohawk Creation," 1989, 32). Most Haudenosaunee keep the version of the bad-tempered Ancient, however, attributing Sky Woman's tumble to his jealousy. In several versions, the Ancient was irrationally jealous of the Aurora Borealis, the Fire Dragon, and especially of Sky Woman, who was more gifted with *uki-okton* than he.

Although unable to climb back up the ledge, she did acquire seeds from the munificent Tree. In her right hand, she garnered the Three Sisters: Corn, Beans, and Squash. Some say she also laid hold of Tobacco in her left hand. A Seneca version claimed that the white Fire Dragon or the Blue Panther—an *okton* spirit jealously sought by the Ancient—was at the root hole just as Sky Woman fell. In this version, it was the Blue Panther who gave her Corn, mortar, and pestle (Hewitt, 1903, 224, and 1928, 481; Cornplanter, 1928, 9, 13). Jesse Cornplanter said that it was the Ancient, himself, who threw the Elder plants (corn, beans, squash, sunflower, tobacco) along with the Elder Animals (Deer, Wolf, Bear, Beaver, etc.) down the abyss after her in a final frenzy of rage ([1938] 1992, 10).

In all versions, however, Skywoman slid down, down, down through space and into the atmosphere of Earth. (The suggestion of tradition is that the strong spirit of Sky Woman's father had foreseen all of these events so necessary to the beginning of human life on earth, and that this was why he had urged his daughter on to such an unfortunate marriage, with all of its character-building trials and tribulations.) Sick of the disruption in Sky World, on her fall through the hole in Sky World, the Sky People set Tooth, the Tree of Light, back into its socket (Hewitt, 1928, 480).

Now, the Elder creatures of earth, alerted first by the far-sighted Eagle, saw Sky Woman falling. For the first time, lightning (the Fire Dragon or Meteor Man) streaked across the sky of earth at her side as she hurtled through the atmosphere (Parker, 1912, 6). Sweeping into action, Heron and Loon caught and held the frightened Sky Woman aloft on their interlocking wings while, in an amusing portion of the tradition, the Great Tortoise sent around a moccasin; that is, he called an emergency council of Elder animals to see what was to be done. (For a sprightly Wyandot version of the Elder animals' Creation Council, see Barbeau, 1915, 38–44.) Knowing that she was a Sky Woman, unable to live on their watery planet, the Elder Spirits of earth creatures all quickly agreed that she should not be dropped into the waters to die.

The Origin of Turtle Island

In every version, the great Snapping Turtle offered his carapace, vowing to carry the earth above him forever as he swam. The idea gained ready assent, and the council of earth Elders assembled its divers. Usually, the divers were said to have been Muskrat, Otter, Toad, or Beaver. In some versions, the Muskrat and Otter die in the attempt to bring up dirt in their mouths, with Beaver finally bringing it up on his tail, or Toad in his mouth. A Mohawk version has poor, dead Muskrat floating to the surface, his mouth smeared with the dirt that was to become earth (Hewitt, 1903, 287). A Seneca version says that it was Sky Woman, herself, who arrived with the dirt of Sky World on her hands and under her fingernails, gathered as she frantically clutched at the tree roots during her fall (ibid., 226). A tad of dirt now ready to accept her, the Birds were able to set Sky Woman down on her new abode, Turtle Island. Looking around forlornly, alone and torn from everything she had ever known, Sky Woman wept bitterly (ibid., 225).

Wherever Sky Woman went, every kind of plant sprouted up before her. Now, she planted the Three Sacred Sisters she had brought from Sky World. Some say that she found potatoes here (Hewitt, 1903, 226), although potatoes are usually attributed to the little daughter, soon born to her on Turtle Island. The land was full with the harvest, on which Sky Woman lived As the land was full of growth, so was Sky Woman. She prepared her birthing hut and delivered herself of an infant daughter. They were at that time, the only two human beings on earth.

The Birth of the Twins: Sapling and Flint

Sky Woman continually refused the Earth Elders as consorts of her daughter until one day the matter passed out of her hands. An engaging man-creature came along, his bark robe tossed rakishly over his shoulder, his black hair pulled up, and his handsome eyes gleaming. He was so gorgeous that the Lynx forgot to ask her mother but lay with him immediately. Some assert that the two did not engage in coitus, but that the young man simply lay an arrow next to her body (Hewitt, 1903, 291–292). In an Onondaga version, Sky Woman consented to, rather than resisted, this final match (Hewitt, 1928, 384–385), but most versions showed Sky Woman was dismayed by the Lynx's unauthorized infatuation.

Young love won out, however, and soon the Lynx was pregnant, a fact that caused her mother to tremble. Sky Woman was fearful of the result of a pregnancy between two such different creatures as a Sky Girl and an earth Man-Being. In the very oldest Keepings of Creation, the Lynx was pregnant not with twins (the common Keeping today), but with quadruplets, analogous to the four sacred messengers of the *Gaiwí:yo* and connected with the Four Winds or cardinal directions (Hewitt, 1928, 468). An interesting, potential echo of this ancient Keeping is found in a Seneca version that told the puzzling story of four children—two male and two female—who were Man-Beings (Hewitt, 1903, 233). The story of the quadruplets, however, is almost completely lost today. The four children of the Lynx were eventually compressed to two, with the personality traits of the four redistributed between them.

As told in modern times, the Lynx overheard twin sons in her womb discussing their plans for the earth life they were about to live. One already knew that he was to create game animals and new trees, but the other was more vague on specifics, merely announcing that he, too, would create in one way or another (Hewitt, 1928, 486). Labor pains overcame the Lynx a few days before her time, and she again overheard her sons holding forth, this time in a discussion over how best to be born because neither precisely knew how to do it. In an Onondaga version, one infant pointed toward the birth canal and said, "I'll go that way," and he did, being first born. The Elder Twin became known as *Tharonhiawakon, Odendonnia, Ioskaha* (Sapling), meaning roughly the Spirit of Life (Hewitt, 1903, 138). Sapling was perfectly formed in the eyes of Sky Woman.

The Younger Twin protested his brother's path. "But this other way is so near," he said, pointing in some versions to the armpit and in others to the navel of his mother. "I shall leave that way," he said, and he did, killing his mother in parturition (Hewitt, 1903, 185). Some Mohawks say that the second son, *Tawiskaro*ⁿ (Flint) was born with a comb of flint on his head, by which means he had cut an exit path through his mother's armpit (ibid., 185). Some Senecas say that he leapt forth from her navel, all covered with warts (ibid., 231).

However it happened, by armpit or caesarean section, when Sky Woman saw that her beloved daughter was dead, she sat on the ground and wept inconsolably. She buried her daughter most tenderly, and from the Lynx's grave sprang all the plants of life: Corn, Beans, and Squash grew from her breasts; potatoes sprang from her toes and tobacco grew from her head (Thomas, 2000). The Lynx had transmuted into Mother Earth, a living entity (Hewitt, 1928, 542). Despite the continued spirit existence of her daughter, Sky Woman's grief almost undid her. It was then that Sky Woman grew suddenly old, becoming known in her turn as the Ancient or Grandmother. Her grief soured into a bitterness of temperament that she had not possessed. She became grumpy and impatient in her old age.

Like Sky Woman and the Lynx before them, the Twins grew rapidly, showing their great spirit power. They soon began to complete the process of creation, although there were many disagreements between the brothers as to what final creation should look like. While Sapling was bringing forth his trademark strawberries, Flint was littering the landscape with brambles and briars. If Sapling created peaceful game animals, Flint responded with a spate of roaring, clawing, dangerous beasts.

Mother Earth. (Courtesy of John Kahionhes Fadden.)

Creation of the Sun, Moon, and Stars

The creation of the sun, moon, and stars is variously attributed to Sky Woman and Sapling. The oldest Wyandot and Onondaga versions give Sky Woman or the Elder Earth animals credit for creating the sun, moon, and stars, especially the Milky Way (Barbeau, 1915, 41). A Seneca version has Sky Woman creating the heavens almost immediately after her arrival on earth (Hewitt, 1903, 226–227). Hewitt also recorded a Mohawk story of Grandmother using dead Lynx's body parts as the material of the heavens (ibid., 295–296), but the Lynx is emphatically Mother Earth in all versions and the Moon is Grandmother, leaving the origin of this version vague and questionable. Yet other versions, following the postmissionary trend of giving Sapling sole credit for creation, showed him hanging the heavens, after the fashion of the Christian god (Hewitt, 1903, 208; 1928, 542–543).

One thing became immediately apparent in nearly every version of Creation: Flint was not nearly as skillful a creator as his brother. This was apparent not only in the animals that each brought forth, but also in their attempts at creating humanity. Some say that whereas Sapling created humankind, Flint in a rival bout of creation only managed to bring forth monkeys (Barbeau, 1915, 51; Hewitt, 1903, 214). Others contend that one day Flint noticed that Sapling had made human beings. Marveling at the feat, he sought to replicate it, going through inferior and unworkable models before he managed a viable version, with the kindly advice of Sapling, who stopped by periodically to check on his little brother's progress.

Flint's first human was mostly made of water and therefore failed to breathe. On his second try, Flint added samples of his own mind, blood, spirit, and breath and finally succeeded in creating a living being, although his creation still lacked luster compared to Sapling's model. It is uncertain just what this creature was intended to have been in the older traditions—perhaps a bear—but postcontact, the Iroquois quickly realized that Flint's water man was the European. By contrast, Sapling had created the True Humans or Native Americans (Hewitt, 1928, 523–525; for a late version of Flint's creation of Europeans, see Parker, 1913, 16–19.)

An older Mohawk version ended the creation story by engaging the brothers in a tit-for-tat spat that escalated into a lethal confrontation. The two lived together in a lean-to, one with a side taller than the other. Flint dwelled at the shorter end and Sapling at the taller. One day, Sapling stoked their shared fire to perilous intensity until it began to chip the chert from Flint's flinty legs. When his complaints did not persuade Sapling to lessen the flames, Flint saw that his brother meant him harm. He ran outside swiftly, looking for a cutting reed and a cattail spear, both of which he knew were harmful to his brother. The fight then spiraled out of control, with the two furiously chasing each other across Turtle Island, leaving huge chasms and water-filled depressions where their feet landed in their hurry. In this version, Sapling killed Flint, whose prone body transmuted into the Rocky Mountains. His spirit dwells to this day inside those mountains (Hewitt, 1903, 328–332).

Flint was not permanently dead, however (Hewitt, 1928, 547). All spirits continue to live, often in renewed bodies (Hewitt, 1903, 218–219). Throughout Iroquoian history, Sapling continued reincarnating, most notably as the Peacemaker, creator of the Haudenosaunee (Iroquois) Confederacy, to aid his favorite creations, human beings; the Lynx became Mother Earth, and Grandmother became the smiling face of the Moon.

~

NEW DEFINITIONS OF AMERICAN ANTIQUITY

How Old Are North America's First Cultures?

A logical starting place in an exploration of American prehistory might be a question: How long have the first Americans been here? From there, our inquiry broadens to the following: Where did North America's first peoples come from and why? These questions are fraught with debate today, which seems to intensify as we learn more about First Nations' cultures. The Bering Strait theory, an assumption that all of the first Native Americans crossed a land bridge over the Bering Strait following the last major Ice Age, perhaps 10,000 to 11,000 years ago, has taken its lumps recently. Given new knowledge, this theory now seems as simplistic and smug as the folk history that maintains a singular "discovery" of America by Christopher Columbus. The reality may be much more complex.

By 2003, the primacy of the Bering Strait theory had been scorched by the discovery that the Siberian site long thought to be the jumping-off point for the peopling of the Americas (at Ushki, Kamchatka) dated later, by about 4,000 years, than its proponents had thought. Thus, the Siberian site was no older, at 13,000 years, than the most ancient Clovis sites in North America, not to mention the Monte Verde sites in South America. Someone may have migrated to America over the Bering Strait, but they were not the first (Goebel, Waters, and Dikova, 2003, 501; Stone, 2003, 450).

Early in 2004, Russian scientists reported the discovery of a 30,000-year-old site where ancient hunters had lived on the Yana River in Siberia, some three hundred miles north of the Arctic Circle. "Although a direct connection remains tenuous, the Yana . . . site indicates that humans extended deep into the Arctic during colder (Ice Age) times," the authors wrote in a study that appeared in *Science* (Pitulko et al., 2004, 52). The researchers found stone tools, ivory weapons, and the butchered bones of mammoths, bison, bear, lion, and hare, all animals that would have been available to hunters during that Ice Age period. The site was twice as old as any previous Arctic settlement, indicating that "people adapted to this harsh, high-altitude, late Pleistocene environment much earlier than previously thought" (Pitulko et al., 2004, 52).

The researchers determined that artifacts were deposited at the site about 30,000 years before the present. That would be about twice as old as Monte Verde in Chile, the most ancient human life known in the American continents. Donald K. Grayson, a paleoanthropologist at the University of Washington in Seattle, said the discovery is very significant because it is so much earlier than any other proven evidence of people living in the frigid lands of Siberia that were used as one path to the Americas (Recer, 2004). "Until this site was reported, the earliest site in Bering land bridge area was dated at about 11,000 years ago," said Grayson. "Every other site that had been thought to have been early enough to have something to do with peopling of the New World has been shown not to be so" (Recer, 2004).

At the time of the Yana occupation, much of the high latitudes on the earth were in the grip of an ice age that sent glaciers creeping over much of what is now Europe, Canada, and the northern United States. The Yana River area was a dry floodplain without glaciers, however. The area was roamed by mammoths, wild horses, musk oxen, and other animals that provided food for the human hunters who survived the Arctic's climate. "Abundant game means lots of food," said Julie Brigham-Grette of the University of Massachusetts, Amherst, in *Science*. "It was not stark tundra as one might imagine" (Recer, 2004).

Among the artifacts found at the Yana site were weapons that resembled some found at a Clovis, New Mexico, site dated around 11,000 years before the present. Grayson and others said, however, that existing evidence linking those implements to the tool and weapon techniques used by the Clovis people is weak. Similar artifacts also have been found in Europe and western Asia, Grayson said. "The similarities [in the tools and weapons] are not enough to prove they were ancestral to the Clovis people in the New World," said Grayson (Recer, 2004).

Native American Arrival Estimates Recede in Time

We do know that America's indigenous cultures evolved for many thousands of years before permanent European settlements began in North America, but we do not yet know for how long. The academically accepted date for original human origin or arrival has been steadily pushed back in time. By 1900, it was acceptable to assert that America's first human occupants had been here 5,000 years. By 1960, for example, an origin or arrival date preceding 8000 B.C. (almost double the 1900 figure) was considered credible. By 1990, that date was considered conservative.

Today, the date of origin or arrival that one is willing to accept depends on the quality of evidence that is demanded. American archeology now reaches roughly 30,000 to 40,000 years into the past, reminding us again that prehistory holds much yet to be discovered. The fact that accepted dates of human arrival in America have receded so rapidly in the recent past has been part of an evolution of knowledge that reflects fieldwork of increasing intensity and sophistication over time. Undoubtedly, more discoveries will enrich this debate in years to come.

The origin date of humanity in the Americas has been debated for centuries. Often, the earliest European settlers thought that the people they met here had resided in the Americas only a few hundred years before their arrival. Fierce debates raged over whether they had migrated from Asia (a view first put forth in 1589 by the Spanish scholar Jose de Acosta), or whether they were the remnants of Israel's ten lost tribes. This interpretation was especially popular between 1600 and 1800; William Penn and Cotton Mather, among others, subscribed to it. James Adair popularized the same idea in a landmark study of American Indians ([1775] 1930).

Science's best guess regarding the date of the first human footfalls in the Americas has always been something of a rubber figure, even as defenders of various sites and dates have, at different times, defended their favorite dates and places with dogmatic intensity. Three decades before the Clovis finds rearranged archaeology's American timeline, some scholarly debate centered on the widely accepted biblical timeline, which held that the earth was created by the Christian God in 4004 B.C.E. At the same time, various academic schools of thought contended that Native Americans might have descended from seafaring Egyptians, Phoenicians, Greeks, Romans, Welsh, Chinese, or Japanese or even from the residents of Atlantis, the lost continent of European imagination.

Thomas Jefferson doubted that all the American Indians could have crossed over the Bering land bridge as recently as the last major Ice Age. As a student of Native languages, Jefferson thought that their variety and complexity required a more complex origin story, covering more temporal territory. By 1800, Jefferson was preparing to publish what would have been the most extensive vocabulary of Indian languages in his time. It also was the year Jefferson became president, so his work was delayed until he left office in 1808. Jefferson packed his research papers at the presidential residence and ordered them sent to Monticello. Contained in the cargo were Jefferson's own fifty vocabularies, as well as several others assembled during the Lewis and Clark expedition. Boatmen piloting Jefferson's belongings across the Potomac River ripped them open and, disappointed that they could find nothing salable, dumped the priceless papers into the river (Boyd, 1982, 20:451–452).

The timeline of human occupation in the Americas has become more fluid as new discoveries shatter earlier assumptions. A few researchers now argue that Native Americans have been present here from 100,000 or more years ago. Support for this thesis is said to come from a site at Calico Mountain in Southern California: crude bits of broken rock that may have served as tools for these ancient peoples. One problem is that the artifacts—if that is what they are—are on the surface of an alluvial fan, soil and debris washed from higher hillsides, and not buried in an undisturbed layer that can be safely dated to an earlier time. The chipped stones found at Calico Mountain may be of much more recent vintage. They are also so crude that they may not be human tools at all.

In 1992, a cave site was discovered in New Mexico that was said to have been occupied by human beings 35,000 years ago, moving back (by 23,000 years at one shot) the arguable date of the earliest occupation of that area by human beings. Richard S. MacNeish of the Andover Foundation for Archaeological Research (Honolulu, HI) reported that the Orogrande Cave contained remains of hearths, butchered bones, stone tools, and even a human palm print. As with most findings of such antiquity, experts disputed MacNeish's finds.

One school of thought held that he had mixed up stratigraphic layers and thus misdated his finds ("Peopling the Americas," 1992).

WHY ARE SOME OF THE OLDEST SITES IN SOUTH AMERICA?

One of the largest credibility problems for the Bering Strait theory may be a growing realization that the oldest human remains are now found, for the most part, in Central and South America, which would have been expected to be the last stop for peoples arriving from the north. In *The Settlement of the Americas* (2000), Thomas D. Dillehay, professor of anthropology at the University of Kentucky, illustrated in rich detail (and in many cases for the first time) the number and complexity of archaeological finds in South America that are undermining long-time support for exclusive diffusion of human cultures in North America from the north. Humanity's prehistory in the Americas, contends Dillehay, is older and more complex than that. Dillehay observed that no major region of South America is without Ice Age sites. In some places, such as the eastern highlands of Brazil, the Andean foothills on the north coast of Peru, and the steppes of southern Chile and Argentina, such sites can be found in profusion (Dillehay, 2000, 89).

Some of these cultures developed sophisticated weapons, including the sling stone and grooved bola stone, both of which can be hurled from a thong or whirled over a hunter's head before release. A number and variety of such weapons have been found in Chilean and Brazilian sites. For scholars seeking projectile points, Dillehay provides a rich variety from across the continent. Some of these points (an example is called the Fishtail Projectile Point) may have diffused from South America to North America.

"Many books have been written about the archaeology of the first North Americans and the process that led to their arrival and dispersion throughout the Americas," wrote Dillehay. "No such book exists for South America" (Dillehay, 2000, xiii). Carrying different assumptions and speaking different languages, North and South American scholars searching for the earliest human origins in the Americas often have failed to communicate with each other. Dillehay's work has removed any excuses for such academic isolation.

Dillehay's book includes a lengthy appendix (2000, 295–321) that lists several hundred significant archaeological finds in South America, several of which pre-date the oldest Clovis sites in North America, first discovered in 1932. Dillehay began his work on one of the best known of these, Monte Verde in southern Chile, during 1976 "after a student at the Southern University of Chile, where I was teaching and doing archaeological research, discovered a large mastodon tooth and other bones" at the site (ibid., xiv). Local men clearing an ox path had found the bones. Monte Verde, an open-air settlement on the banks of a small freshwater creek surrounded by sandy knolls, a narrow bog, and forest, soon became an active archaeological dig.

Artifacts from Monte Verde subsequently were radiocarbon dated as old as 12,500 years before the present (at a minimum), making them the oldest known links to human settlement in the Americas. (To date, no site in North America has been dated earlier than 11,200 years before the present.) Over the years, Dillehay has directed up to eighty professionals at a time excavating Monte Verde.

Dillehay, with scholarly contacts on both continents, is superbly qualified to describe this story's scientific side as well as the political struggle to convince English-speaking North American specialists that Monte Verde was not a fraud because the new range of dates contradicted the assumptions of "stringent Clovis loyalists who had spent their entire careers defending the theory against one pre-Clovis candidate after another" (2000, xvi).

After ten years of research, Dillehay and his colleagues at Monte Verde had found traces of people living at Monte Verde at least 12,500 years ago who practiced a generalized hunting-and-gathering style of life, not just big game hunting (Dillehay, 2000, xvi). "It is now apparent," wrote Dillehay, "that humans were in the Americas much earlier than we previously thought.... We are also realizing that the first immigrants probably came from several different places in the Old World and that their genetic heritage and physical appearance were much more diverse than we had thought" (2000, xiv). Previous North American sites are now being pre-dated by several others in addition to Monte Verde, including Meadowcroft Rockshelter in Pennsylvania, Cactus Hill in Virginia, Topper in South Carolina, and several others in eastern Brazil, Venezuela, and Colombia.

"We have enough evidence to be sure that virtually all parts of the continent [South America] were at least traversed, if not occupied, by the end of Pleistocene, around 10,500 B.P. [before the present]," wrote Dillehay (2000, 216). Our knowledge of societies at such an early date is limited by what nature leaves behind. "We are extraordinarily ignorant about certain aspects of the first immigrants to the Americas: their anatomical features, their religious beliefs, when and how they buried their dead, the kinds of languages they spoke," Dillehay wrote. Direct evidence on the physical and genetic makeup of the first Pleistocene Americans, especially South Americans, is scant or entirely missing (ibid., 227).

Dillehay (2000) makes a case that the image of early Americans as principally big game hunters is more a stereotype than a reality, more a reflection of the assumptions of capitalism than a residue of accurate scholarship. He cites Kathleen Gordon, a biological anthropologist:

This preoccupation with hunting as the "master behavior pattern of the human species"...has been fueled by many factors: the indisputable evidence of large-scale game hunting in Upper Paleolithic Europe; the visible archaeological record, with its emphasis on stone "weapons" and animal bone fragments, and also (perhaps subliminally) the high value accorded meat and hunting as a leisure activity in Western society. (pp. 28–29)

According to Dillehay (2000), recent excavations in South America indicate that Native Americans may have begun to domesticate plants and form the basis of agriculture that eventually would supply half the world's staple crops as early as 8,000 to 10,000 years ago, earlier than any other present-day evidence. A picture emerges from *The Settlement of the Americas* that human beings not only arrived in the New World earlier than previously thought, but also very quickly thereafter began utilizing all the food sources nature offered them, plant and animal. This picture contradicts the Clovis theory's implicit assumption that ancient Americans lived mostly by hunting big game. Dillehay criticizes defenders of the Clovis theory for being unable (and unwilling) to take seriously any archaeological find that does not occur in a dry location. Different techniques are required in humid sites (such as Monte Verde), wrote Dillehay.

Dillehay did much more than describe archaeological finds in *The Settlement of the Americas* (2000). He also probed the environment in which the earliest American peoples lived. Dillehay's speculations ranged from various aspects of geology to ecology and paleoclimatology. In his own words, Dillehay did his best to reconstruct the complexity of the mutual interaction between society and environment that creates the cultural landscape (ibid., 78).

Dillehay was fascinated by the rapid development of cultures and technologies among the earliest peoples of the New World. He asserted that some of the "first pulses of human civilization," including permanently occupied sites, the appearance of architecture and art, and the use of domesticated plants and animals, developed only five to ten millennia after people first arrived (2000, 275). By contrast, Asia, Africa, and Europe were inhabited for hundreds of thousands of years before the same attributes of culture appeared.

How long ago can a credible archaeologist argue that human beings arrived in the Americas? Dillehay's answer (2000, 283) to that question seems to be 15,000 to 20,000 years ago if one assumes that the primary early migration came from the north and that it reached Monte Verde about 12,500 years ago. Dillehay provided a caveat with this figure, indicating that Monte Verde may place human traces in areas dating 20,000 to 50,000 years before the present. We are reminded again that the date of human origins in the Americas is historically pliable, its boundaries restricted at any time not only by the methods of available science, but also by the dominant cultural and political attitudes of those who decide what is acceptable as general knowledge. If a generally accepted date a century ago was 4004 B.C.E. and now it is 15,000 to 20,000 years, what might science and society tell a curious student a century or two from now?

The archeological record supporting theories of human migration to the Americas is in constant flux. Late in 2002, a 13,000-year-old skull was found in Mexico that may help support theories that some of the New World's first settlers arrived along a Pacific Coast route from Japan instead of across the Bering Strait. This skull was one of the oldest thus far discovered in the

Americas, according to Silvia Gonzalez, a leading world authority on prehistoric humans and mammoths. She said the skull is similar to others found belonging to the now-extinct Pericues people, who populated the southern tip of Mexico's Baja California state, along the Pacific Coast route, until the eighteenth century. "The question is, we have these very ancient individuals, but where did they come from?" said Gonzalez, an earth sciences lecturer at Liverpool's John Moores University in England ("Mexican Skull," 2002).

Within days of the Mexican skull's discovery, news reports described 10,000-year-old human remains found at Boardman State Park on the Oregon Coast at a site roughly 12 miles north of Brookings, excavated the previous August by a team of researchers from Oregon State University led by professors Roberta Hall and Loren Davis. The remains, 2,000 years older than anything previously found in the area, were said to "lend weight to the theory that early inhabitants of the area might have arrived by sea, rather than by land" (Frazier, 2002). According to this account, "The discovery puts their arrival at about the time inland inhabitants arrived, bringing into question the theory that all of the earliest inhabitants crossed the Bering Strait and moved south overland to what is now the United States." The findings are about the same age as those found at a few sites in coastal Alaska, British Columbia, and California.

Dillehay wrote in *Nature* that "more recent archaeological discoveries suggest that there were several different founding populations" (2003, 23); he discussed a study of thirty-three ancient skulls excavated from Mexico that suggests the first Americans' links with southern Asian populations. Writing in the same issue of *Nature*, Gonzalez-José et al. present a comparative study of early historic human skulls from Baja California, Mexico (2003, 62), and their findings lend weight to the view that not all early American populations were directly related to present-day Native Americans.

By late 2004, radiocarbon findings had been presented for a site in present-day South Carolina that may be 50,000 years old, which could rewrite the history of how the Americas were first settled by humans. The new findings were raising considerable controversy among archaeologists. If the dates hold up to scrutiny, they would push back the first date of human occupancy in the Americas by about 25,000 years. "Topper is the oldest radiocarbon-dated site in North America," said Albert Goodyear of the University of South Carolina Institute of Archaeology and Anthropology (Walton and Coren, 2004). Goodyear has been excavating the Topper dig site along the Savannah River since the 1980s. The items that he believes to be 50,000 years of age were found in May 2003.

Theodore Schurr, an anthropology professor at the University of Pennsylvania in Philadelphia and a curator at the school's museum, said that conclusive evidence of stone tools similar to those in Asia and uncontaminated radiocarbon-dating samples are needed to verify that the Topper site is actually 50,000 years old. "If dating is confirmed, then it really does have a significant impact on our previous understanding of New World colonization," he said

(Walton and Coren, 2004). Some scientists expressed skepticism whether Goodyear's findings represented human presence. Stone shards that Goodyear believes to be human may be natural, according to Michael Collins of the Texas Archeological Research Laboratory at the University of Texas at Austin.

KENNEWICK MAN: ARCHAEOLOGY'S RACIAL POLITICS

The discovery during 1996 of a nearly complete human skeleton that came to be called Kennewick Man also threw neat, simple theories of the human occupancy of the Americas into disarray, in large part because the remains seemed not to resemble clearly any present-day ethnic group. Was Kennewick Man European? Norse, perhaps? Was he Asiatic, perhaps Ainu, the indigenous people of Japan? Was he Native American, from the earth of Turtle Island (North America)? Is Kennewick Man, perhaps, a combination of the worldly elements of his own time, a reminder in our time that human origins in the Americas are much more complex (and much more multicultural) than has been commonly supposed?

Kennewick Man is one anecdote in a long story, one reminder of the increasing complexity of our knowledge about human origins in the Americas. The discovery of Kennewick Man is part of an ongoing rewriting of the story of human origins in the Americas. A number of archaeological discoveries (and speculations) during the past generation have effectively jettisoned the neat-and-tidy myth popular in the 1950s that one group of Asiatic people traversed the Bering Strait more or less at one time and populated the continents of the Western Hemisphere in one fell swoop. The racial politics evoked by the discovery of Kennewick Man (and other, similarly ancient, remains) have presented us with a number of very diverse opinions, but one thing that nearly all serious observers of human antiquity in the Americas now share is this: Human origins in the Americas are much more diverse, and cover a much greater time span, than the simplistic Bering strait theory allows.

Some present-day Native American peoples do not fit century-old racial classifications. Many Haudenosaunee are light skinned, for example. It takes some imagination to assign a Lakota Sioux and a Maya to a single 10,000-year-old ancestor. Many Native nations adopted people who were not racially similar to them. The texture of the debate changes when it is viewed through this lens. Kennewick Man could have Asian (or even European) facial features and still be defined as a member of a Native American nation using criteria accepted by many Native peoples.

At the same time that Kennewick Man has thrown some assumptions of mainstream academia into doubt, the skeleton has become a stalking horse for non-Indian academics who have an interest in limiting Native American nations' legal rights to newly discovered human remains. Kennewick Man has become the first significant legal test of attempts to limit the Native American Graves Protection and Repatriation Act (NAGPRA; 1990) to allow, for example, inspection of remains found on federally owned land, including Kennewick Man, before (or instead of) reburial by Native American peoples.

Assertions that Kennewick Man migrated to America from Europe have made him something of a hero to non-Indians who would like to abrogate treaties and limit Native American sovereignty in our time. Architects of racial fantasies have built an entire racial pedigree for this skeleton on scant evidence and used claims that he was "white" to support a theory that he and his kind were the first human immigrants to the Americas. The more extreme variations of these tales assert that Kennewick man and his kin were slaughtered by the ancestors of present-day Native Americans.

The remains that would come to be called Kennewick Man were stumbled on (literally) by two college students, Will Thomas, 21 years old, and Dave Deacy, 20 years old, on July 28, 1996. The two residents of nearby West Richland, home for the summer, were looking for a spot on the banks of the Columbia River from which to view the annual hydroplane races.

James Chatters of Applied Paleoscience (Richland, WA), who routinely conducted skeletal forensics for Benton County Coroner Floyd Johnson, helped police gather a skeleton that was complete except for its sternum and a few small bones in the hands and feet. Recent flushing from Columbia River Dams, an attempt to preserve salmon runs for commercial and Native fishing, had disturbed the sediments and exposed the human remains, which soon became known as Kennewick Man (Johansen, 1999).

The skeleton seemed to Chatters to have belonged to a man who was old (between 40 and 55 years) by the standards of his time; who was about five feet nine or ten inches, tall for a human being that old; who had led a rough life. He had compound fractures in at least six ribs and damage to his left shoulder, which probably caused his arm to wither. He also had a healed-over skull injury. Kennewick Man, whose dietary staple may have been fish, probably died of injuries sustained after a stone projectile point pierced his thigh and lodged in his pelvis. The projectile probably caused a fatal infection that may have festered for as many as six months. Kennewick Man also suffered from advanced osteoporosis in one of his elbows and minor arthritis in his knees, according to Chatters.

Kennewick Man had a long, narrow skull; a projecting nose; receding cheekbones; a high chin; and a square mandible. The lower bones of the arms and legs were relatively long compared to the upper bones. These traits are not characteristic of modern American Indians in the area, although many of them are common among Caucasoid peoples, said Chatters.

A skeleton can reveal only so much about race, not to mention culture. From a skeleton, no one knows the form and color of eyes, color of skin and hair, whether the lips were thin or broad, and whether the hair was straight, wavy, or curly. No one at present knows what language Kennewick Man spoke or anything about what type of religion, if any, he practiced. In other words, the game of racial classification that so preoccupied much of the popular discourse about Kennewick Man was constructed on a very scant evidence base. On such small foundations, however, castles of imagination have been built.

Anthropologist Grover S. Krantz of Washington State University examined the bones at Chatters's request. The skeleton "cannot be anatomically assigned to any existing tribe in the area, nor even to the western Native American type in general," he wrote to Chatters (Slayman, 1997, 17). "It shows some traits that are more commonly encountered in material from the eastern United States or even of European origin, while certain other diagnostic traits cannot presently be determined" (ibid., 17).

According to many who claim Kennewick Man to be a long-lost Caucasian brother, seven skeletons with similar features have been discovered in North America since 1938. The first such discovery, at Fork Rock Cave, Oregon, was radiocarbon dated to about 9,000 years of age. Spirit Cave Man was caught in the same sort of crossfire as Kennewick Man; the Northern Pauites filed a claim for his remains that was contested by several non-Indian scientists. Researchers also contested the return to the Shoshone-Bannock tribe of a skeleton found near Buhl, Idaho. This set of remains was radiocarbon dated to roughly 10,600 years before the present. Most of the skeletons and associated artifacts were found in the western reaches of North America because the eastern side of the continent is much more humid and acidic, which makes long-term preservation of bones more difficult.

To David Hurst Thomas, writing in *Skull Wars* (2000), the present-day "custody battle" over Kennewick Man's remains tells us less about the world in which he lived than it does about the racial politics of our own time. The central theme of Thomas's book is that the struggle over Kennewick Man

> is not about religion or science. It is about politics. The dispute is about control and power, not philosophy. Who gets to control ancient American history?.... In a nutshell, then, *Skull Wars* explores the curious and often stormy relationship between American Indians and the non-Indians bent on studying them. (p. xxv)

How can an old human skeleton fire such passion of possession? In *Skull Wars* (2000), Thomas, long-time curator of anthropology at the American Museum of Natural History in New York City, describes five centuries of racial politics behind the contemporary debate regarding Kennewick Man's remains. The most intriguing part of the story is that Kennewick Man's remains fully fit no single present-day racial classification. Although some people believe Kennewick Man may have resembled the actor Patrick Stewart, Vine Deloria Jr. made a case in *Skull Wars* that Kennewick Man may have resembled the Sauk-Fox chief Black Hawk as painted in 1833 by John Jarvis. Kennewick Man may be a multicultural reminder that notions of race are present-day human constructs overlaid on a vastly more complicated natural record.

Self-definition, wrote Thomas (2000), walks hand-in-hand with self-determination. The power to name is key to nation building in contemporary

Native America, as well as to the identity politics of the Asatru Assembly and several groups of neo-Nazis who have claimed the remains of Kennewick Man. Thus far, the federal courts at the district and circuit levels have held that the remains should be held by the government and released for study by archaeologists. Federal judges to date have refused all other claims.

PREHISTORIC TIME PERIODS

Academics have designated certain prehistorical periods before sustained Native American contact with Europeans. These periods have had various names at various times and are subject to blurring into one another as we discover more about individual prehistorical cultures in America. In the language of contemporary archaeology, most of the time that human beings are now believed to have occupied North America—possibly as long ago as 40,000 to 8,000 years ago—is classified as the Paleo-Indian Tradition. Before about 8000 B.C.E. (or 10,000 years before the present), the indigenous cultures that existed in North America are generally believed to have been relatively uniform in cultural level and ways of life. Such uniformity may be more in the eye of the beholder than real; at this stage, evidence is scant and often restricted to the sort of hunting projectiles that were used at the time. The oldest (possibly 40,000 to roughly 10,000 years ago) artifacts are classified as from "preprojectile point" cultures. Stones that may have been chipped by human hands were unearthed at the Orogrande Cave in southern New Mexico dating to 38,000 B.C.E. or 40,000 years ago; a bone tool made from the carcass of a caribou has been dated to 25,000 B.C.E. at Old Crow Flats, Yukon Territory.

Before roughly 25,000 years ago, tools (such as chipped stones) were usually quite crude. Several sites in the western parts of the present-day United States have yielded simple materials, such as stone tools and debris from fires, believed by some to have been left behind by people 30,000 to 40,000 years ago. Most of these remains fail many archaeological tests meant to verify that they actually were created by human beings, so they remain, for our time, within the realm of the possible.

By about 25,000 years ago, hunters' technology was improving, with projectile points often made of chert or flint. Human bones found at La Jolla and elsewhere in southern California indicate possible human antiquity in that area from at least 27,000 B.C.E., and possibly as early as roughly 40,000 B.C.E., although the dating methods used in these studies have been subject to debate. A site near Midland in western Texas and the Marmes site in eastern Washington yield an antiquity of 16,500 B.C.E. to 9000 B.C.E. Crude tools and other artifacts of similar age have been found at many other sites. Several sites in Mexico date to roughly 20,000 B.C.E. as well (Kehoe, 1981, 1–11). In the Sandia mountains of New Mexico, archaeologists in 1936 found flint knives, scrapers, and other artifacts that have been dated to between 25,000 and

15,000 B.C.E. From these discoveries, the cultures that evolved in this area at that time have become known as the Sandia phase.

Artifacts are more widespread, more easily identified, and more technologically advanced from 11,000 years ago. Thus, the emphasis on the Folsom, Clovis, and Plano (or Plainview) points (all first found at sites in present-day New Mexico and Texas). Each dates to between 5000 and 10,000 B.C.E. The Clovis points seem to be the oldest, dating to about 12,000 B.C.E., with Folsom points dating to 8000 B.C.E., and Plano points recognizable at 7500 to 4500 B.C.E. Each type of point is used to identify the culture that used it. By the time of the Clovis culture, weapons were becoming much more sophisticated. For example, some hunters used an *atlatl*, a device allowing thrust of a spear with greater speed and accuracy than a hunter could achieve simply by throwing it. With such a device, which combined a spear of older design with a throwing device made from animal skin, hunters could attack game from distances of up to 100 yards. A weapon point of distinctively American design, found in Fort Rock Cave, Oregon, has been radiocarbon dated to 11,000 B.C.E. A site at Debert, in Nova Scotia, has yielded fluted points of a slightly different design, also dating to 8500 B.C.E.

Archeologists have found evidence that by 9000 B.C.E. different cultures were evolving. The Cascade (or Old Cordilleran) style of point, for example, was being used in the Pacific Northwest. Its design differed slightly from the Folsom points used in other areas. Similarly, a distinct culture was evolving at this time in some areas of the Great Basin in Arizona and Utah; today, these peoples usually are called the desert cultures. Even at 5000 to 10,000 B.C.E., the use of a single timeline seems to obscure the differing ways in which cultures developed, but it can be a useful tool given the scarcity of other evidence. Even 5,000 to 7,000 years ago, examples of very distinct cultures arise, such as the copper culture of present-day Wisconsin, in which people forged lance points and other articles from the copper that is common in the region. This was one of the earliest metal-working cultures in the world.

More recently than 5000 B.C.E., individual cultures are best treated on their own in most cases. Generally, a drier and warmer climate, as well as technological advances, allowed many Native cultures to move away from hunting as a sole means of survival. Native peoples began to forage and gather food. This eventually led to domestication of plants and animals, as well as other forms of sedentary agriculture and (in some cases) civilizations with large urban concentrations of population supported by forms of agriculture that present-day scholars are still rediscovering.

As older Native American settlements of greater complexity are found throughout the Americas, we may ask, as Thomas Jefferson did two centuries ago, how peoples assumed to have crossed the Bering Strait so recently could have diffused so rapidly, become so diverse, and (in some cases) built civilizations and spoken languages of such complexity over such a short time. All migrations have causes; there seems to have been no singular reason that propelled great numbers of people across the Bering Strait during one short period and no other. "Migration" may be a misleading term because many of the people who crossed the Bering Strait probably were not consciously moving from one continent to another but were following the animals that gave them sustenance, seeking new land, moving a few miles at a time.

WRITTEN LANGUAGES IN PREHISTORIC AMERICA

A century and a half ago, when American anthropology was born, many academics commonly delineated races as "civilized," "barbarian," and "savage," a system developed by Lewis Henry Morgan, who is widely known as the father of the discipline in the United States. One of the main determinants of civilization was often said to be a culture's development (or lack) of written communication. Until early in this century, many "experts" assumed that America's indigenous peoples had only the slightest inkling of written communication, that their cultures were for the most part singularly oral. Considering such distinctions, many people forgot that in Europe, at the time of Columbus' first voyage, the invention of movable type was within living memory. The number of published books at the time was miniscule, and the practice of writing (and even reading) was isolated generally to people of high economic class and members of religious orders. Barely one in every twenty people in Europe was able to read in 1492. Fewer still had a competent command of written language. For the average person at that time, life and history were mainly oral in Europe.

During the past few decades, deeper study of many ancient cultures in the Americas has revealed that many of them did indeed communicate using written symbols, some of them even phonetic—a system, like the languages of Europe, in which the written symbols may stand for ideas or "words." Such discoveries bring into question the common nomenclature of the periods into which scholars have long divided Native history in the Americas. The word *prehistory* itself implies a lack of written communication, which comprises history in the European sense. Even today, some accounts equate prehistoric with "precontact [with Europe]." Although the indigenous cultures of America may have been prehistoric in the sense that Europeans could not decipher their languages, they did maintain historical records.

Olmec Writing

The earliest form of written communication in the New World may have been a language used by the Olmecs. Several years of research in the Mexican state of Vera Cruz has turned up a number of indications that the Olmecs operated an organized state-level political system that utilized written communication (O. Moore, 2002; M.E.D. Pohl, Pope, and Nagy, 2002, 1,984; Stokstad, 2002, 1,872).

Late in 2002, a team of archeologists led by Mary Pohl of Florida State University described two artifacts containing portions of script found in Olmec ruins that date to about 650 B.C.E., about 400 years earlier than any previously discovered Mayan writing. Fragments of stone plaques and a cylindrical seal bearing glyphs resembling later Mayan writing lend support to the idea that the Olmecs were a "mother culture" pre-dating the writing and calendar systems of both the Maya and the Aztecs (as well as cultures pre-dating the Aztecs in the Valley of Mexico). The cylindrical seal is thought to have been used to imprint clothing with symbols, and the stone plaques were used as a form of jewelry. Both of them may have indicated rank or authority within a hierarchical society.

Other finds included human and animal bones, food-serving vessels, and hollow figurines (O. Moore, 2002). The connection among Olmec writing, their calendar, and kingship is indicated in these communications, dating to 650 B.C.E., "which makes sense, since the Olmecs were the first known peoples in Mesoamerica to have a state-level political structure, and writing is a way to communicate power and influence," said Pohl (O. Moore, 2002).

The new Olmec discoveries depict a bird's beak spewing two diverging lines of symbols that are believed to depict a system of communication that is not purely iconographic, one that must be learned, a hallmark of true writing. Later inscriptions show similar symbols emerging from human mouths (Stokstad, 2002, 1,873). According to M.E.D. Pohl and colleagues, writing in *Science* (2002), the symbols "imply that Mesoamerican writing originated in the La Venta polity" of the Olmec culture near Tabasco, in southern Mexico (p. 1,984).

These discoveries led to speculation that three ancient languages (Mayan, Isthmian, and Oaxacan) could have shared a common origin in the script of the Olmecs. "It was generally accepted that Mayans were among the first Mesoamerican societies to use writing," said John Yellen, an archeologist and program manager for the National Science Foundation. "But this find indicates that the Olmecs' form of written communication led into what became forms of writing for several other cultures" (O. Moore, 2002). Pohl, who led the excavations at San Andres, near La Venta, has worked for years to analyze and fine-tune the estimated dates of the artifacts discovered in the initial dig. "We knew we had found something important," she said. "The motifs were glyph-like but we weren't sure at first what we had until they were viewed more closely" (O. Moore, 2002).

Wampum Belts as Written Language

Indigenous Americans sometimes communicated through pictorial signs and symbols that may be likened in some ways to the hieroglyphs of Egypt. The Iroquois fashioned pictographs into wampum belts that were used to jog memory for oral historians. Replicas of some of these story belts may be examined today, for example, at the Six Nations Indian Museum in Onchiota, New York. The wampum belts that Iroquois diplomats gave and received during meetings with colonial representatives in the seventeenth and eighteenth centuries are adapted on the same model. Like written contracts, they were evidence that certain actions had been taken at a given place and time (B. Mann, 1995, 40–48).

Wampum are strings or arrayed patterns made of seashells and have been used by many American Indians in the Northeast to preserve accounts of history, to conduct diplomacy, and to complete some commercial transactions. Nearly every important treaty negotiated in the eighteenth century was sealed with the presentation of wampum belts. The shells that comprised the belts were harvested and traded to inland peoples by Native American peoples who lived on the coast.

Peace among the formerly antagonistic Iroquois nations was procured and maintained through the Haudenosaunee's Great Law of Peace (*Kaianerekowa*), which was passed from generation to generation by use of wampum belts that outlined a complex system of checks and balances between nations and genders. A complete oral recitation of the Great Law can take several days. The wampum belts, complex designs of purple (or sometimes black) and white shells, were used to prompt the memory of a speaker.

According to the Iroquois Great Law, the blood feud was outlawed and replaced by the Condolence Ceremony. Under the new law, when a person killed someone, the grieving family could forego the option of exacting clan revenge (the taking of the life of the murderer or a member of the murderer's clan). Instead, the bereaved family could accept twenty strings of wampum from the slayer's family (ten for the dead person and ten for the life of the murderer himself). If a woman was killed, the price was thirty wampum strings because women bore life.

Although wampum was used principally in diplomacy, the settlement of disputes, and the recitation of history, it also was used sometimes as currency. In 1612, John Smith of Virginia visited the Susquehannocks in the northern regions of the Chesapeake Bay. He encountered the use of wampum and found hints of the existence of the Iroquois Confederacy. During the course of their meeting, the Susquehannocks implored Smith to defend them against the "Atquanahucke, Massawomecke and other people [that] inhabit the river of Cannida." The Susquehannocks draped "a chaine of white beads (waighing at least 6 or 7 pound) about" Smith's neck while reciting an "oration of love" (Johansen, 1997, 1,353).

The Cherokees used wampum in a ceremony meant to provide for the poor. During a special war dance, each warrior was called on to recount the taking of his first scalp. During the ceremony, anyone with something to spare, according to Henry Timberlake, "a string of wampum, piece of [silver] plate, wire, paint, lead" heaped the goods on a blanket or animal skin placed on the ground (Johansen, 1997, 1,353). Afterward, the collection was divided among the poor of the community, with a share reserved for the musicians who had provided entertainment during the ceremony.

Haudenosaunee (Iroquois) wampum strings. (Courtesy of John Kahionhes Fadden.)

Aztec and Mayan Picture-Writing

The Spanish warmed their hands over fires built from entire Mexica (Aztec) libraries during the early years of the conquest, little realizing what they were burning because Aztec writing did not resemble Spanish. One of the Aztec books that survived this holocaust relates its anguish:

> Broken spears lie in the roads;
> We have torn our hair in our grief
> The houses are roofless now, and their walls
> are red with blood...
> —Portilla, 1962, frontispiece

The Aztecs also used a form of pictograph writing that was conceptually similar in some ways to the Iroquois' "story belts." The historical record of Aztec culture was compiled in books and scrolls by priest-scribes. The result was writing that looked something like present-day cartoon strips. Some of these books folded into large screens stacked like an accordion, bound in animal skins. One of these, today called the *Codex Egerton*, recounts the lives of 26 generations of rulers, "symbolized by husbands and wives seated on thrones and passing mysterious presents to one another" (Morison, 1993, 54).

The development of knowledge related to indigenous writing is yet another indication that, after five centuries in the Americas, immigrants from Europe who followed Columbus are still "discovering America." In late 1991, for example, Marilyn M. Goldstein, a professor of art history at the C. W. Post campus of Long Island University in Brookville, New York, announced discovery of a ceramic Mayan vessel bearing rows of glyphs and scenes from mythological events that represented pages from a Mayan book created before the year 900 C.E., at the end of the period in Mayan history that scholars usually refer to as the late classic. This book dated 500 years earlier than similar, earlier finds. Professor Goldstein estimated that, based on the sophistication of these symbols, the Maya probably composed elementary books of this type as early as 300 to 600 C.E.; written symbols have been found on Mayan stone monuments and tombs dating to a century or two before the birth of Christ. The Mayan books could perhaps be compared to the written records kept by monks and others in Europe before the invention of movable type, when literacy was limited to a small fraction of the population. The Mayan vessel, called the Wright codex, was found in a United States private collection.

A Mayan piece, from a book in their language dated to the sixteenth century, idealizes the time before contact with Europeans as a disease-free paradise:

> There was then no sickness;
> They had then no aching bones;
> They had then no high fever;
> They had then no smallpox;
> They had then no burning chest . . .
> They had then no consumption . . .
> At that time the course of humanity was orderly,
> The foreigners made it otherwise when they arrived here.
> —Wright, 1992, 14

According to John S. Henderson (1981), the system of symbols that the Maya used for written communication was a

limited, special-purpose system . . . that directly represents not [only] units of meaning, but sounds of language. With these signs, they could write any message that could be spoken. With phonetic signs, the Maya carried the elaboration of graphic symbols to a degree unmatched in the Americas. [This was written before more recent discoveries about Inca writing, discussed below.] Maya hieroglyphic writing is just that—a true writing system, capable of expressing an unlimited range of information. (pp. 87–88)

Although Mayan civilization was generally well past its peak when the Spanish arrived, the Maya still possessed several thousand handwritten books that included collections of songs, volumes describing their sciences, biographies, genealogies, accounts of ritual, and other historical material. Spanish religious authorities, who were well aware of the spiritual significance that the Maya vested in these books, destroyed nearly all of them. Today, only four of these ancient volumes are known to have survived the Spanish pillage. In the time of the conquest, possession of native writing could put its holder in peril of his or her life if church authorities learned of them. Diego de Landa, a bishop of Yucatan during the sixteenth century, wrote: "We found a large number of books in these characters [hieroglyphs], and they contained nothing in which there were not to be seen superstition and lies of the devil[;] we burned them all, which they regretted to an amazing degree, and which caused them much affliction" (Tozzer, n.d., 169).

Beginning during the 1970s, scholars translated the Maya's writing for the first time, standing on its head a century or more of archaeological speculation about Mayan society. Until this writing was translated, many archaeologists had thought that the Maya were a relatively peaceful, rural people who lived in a benign theocracy governed by priest-kings. Today, we still know the Maya as people who built complex cities, studied astronomy, and were probably the first in the world to use negative numbers. We now know them also as very violent.

Demarest said that evidence from stone art and texts indicate that "the Maya were one of the most violent state-level societies in the New World, especially after 600 c.e." (Wilford, 1991, 7-L). Sometimes, losing rulers were decapitated with great ceremony. The Maya's writing depicts repeated raids by the elites of adjoining city-states, as well as ritual bloodletting and human sacrifice, all used to build the prestige of ruling families. Linda Schele, a Maya scholar at the University of Texas at Austin, said: "We don't know if early Maya went to war mainly to acquire territory, take booty, control conquered groups for labor, take captives for sacrifice . . . or a combination of these" (1991, 7).

The Maya's written records describe wars that began before 400 c.e. The first recorded Mayan war was fought in the jungles of what is now northern Guatemala in 378 c.e. A stone monument was later erected that gave the date of the conflict and the victorious general, Smoking-frog. Another monument observes that Great Jaguar-paw, the ruler of Tikal, the winning city-state, observed the victory "with a ceremony of bloodletting from his genitals" (Wilford, 1991, 7-L).

In 1990, a treasure trove of Mayan history was uncovered at Dos Pilas, a settlement begun in the seventh century, possibly by emigrants from Tikal, who seemed to have conquered several other Mayan city-states. At Dos Pilas, archaeologists have uncovered a large stairway lined with carved images of warfare, including the torture and execution of captives. The carvings are explained by Mayan writing describing a series of wars in which the army of Dos Pilas subdued the peoples of Tikal in 678 c.e.

During the next century, Dos Pilas grew further by conquest to a size of about two thousand square miles of rain forest, possibly (according to Arthur A. Demarest [1993, 95], an archaeologist at Vanderbilt University), the largest single Mayan kingdom. After its string of conquests, the recorded history indicates that Dos Pilas dissolved into a gaggle of feuding warrior-states. Continual warfare caused the Maya generally to abandon dispersed, undefended settlements that had allowed them to exploit the fragile rain forest ecosystem successfully. Some farmers devastated the forest, trying to produce more food, as others fled to the armed cities. The society's ability to support itself agriculturally declined as warfare intensified, ultimately destroying the civilization.

The written history of Mayan culture (which reached its peak between 200 and 900 C.E.) indicates that it may have declined because increasing militarization (including siege warfare) forced people into urban areas, interrupting agriculture that had fed the cities. Siege warfare also devastated countryside around the urban areas, stripping it of trees (which were used for firewood) and destroying crops. Once soils were laid bare, heavy tropical rains leached them of vital nutrients, further harming agriculture.

Because the Maya are finally telling history to us in their own words, said Demarest, "It's a very exciting time in Maya studies. It's a time for new editions of all the textbooks" (Wilford, 1991, 7-L). According to David Freidel, an archaeologist at Southern Methodist University (Dallas, TX), "No Egyptian tomb's discovery was ever more exhilarating than the decipherment process underway today" (Wilford, 1991, 7-L).

For more on Mayan civilization, including their writing system, see chapter 2.

The Incas' Writing System

Discoveries regarding the writing of the Incas have paralleled those about the Maya. By the 1980s, after more than thirty years of examining ancient Inca textiles, British-born William Burns was piecing together a phonetic writing system that was used in the Andes long before the Spanish conquest. In his book, *Ancient Peru*, Federico Kauffmann Doig wrote that Burns had made "the most revolutionary contribution to the study of the writings of ancient Peru. Given the evidence in [Burns'] work, we should change the idea that ancient Peru did not have an authentic writing system, meaning one with phonetic symbols" (*La Republica*, 1991, 50).

Working as a textile engineer for a Peruvian company, Burns's examination of about four hundred rectangular patterns (called *tocapus*) on Inca textiles convinced him that he was actually dealing with a written language, not random designs. Burns also studied strings of knots in variously colored cords (called *quipus*) that had been previously acknowledged as a system for counting. According to Burns, the Inca *quipus* also utilized the elements of a language that seemed to have been used with some degree of secrecy to describe historical events. Burns also found such a system referenced in the writings of chroniclers who accompanied the Spanish conquistadors. He noted that the Simi Runes (or *Kicwa*, as the Spanish called them), the earliest works describing Peru's aboriginal languages, contained dictionaries with words in them such as *quillcanigui* (to write), *quellca* (paper, letter, or writing) and *quellcascacuna* (the letters). This writing system, which utilized ten consonants and no vowels, could have been used to construct more than 3 million words.

The discovery of phonetic writing among the Incas, together with other work, indicates that human society in the Andes was probably as complex as Egypt's during the time of the Great Pyramids. Ruins have been found of a warehouse believed to be between 3,500 and 3,800 years old that probably contained food stores for very large urban settlements. The building itself was more than 100 yards long and as tall as a present-day three-story building and is divided into dozens of individual compartments. The age of this building places it roughly at the time the Great Pyramids were constructed. In other words, evidence is accumulating that New World civilizations evolved on a timescale rather similar to those of Europe and Asia. In the Andes, archaeologists have been finding evidence of stepped pyramids and very large, U-shaped temples more than ten stories high.

A New York *Times* report described discovery of "bright, multi-colored friezes with jaguar and spider motifs and broad plazas flanked by residential areas" (Stevens, 1989, C-1). Many of the sites have been well preserved by the arid climate of the area, so that "adobe friezes and sculptures that might have been destroyed in another climate are preserved almost intact, with their vivid reds, blues and blacks still showing. Seeds, pollen and animal skeletons are not fossils, but real" (ibid., C-1). Some of these sites dated to 5,000 years ago, at least a thousand years earlier than ruins in Central America, which previously had been thought to be the oldest in the hemisphere. The earliest sites seem to have had economies tied to the sea. Later, for unknown reasons, the settlements moved upward in elevation along more than fifty river valleys along the coast of Peru and sustained themselves on irrigated agriculture that flourished despite the arid, harsh highland climate, providing the basis for the later Incan civilization.

The following elegy was written in Quechua (the Incan language) near the present-day site of Quito, Ecuador, during the conquest. It was titled "Atawallpa Wanuy," meaning "The Death of Atawallpa," the Father Inca to whom the poem refers, at the hands of invading Spanish conquistadors.

> Like a cloud, the wiraqochas,
> the white men,
> Demanding gold,
> Invaded us.
> After seizing
> Our Father Inca;
> After deceiving him,
> They put him to death.
> He with the heart of a puma
> The adroitness of a fox,
> They killed
> As if he were a llama.
> Hail is falling,
> Lightning strikes,
> The sun is sinking;
> It is becoming night.
> And in their terror,

> The elders
> And the people
> Have buried themselves alive.
> —Lara, n.d., 193–194

CAHOKIA: AN ANCIENT TRADING CENTER

Archaeology has been, piece by piece, providing us with a picture of human ingenuity in the Americas. Witness, for example, the development of a major trading center that was home to about 30,000 people at the confluence of the Mississippi and Missouri Rivers roughly at the same time that London, England, housed a similar population. Other urban centers in Mesoamerica (see chapter 2) ranked among the largest cities of the world many centuries before sustained contact with Europeans.

Only a few miles from present-day St. Louis, Missouri, one may find the ruins of a ten-story ceremonial mound that covered fifteen acres, two acres more space than the base of Egypt's Great Pyramid. Archaeological inference has it that an ancient ruler called the Great Sun stood on top of that mound and chanted ritually as the sun rose over Cahokia, a six-square-mile city containing 120 mounds, as well as dwellings and places of business. This temple is believed to have been the center of a city that served a trade network reaching from the present-day Dakotas to the Gulf of Mexico, roughly the European distance between Paris and Moscow.

Cahokia was the largest of several population centers that developed in the Mississippi Valley (archaeologists call them the Mississippian culture) around the year 1000, possibly influenced by the civilizations of Mesoamerica through the travels of the *pochtecas*, wide-ranging Mesoamerican traders. The temple mounds of the Mississippians resembled the constructs of the civilizations to the south, as did their social structure, remnants of which survived into the period of European contact among the Natchez.

Cahokia and other ceremonial centers usually were situated at the center of a larger cluster of villages, housing from one hundred to nearly one thousand people each in orderly rows of thatched-roof houses. The people of this hinterland intensively farmed corn and tobacco, as well as several varieties of squash and beans. They also hunted, fished, and gathered other foodstuffs. Doubtless, at least some of the food raised and gathered in these rural hinterlands was taxed for consumption by the elites inside the ceremonial centers.

European immigrants long thought that Natives of America could not have constructed such a city. They attributed the ruins to the lost tribes of Israel, the Phoenicians, the Vikings, or any number of European peoples. This theory held that these obviously enlightened Old World immigrants had been slaughtered by the indolent savages (who must have been very patient as the immigrants somehow constructed a large urban area). The theory finely suited immigrants from Europe, who had convinced themselves that they were putting to good use a continent that the Native peoples were presumed to have left idle.

Native American intelligence built Cahokia, which functioned somewhat as the Aztecs' Tenochtitlan but probably without as a heavy military and political hand on surrounding peoples. The inhabitants of Cahokia also understood basic geometry and astronomy because here (and at other ruins in the eastern United States) the sun lines up with human constructions at the two equinoxes as it does at England's Stonehenge. The city appears to have declined not by conquest but from environmental exhaustion. The people of Cahokia learned that farming a single crop (in this case, corn) on the same land year after year depletes the soil. They also harvested trees for cooking fires and warmth much faster than nature could replace them, altering the topography of their land, the same fate that befell some Mayan urban areas (Weatherford, 1991, 14).

NATIVE AMERICAN AGRICULTURE

Although popular imagination sometimes stereotypes them solely as nomadic hunters, many, if not most, of North America's Native American peoples practiced agriculture, the domestication of plants for human consumption. At least half of the earth's staple vegetable foods, the most important being corn and potatoes, were first cultivated by indigenous peoples in the lands Europeans came to call America; these indigenous people often drew their sustenance from hunting, gathering, *and* agriculture. Agriculture was an established way of life for many Native peoples in North America. At first sight, many immigrating Europeans did not recognize Native American agriculture because it did not resemble their own. Indians did not domesticate draft animals and only rarely plowed their fields. Sometimes, crops were grown in small clearings amid a forest.

Native Americans first cultivated many of the foods taken for granted as everyday nourishment today. The main ingredients of Crackerjacks (peanuts and popcorn), for example, are both indigenous to the Americas, as are all edible beans except horse beans and soybeans, all squashes (including pumpkins), Jerusalem artichokes, the "Irish" potato, the sweet potato, sunflowers, peppers, pineapples, watermelons, cassava, bananas, strawberries, raspberries, gooseberries, and pecans.

Corn was first domesticated in the highlands of Mexico about 7,000 years ago from a wild grass called *teosinte*. The first corn cobs were the size of a human thumbnail. As the use of maize (Indian corn) spread north and south from Mexico, Native peoples domesticated hundreds of varieties and bred them selectively so that the edible kernels grew in size and number.

Corn, the major food source for several agricultural peoples across the continent, enjoyed a special spiritual significance. Often, corn and beans (which grow well together because the beans, a legume, fix nitrogen in their roots) were said to maintain a spiritual union. Some peoples, such as the U'ma'has (Omahas) of the eastern Great Plains, "sang up" their corn through special rituals.

In addition to "singing up the corn," the Pueblos cleaned their storage bins before the harvest so the corn would be happy when they brought it in. The

Pawnees grew ten varieties of corn, including one (called "holy" or "wonderful" corn) that was used only for religious purposes and never eaten. The Mandans had a Corn Priest who officiated at rites during the growing season. Each stage of the corn's growth was associated with particular songs and rituals, and spiritual attention was said to be as important to the corn as proper water, sun, and fertilizer. Among the Zuni, a newborn child was given an ear of corn at birth and endowed with a "corn name." An ear of maize was put in the place of death as the "heart of the deceased" and later used as seed corn to begin the cycle of life anew. To Navajos, corn was as sacred as human life.

Corn is intertwined with the origin stories of many Native American peoples. The Pueblos say that corn was brought to them by Blue Corn Woman and White Corn Maiden, who emerged to the surface of the earth from a great underground kiva, a sacred place. At birth, each infant is given the seed from an ear of corn as a fetish to carry for life as a reminder that the Corn Mothers brought life to the Pueblos. The corn fetish has a practical side as well: Should a harvest completely fail for drought or other reasons, the fetishes may become the seed corn for the next crop.

When colonists arrived in eastern North America, many of the Native American peoples they met farmed corn in large tracts. John Winthrop, governor of the Massachusetts Bay Colony, admired abandoned native cornfields and declared that God had provided the epidemics that killed the people who had tended them as an act of divine providence, clearing the land for the Puritans. Native Americans taught the Puritans which seeds would grow in their territories. Most of the seeds that the Puritans had brought from England did not sprout when planted in the area that the colonists called New England.

Native American agriculture has influenced eating habits around the world so completely that many people forget their culinary origins. Before the voyages of Columbus, Italian food that depends on tomato-based sauces was unknown. The Irish prepared their food without potatoes. Europeans satisfied a sweet tooth without chocolate. Corn was unknown outside the Americas. These crops were produced by experimentation of many Native American cultures over thousands of years. Knowledge of plant life was passed along from generation to generation with other social knowledge, usually by the elder women of a native tribe or nation.

The production of food is woven into Native American spiritual life. Among the Iroquois and many other Native peoples, for example, festivals point to the role of the "Three Sisters" (Corn, Squash, and Beans). The food complex of corn, beans, and squash was transferred northward from Mexico as a set of rituals before it became the basis of an agricultural system. By practicing the rituals, Native Americans in the corn-growing areas of North America became farmers. Corn requires a 160-day, frost-free growing season; the northern limit of corn cultivation also often marks the limit of intensive Native agriculture.

Agriculture among Native American peoples enabled higher population densities than hunting and gathering. According to William Cronon, Native peoples in Maine who did not use widespread agriculture sustained an average density of about 40 people per hundred square miles, and indigenous peoples in southern New England, who raised crops (corn being their major staple), averaged 287 people (seven times as many) on the same amount of land (Cronon, 1983, 42).

Native American agriculture often seemed disorderly to European eyes accustomed to large monocultural fields comprising one crop. Native American fields showed evidence of thought and practice, however. Samuel de Champlain described how Natives planted corn on small hills mixed with beans of several types. "When they grow up, they interlace with the corn, which reaches to the height of five to six feet; and they keep the ground free from weeds," Champlain wrote (Cronon, 1983, 43). John Winthrop, describing Indian fields in Massachusetts within a generation of the Pilgrims' arrival, said that their agriculture "load[ed] the ground with as much as it will beare" (Cronon, 1983, 44). Indian farming methods (usually the responsibility of women, except when growing tobacco) not only kept weeds at a minimum, but also preserved soil moisture.

Many Native peoples offer their thanks to the plants as well as the animals that they consume out of a belief that the essence of life that animates human beings also is present in the entire world, even in the rocks under one's feet. Long before a science of "sustained yield" forestry evolved, Native American peoples along the northwest coast harvested trees in ways that would ensure their continued growth, associating such practices with a belief that trees are sentient beings. Some Native Americans charted farming cycles through complicated relationships with the sun and moon. In addition to domesticating dozens of food plants, they also harvested the wild bounty of the forests for hundreds of herbs and other plants used to restore and maintain health.

Although the Maya are known for their temples in such places as Tikal, Copan, and Palenque, most Maya were commoners (who supported a small elite that maintained the temples) and spent most of their working lives cultivating food, principally corn. Most of the Maya's ceremonial centers were surrounded by earthworks. These artificial ramparts were not discovered by modern archaeologists until they started using satellite images of the land because today the earthworks often are submerged in jungle and thus are very difficult to locate from ground level. The earthworks included complex irrigation channels and raised fields, often hewn from reclaimed swampland. The Maya dredged nutrient-rich soil from the bottoms of the irrigation ditches to fertilize fields that they raised above the flood level of the rainy season. The fields were so rich that they produced several crops a year to feed the people of the urban ceremonial centers.

The discovery of complex agricultural earthworks among the Maya caused scholars to question earlier assumptions that the Maya had practiced slash-and-burn agriculture, which was said to have deforested the land, exhausted and eroded the topsoil, and played a role in the collapse of the "classic" age of the Maya. Today, the collapse of the Maya is usually ascribed not to deforestation caused by agriculture but to ecological damage and social disorganization caused by dense populations and escalating warfare between city-states. Not all of the Maya's earthworks were constructed to aid agriculture. Some ramparts were defensive, and as war became more common and deadly, the Maya's complex agricultural system suffered immensely.

About the same time that Mayan civilization collapsed, the ancestors of today's Pueblos were building a corn-based culture in the Chaco Canyon of present-day New Mexico. The Pueblos of the Rio Grande are cultural and economic inheritors of the Mogollon, Anasazi, and Hohokam communities to the west and southwest of the upper Rio Grande valley. Cultivation of corn was introduced into the area about 3000 B.C.E. About 2000 B.C.E., beans and squash were added. Cotton later became another staple crop.

About 2,000 years ago, irrigation was introduced to supplement dry farming in the same area. The Pueblos used brief, heavy precipitation to advantage by constructing some of their irrigation works at the bases of steep cliffs and collected runoff. The residents of this area constructed roads that often ran for hundreds of miles so that they could share food surpluses. If one pueblo had a bad harvest, others, using the roads, would share what they had. The cultivation of corn in Chaco Canyon supported a civilization that constructed the largest multifamily dwellings in North America before twentieth century high-rise apartments. Such a high degree of agricultural organization supported a culture that dominated the turquoise trade in the area. Turquoise was important as a "liquid asset," a medium of trade. Pueblo centers, such as Pueblo Bonito, became centers of trade, manufacturing, and ceremony.

The vital role of water and irrigation in Pueblo agriculture is illustrated by the fact that the great classic Pueblo civilizations were destroyed by a drought so severe that not even ingenious water management could cope with it. In the thirteenth century C.E., most Pueblo settlements outside the Rio Grande valley had been abandoned after fifty years of nearly rainless drought that destroyed their agricultural base.

Following the Spanish colonization of New Mexico, access to water became a crucial cause of conflict. Land without water is worthless in the arid Southwest. Paradoxically, the Pueblos in 1680 used the waters of the Rio Grande River to defeat the Spanish; they staged their revolt while the river was flooding to keep Spanish reinforcements out.

Irrigation of farmland was *the* key factor in Pueblo agricultural land use. To plan, construct, and maintain elaborate land systems, cooperation between several villages was crucial. Irrigation systems needed routine maintenance that rendered clans inefficient, so nonkinship associations were created to cope with such work. This organizational framework had other community functions, and it revolved primarily around the spiritual life of the Pueblos. The basic rationale for the nonkinship associations was irrigation, however.

Some Native peoples used fire to raze fields for farming and to drive game while hunting. These were not fires left to blaze out of control, however; Navajos who used

Hopi dwelling. (Courtesy of the Nebraska State Historical Society
Photograph Collections.)

range fires customarily detailed half of their hunting party to contain and control
the flames and to keep the blaze on the surface, where the flames would clear old
brush so that new plant life could generate instead of destroying the forest canopy.
When Europeans first laid eyes on North America, it was much more densely
forested than today. In some places, the parklike topography of many eastern forests
was a result of Native American peoples' efforts to manage plant and animal life.

NATIVE AMERICAN FAMILY LIFE

European American immigrants to North America sometimes were con-
founded by ways in which Native American family life differed from their
own. For one thing, women often were (as they continue to be) influential in
family life as well as the political and economic lives of many Native American
peoples. Gender relations that some Europeans thought to be deviant (such as
the *berdache* or homosexual) were accepted in some Native cultures. Many
Native Americans formed and broke marital bonds more quickly and easily
than most European Americans as well. Bonds other than marriage also were
highly significant for many Native Americans. Clan relationships were often

so strong that (even today) relatives that Anglo-Americans call cousins are regarded as brothers and sisters.

Following are capsule descriptions of a few specific Native American family structures and customs. For the most part, practices noted by historical observers are still evident today, along with modifications compelled by association with European American cultures.

The Iroquois

The Iroquois Confederacy is fundamentally a kinship state. The Iroquois are bound together by a clan and chieftain system that is supported by a similar linguistic base. Through the *hearth*, which consists of a mother and her children, women play a profound role in Iroquois political life. Each hearth is part of a wider group called an *otiianer*, and two or more *otiianer* constitute a clan. The word *otiianer* refers to the female heirs to the chieftainship titles of the League, the fifty authorized names for the chiefs of the Iroquois, passed through the female side of the *otiianer*. The *otiianer* women select one of the males within their group to fill a vacated seat in the League.

Such a matrilineal system was headed by a clan mother. All the sons and daughters of a particular clan are related through uterine families. In this system, a husband lives with his wife's family, and their children become members of the mother's clan by right of birth. Through matrilineal descent, the Iroquois form cohesive political groups that have little to do with where people live or from which village the hearths originate.

The oldest daughter of the head of a clan sometimes, on the judgment of the clan, succeeds her mother at the mother's death. All authority springs from the people of the various clans that make up a nation. The women who head these clans appoint the male delegates and deputies who speak for the clans at tribal meetings. After consultation within the clan, issues and questions are formulated and subsequently debated in council.

The Iroquois are linked to each other by their clan system, in which each person has family relations with every other nation of the federation. If a Mohawk of the Turtle Clan had to travel, he or she would be cared for by Turtles in each other nation: the Oneidas, the Onondagas, the Cayugas, and the Senecas.

Iroquois political philosophy is rooted in the concept that all life is unified spiritually with the natural environment and other forces surrounding people. The Iroquois believe that the spiritual power of one person is limited but may be enhanced when combined with other individuals in a hearth, *otiianer*, or clan. Whenever a person dies, by either natural causes or force, through murder or war, this power is diminished. To maintain the strength of the group, families in the past often replaced the dead by adopting captives of war. This practice of keeping clans at full strength through natural increase or adoption ensured the power and durability of the matrilineal system as well as the kinship state.

Childrearing is an important way to instill political philosophy in the youth of the Iroquois. The ideal Iroquois personality demonstrates not only loyalty to the group, but also independence and autonomy. Iroquois people were trained to enter a society in which power is shared between male and female, young and old, more so than in European American society. European society emphasizes dominance and command structures; Iroquois society is more interested in collaborative behavior.

The Wyandots (Hurons)

Native Americans living near the eastern edge of Lake Huron in present-day Ontario called themselves Wyandots. The French called them Hurons, a French reference to the bristles on a boar's head, probably because the first Wyandots they met wore their hair in a style that today is called a Mohawk.

As with the Iroquois, the Wyandot clans—Porcupine, Snake, Deer, Beaver, Hawk, Turtle, Bear, and Wolf—create familial affinity across the boundaries of the four confederated Wyandot nations. Members of each clan can trace their ancestry to a common origin through the female line. In each village, clan members elect a civil chief and a war chief. The titles are carried through the female family line but are bestowed on men, a practice again resembling that of the Iroquois. Although the titles are hereditary in that sense, they do not pass from head to head of a particular family as in most European monarchies.

As among the Iroquois, economic roles among the Wyandots are determined by gender. Women usually tend gardens, gather plants from the forests, and manage the home. Men participate in agriculture mainly by clearing fields for women to work and contribute to subsistence by hunting. Men are the main visible participants in trade and diplomacy, but women contribute trade goods and political advice, usually behind the scenes.

The Apaches

Traditional Apache society is centered around groups of two to six matri-local extended families, called *gotas*. Members of the *gota* live together, and members of the different households cooperate in the pursuit of game and raising of crops. A *gota* is usually led by a headman, who assumes his status over several years by general consensus of the extended families in the *gota*. The headman in some cases inherits the title of "true chief." He will not retain the position, however, unless he displays leadership. If no qualified headmen are raised through inheritance, a consensus may form in favor of another leader, who will be informally "elected" by members of the *gota*. Headmen are invariably male, but women exercise influence as political advisers. Their society and kinship lineages maintain the Apaches' matrilineal society.

A headman may wield considerable influence, but only if the people in the extended families are willing to follow his advice, which includes detailed lectures on how to hunt, the techniques of agriculture, and who should work with whom. He also coordinates labor for hunting and foraging, advises parties engaged in disputes, and offers advice regarding who should marry whom. At times, the wife of a chief may become, in effect, a subchief. As a chief ages, he is charged not only with maintaining exemplary behavior, but also with identifying young men who may become leaders in the future. He is expected to tutor younger men in the responsibilities of leadership. A chief is also charged with aiding the poor, often by coordinating distribution of donations from more affluent members of the *gota*. If two or more *gotas* engage in conflict, their headmen are charged with resolving the dispute.

Each traditional Apache is a member not only of a *gota*, but also of one of sixty-two matrilineal clans that overlap individual settlements. Members of one's clan (and, in some cases, others identified as being close to it) help each other in survival tasks and usually do not intermarry. Such a system resembles that of many peoples in the eastern woodlands (e.g., Cherokees, Wyandots, and Iroquois).

The Crees

Before challenges from the outside forced them to convene a central council, the Crees, who live in present-day Quebec, had no unified political organization as among the Iroquois and Wyandots (Hurons) to the south. Even the individual bands or hunting parties had little or no organized political structure. Such a lack of structure is sometimes called *atomistic* by scholars; it is the closest that actual Native governance comes to the stereotype of the "noble savage." Instead of a formal council, Cree bands, which were groups of families, informally select a wise elderly man, usually the head of a family, as a source of advice. He exercises informal, limited influence. As with the sachems of the more organized farming and hunting peoples to the south, these informal leaders usually do not relish the exercise of power, probably because most of the people who seek their advice resent any attempt to dictate.

Cree life is marked only rarely by multifamily celebrations or rituals. Social life and social control are usually a function of the extended family. Outside the family, a Cree might appear ambivalent or reticent, usually out of respect for others' autonomy. People who transgress social norms of interpersonal behavior became targets of gossip or sorcery of a type that was used widely across the continent. Although their society is family based, the Crees recognize no clan or other kinship system between different bands. The society thus does not have the interconnections between settlements similar to those offered by the clans of the Iroquois, Wyandots, Cherokees, and others.

Northwest Coast Peoples

Native Americans who live along the northwest coast of North America also do not maintain the strong clan systems that characterize many other Native

American societies. Instead, they have a very class-conscious social system in which family economic status means a great deal.

Northwest coast peoples from the Alaska panhandle to northern California traditionally recognize three social classes that seem as imperishable as the red cedar from which they constructed their lodges: nobility, commoners, and slaves. The nobility includes chiefs and their closest relatives; the eldest son is the family head. He, his family, and a few associates live in the rear right-hand corner of the family longhouse, with people of lower status on each side. These people are said to be "under the arm" of the chief. The next-highest-ranking chief, usually a younger brother of the head chief, invariably occupies the rear left-hand corner of the house with his family. He, too, has a number of people under the arm. The other two corners are traditionally occupied by lesser chiefs' families.

NORSE EXPLORATION OF NORTH AMERICA

Before Columbus's voyages on both sides of the Atlantic, sporadic contacts left a residue of myth transmitted from generation to generation in oral histories. American Indians from Nova Scotia to Mexico told their children about pale-skinned, bearded strangers who had arrived from the direction of the rising sun. Such myths played a large part in Cortes's conquest of the Aztecs, who were expecting the return of men who looked like him. The natives of Haiti told Columbus they expected the return of white men; some Mayan chants speak of visits by bearded strangers. The Lenape (Delaware) told Morovian missionaries that they had long awaited the return of divine visitors from the East. These premonitions, among others, suggest that the peoples of the Old and New Worlds communicated with each other on a sporadic basis centuries before Columbus.

In the realm of what critic Stephen Williams calls "fantastic archaeology" (Williams, 1991), theories establishing European origins for Native American peoples have long historiographic pedigrees. Evidence that meets the strictest standards of professional archaeology is scant in support of any of them.

One exception is the pre-Columbian landfall of the Vikings. Norse sagas (oral histories) and scattered archaeological evidence indicate that, beginning about 1000 C.E., Viking explorers who had earlier settled Iceland and Greenland conducted several expeditions along the East Coast of North America. At three locations—Newfoundland as well as possibly Cape Cod and the James River of Virginia—some evidence exists of small-scale, short-lived Viking settlement. According to the sagas, one Viking (the word is from the Norwegian *viks*, for fjord dweller), Thorfinn Karlsefni, explored 3,000 miles of North American coast in the early eleventh century.

The technical capability of the Vikings to reach North America is not in doubt. They were capable seafarers and built sturdy longships capable of easily reaching Iceland from Norway, a distance much greater than the voyage from Greenland to North America. In 1893, Magnus Andersen, a Norwegian, sailed a reconstructed Viking ship from Norway to Newfoundland.

Vikings may have followed the St. Lawrence River and Great Lakes as far inland as the vicinity of Kensington, Minnesota, where in 1898 a large stone was found inscribed with Norse runic writing that described the ambush and killing of ten men. The runes have been tested as weathered (as would be expected) but authentic. The Norse may have been looking for new sources of furs after the German Hanseatic League captured their trade in Russian furs during 1360 (Kehoe, 2002, 217).

Indisputable proof of Viking landings in North America have been found on the northern tip of Newfoundland. These discoveries began with the explorations of Helge Ingstad, at L'Anse aux Meadows, about 1960. The site has since been excavated and part of it turned into a public park. The evidence there is conclusive—right down to such things as a soapstone spindle whorl, nails, and even the remains of an iron smelter, along with hundreds of other artifacts, many of which have been carbon-14 dated to about 1000 C.E. Most other supposed Viking visits to North America (one in the unlikely venue of Tuscon, Arizona) still reside in the realm of archaeological speculation. According to Frederick Pohl (1972), a science fiction novelist who also has written three books on Norse exploration of North America, eighty-nine locations of Norse landfall have been asserted in North America. Some of these locations are as far apart as present-day Minnesota and New Orleans, Louisiana.

Piecing together evidence found in the Viking sagas, it is likely that about 985 C.E. the Viking sailor Bjarni Herjulfsson sighted land (probably Cape Cod) after several navigational errors led him astray on a voyage to Greenland. He finally reached his destination by sailing northeastward along the North American coast. In Greenland, his story of three land sightings to the southwest excited the imagination of Leif Erickson, who interviewed Bjarni and purchased his ship.

According to the Norse sagas that were told (which have been written and translated into English) after his voyages, Erickson made landfall at three places. He called the first "Helluland," probably Baffin Island; the second was "Markland," possibly Labrador or Newfoundland. The third landing, where Erickson established a small winter settlement, may have been on Cape Cod, near Follins Pond. The sagas tell of their ship being beached and stored, a house being built, and salmon caught that were larger than any the Vikings had ever seen. Although the Viking settlement in Newfoundland lasted several years and left behind many artifacts, the visit to Cape Cod seems to have been more of a temporary stop, leaving little evidence that survived ensuing centuries.

Thorvald Erickson, a brother of Leif, set out on his own voyage of discovery shortly afterward, in 1007 C.E. His plan was to explore the coast north and south from Cape Cod. Along the way, Thorvald's thirty-man crew seized and killed eight American Indians (they called them *Skraelings*, meaning "screamers," after their war-whoops). Thorvald later was killed in revenge for those murders. His crew sailed back to Greenland without him.

A few years later, in 1010 C.E., Thorfinn Karlsefni sailed from Iceland to Leif's settlement on Cape Cod, after which he probably explored the Atlantic Coast southward to the James River of present-day Virginia. The trip took four summers. The first winter was spent along the Hudson River of New York State, where the Vikings were surprised by the depth of snowfall for a place so far south. The second winter was spent along the James River of Virginia. The sagas tell of a voyage up the river to the rapids, far enough upstream to have seen the peaks of the Blue Ridge Mountains. At one point, according to the sagas, Karlsefni's crew was attacked by Native Americans, who used a large hornet's nest as a weapon. In all, the Karlsefni expedition probably logged about 3,000 miles along the coast and adjoining rivers.

Leif Erickson died about 1025 C.E., and his Labrador settlement withered, but not before Karlsefni and Gudrid, his wife, had given birth to a son they called Snorri, the first child believed to have been born in America of European parents. After that, voyages continued from time to time through the thirteenth and fourteenth centuries. King Magnus of Norway and Sweden authorized the Paul Knutson expedition, which sailed in 1355 to explore conditions in Greenland and Vinland. Knowledge of North America was apparently still being recalled in Iceland during 1477, when a young Italian sailor, Cristoforo Colombo, visited and became excited by sailors' gossip of land to the south and west of Greenland.

THE PERILS OF MILKING BUFFALO

Attempts to reconcile new information with old theories can have comical effects in academia. To provide one small but poignant example, a debate arose some years ago among archaeologists regarding the origins of tuberculosis in America. Excavations of Native bones indicated that an epidemic of the disease had begun on Canada's East Coast about the year 1000. Evidence indicated that the disease had spread rapidly down the St. Lawrence Valley, then overland as far as the present-day states of North and South Dakota.

One way to explain this outbreak would have been to acknowledge that Leif Erickson and other Vikings had introduced it. For archaeologists who were not prepared to acknowledge European contact before Columbus, another explanation had to be found. One alternative that was debated for a time had it that Native people had caught a mutated form of tuberculosis from buffalo. How had the buffalo passed the disease? One faction maintained that the Native people had caught it by milking the buffalo. This faction now had to explain why there is no reference in Native oral histories to the use of buffalo milk. Even the notion of "milking" a wild animal seemed a little silly to anyone who had ever contemplated it (Grinde, 1991, 36).

DISPUTES REGARDING NATIVE POPULATION DENSITY

As with theories of Native American origins, questions regarding the number of peoples who lived in the Americas prior to sustained contact with Europeans provoked a lively debate during the last third of the twentieth century. This debate involves two very different ways of looking at historical and archaeological evidence. One side in the population debate restricts itself to strict interpretation of the evidence at hand. Another point of view accepts the probability that observers (usually of European ancestry) recorded and gathered evidence from only a fraction of phenomena that actually occurred in the Americas.

The fact that disease was a major cause of Native depopulation is not at issue; both sides in this debate agree on the importance of disease. Disease ravaged Native Americans to such a degree that many early European immigrants (who at the time had no understanding of how pathogens spread disease) thought they had come to a land that had been emptied for them by their God. The debate is over the *number* of native people who died. There also seems to be little disagreement on indications that the plagues loosed on the Americas by contact with the Old World have not ended, even today. For example, between 1988 and 1990, 15 percent of the Yanomami of Brazil, who had only limited contact with people of European descent until this time, died of malaria, influenza, and even the common cold (Wright, 1992, 14).

Henry F. Dobyns has estimated that about 16 million Native Americans lived in North America north of Mesoamerica, the area populated by the Aztecs and other Central American Native nations, at the time of Columbus's first voyage (1983, 42). Because population densities were much greater in Central America and along the Andes, an estimate of 16 million north of Mesoamerica indicates to Dobyns that 90 to 112 million native people lived in the Americas before the year 1500, making some parts of the New World as densely populated at the time as many areas of Europe and Asia.

Smallpox created such chaos in the Incan empire that Francisco Pizzaro was able to seize an empire as large and populous as Spain and Italy combined with a force of only 168 men (C. C. Mann, 2002, 43). By the time imported diseases were done with Native Americans, according to Dobyns, 95 percent of them had died, the worst demographic collapse in recorded human history (ibid., 43). All across America, "Languages, prayers, hopes, habits, and dreams, entire ways of life hissed away like steam" (ibid., 46).

One of the deadliest vectors of disease was pigs brought across the ocean by explorers such as Hernando de Soto to provide members of their expeditions with food on the hoof. The pigs multiplied rapidly and spread European diseases to deer, turkeys, and eventually Native human beings as well. De Soto recorded having seen many well-populated villages; explorers a century later found forests largely bereft of people. According to Charles C. Mann, writing in the *Atlantic Monthly* (2002), "The Coosa city-states, in Western Georgia, and the Caddoan-speaking civilization centered on the Texas-Arkansas border, disintegrated soon after de Soto appeared.... The Caddoan population fell from about 200,000 to about 8,500, a drop of 96 per cent. In the eighteenth century the tally shrank further, to 1,400" (p. 45).

Dobyns's population estimates have risen over time from his initial estimate of 12.5 million in North America north of the Rio Grande (1966, 395). Scholars other than Dobyns agree with his hemispheric estimate of about 100 million (Borah, 1976; Cook and Simpson, 1948). In the meantime, the Smithsonian Institution, under pressure from rising population estimates elsewhere, raised its own estimate of aboriginal population, doubling the population north of the Rio Grande to 2 million from half that number.

Dobyns's estimate of indigenous population at contact represents a radical departure from many earlier estimates, which depended for the most part on actual historical and archaeological evidence of the dead, assuming that Euro-American scholars (and others, such as missionaries) were capable of counting native people who had in some cases been dead for several centuries. Although anthropologists usually date the first attempt at measuring Native populations to Henry Schoolcraft (during the 1850s), Jefferson's *Notes on the State of Virginia* (published in several editions during the 1780s) contained an extensive (if fragmentary) Native American "census." Jefferson did not attempt to count the number of Native people inhabiting all of North America during his time—no one then even knew how large the continent might be, not to mention the number of people inhabiting it. Jefferson prudently settled for estimates of the Native nations bordering the early United States.

The first "systematic" count was compiled during the early twentieth century by James Mooney, who estimated that 1,153,000 people had lived in the land area now occupied by the United States when Columbus made landfall. Mooney calculated the 1907 Native population in the same area at 406,000. Dividing the country into regions, he calculated the percentage of population loss between 1492 and 1900 at between 61 percent (in the North Atlantic states) and 93 percent in California (Mooney, 1910, and Mooney, 1928).

Subsequent to the work of Mooney, the most widely followed population estimates were provided beginning in 1939 by A. L. Kroeber in his *Cultural and Natural Areas of Native North America*. By Kroeber's determination, only about 900,000 native people had occupied North America north of Mexico before sustained European contact. According to Ann F. Ramenofsky (1987, 9), Kroeber did not consider disease a factor in depopulation because he feared that such an emphasis would lead to an overestimation of precontact population sizes. One may speculate whether this was a case of deliberate scientific oversight or simple academic prudence, but the fact was that after nearly a half century of authority for his conservative figures (a time when one could appear "radical" by arguing that perhaps 2 million native people occupied the area now occupied by the United States in 1492), a challenge was likely to arise. Dobyns, who *did* consider disease (some say he overemphasized it), stepped into that role along with others to initiate the present debate.

Defending his pre-Columbian population estimates, Dobyns argued that "absence of evidence does not mean absence of phenomenon," especially when written records are scanty, as in America before or just after sustained

European contact (Dobyns, 1989, 286). Dobyns's position is that European epidemic diseases invaded a relatively disease-free environment in the Americas with amazing rapidity, first in Mesoamerica (via the Spanish), arriving in eastern North America along native trade routes long before English and French settlers arrived. The fact that Cartier observed the deaths of fifty natives in the village of Stadacona in 1535 indicates to Dobyns that many more may have died in other villages that Cartier never saw. Given lack of evidence, conclusions must be drawn from what little remains, according to Dobyns, who extended his ideas to other continents as well: "Lack of Chinese records of influenza does not necessarily mean that the Chinese did not suffer from influenza; an epidemic could have gone unrecorded, or records of it may not have survived" (ibid., 296).

Critics of Dobyns's estimates assert that "there is still little certain knowledge about pre-1500 population levels," and that "on a historiographic level, Dobyns has been accused of misusing a few scraps of documentary evidence we have in an effort to sustain his argument for widespread sixteenth-century epidemics" (Snow and Lanphear, 1989, 299). To the critics of Dobyns, the fact that fifty native people were recorded as dying at Stadacona means just that: Fifty natives died, no more, no fewer. To Dobyns, however, such an argument "minimizes Native American population magnitude and social structural complexity" (1989, 289).

Although Dean Snow and Kim M. Lanphear, both strident critics of Dobyns, maintained that "there were often buffer zones between population concentrations or isolates that would have impeded the spread of diseases" (1989, 299) Dobyns replied that the practice of trade, war, diplomacy, and other demographic movements obliterated such "buffer zones" and aided in the spread of disease (1989, 291). Snow and Lanphear also asserted that the sparseness of native populations in North America itself impeded the spread of disease, a point of view that does not account for the speed with which smallpox and other infections spread once history recorded them as having reached a particular area.

Dobyns not only denied that buffer zones existed, but also maintained that smallpox was the most virulent of several diseases to devastate New World populations. The others, roughly in descending order of deadliness, included measles, influenza, bubonic plague, diphtheria, typhus, cholera, and scarlet fever (1983, 11–24). According to Dobyns (1983):

> The frontier of European / Euro-American settlement in North America was not a zone of interaction between people of European background and vacant land, nor was it a region where initial farm colonization achieved any "higher" use of the land as measured in human population density. It was actually an interethnic frontier of biological, social, and economic interchange between Native Americans and Europeans and/or Euroamericans. (p. 43)

The most important point to Snow and Lanphear (1989), however, was "where one puts the burden of proof in this argument, or, for that matter, in any argument of this kind.... We cannot allow ourselves to be tricked into assuming the burden of disproving assertions for which there is no evidence" (p. 299).

Given the evidence they had in hand, however, even Snow and Lanphear acknowledged (1988) that between 66 and 98 percent of the Native peoples inhabiting areas of the northeastern United States died in epidemics between roughly 1600 and 1650. The Western Abenaki, for example, are said to have declined from 12,000 to 250 (98 percent), the Massachusett (including the Narragansett) from 44,000 to 6,400 (86 percent), the Mohawk from 8,100 to 2,000 (75 percent), and the Eastern Abenaki from 13,800 to 3,000 (78 percent) (p. 24).

Given the number of people killed and the lengthy period during which they have died, the world has probably not again seen such continuous human misery over such a large area. Tenochtitlan, the Aztecs' capital city (which occupied the site of present-day Mexico City), struck Hernan Cortes as a world-class metropolis when he first looked out over it shortly after the year 1500. The Aztec metropolis is estimated to have contained 250,000 people at a time when Rome, Seville, and Paris housed about 150,000 each. Before he destroyed it, Cortes stared at the splendor of the Aztecs' capital and, sounding something like a country bumpkin, he called Tenochtitlan the most beautiful city in the world.

Spanish chronicler Bernal Diaz del Castillo stood atop a great temple in the Aztec capital and described causeways eight paces wide, teeming with thousands of Aztecs, crossing lakes and channels dotted by convoys of canoes. He said that Spanish soldiers who had been to Rome or Constantinople told Diaz that "for convenience, regularity and population, they have never seen the like" (McDowell, 1980, 753). The comparisons of life among the Aztecs with what the Spanish knew of Europe acquire some substance as one realizes that, in 1492, the British Isles were home to only about 5 million people, and Spain's population has been estimated at 8 million (Wright, 1992, 11). Even almost three centuries later, at the time of the American Revolution, the largest cities along the eastern seaboard of the new United States—Boston, New York, and Philadelphia—housed no more than roughly 50,000 people each.

Within a decade of Cortes's first visit, Tenochtitlan was a ruin. Ten years after the Aztec ruler Mochtezuma had hailed Cortes with gifts of flowers and gold (and had paid for such hospitality with his life), epidemics of smallpox and other diseases carried by the conquistadors had killed at least half the Aztecs. One of the Aztec chroniclers who survived wrote the following: "Almost the whole population suffered from racking coughs and painful, burning sores" (Portilla, 1962, 132).

The plague followed the Spanish conquest as it spread in roughly concentric circles from the islands of Hispanola and Cuba to the mainland of present-day Mexico. Bartolome de las Casas, the Roman Catholic priest who questioned Spanish treatment of the natives, said that when the first visitors found it, Hispanola was a beehive of people. Within one lifetime, the forests were silent. Within thirty years of Cortes's arrival in Mexico, the Native population had fallen from about 25 million to roughly 6 million. After Spanish authorities set limits on money wagers in the New World, soldiers in Panama were said to have made bets with Indian lives instead. Native people who were not killed outright by disease died slowly as slaves under the conquerors' lash.

Las Casas ([1542] 1974), who had arrived in the New World ten years after Columbus, described one form of human servitude, pearl diving: "It is impossible to continue for long diving into the cold water and holding the breath for minutes at a time ... sun rise to sun set, day after day. They die spitting blood ... looking like sea wolves or monsters of another species" (p. 15). Other conquistadors disemboweled native children. According to Las Casas, "They cut them to pieces as if dealing with sheep in a slaughterhouse. They laid bets as to who, with one stroke of a sword, could cut off his head or spill his entrails with a single stroke of the pike" (ibid., 43).

A century later, entering North America, the Puritans often wondered why the lands on which they settled, which otherwise seemed so bountiful, had been emptied of their Native American inhabitants. Four years before the Mayflower landed, a plague of smallpox had swept through Native villages along the coast of the area that the immigrants renamed New England. The disease may have been brought ashore by visiting European fishermen, who had been exploiting the rich coastal banks for many years. John Winthrop admired abandoned Native cornfields and declared that God had emptied the land for his fellow voyagers as an act of divine providence.

As European immigrants spread westward, Native peoples learned to fear the sight of the honeybee. These "English flies" usually colonized areas about a hundred miles in advance of the frontier, and the first sight of them came to be regarded as a harbinger of death. The virulence of the plagues from Europe may be difficult to comprehend in our time. Even in Europe, where immunities had developed to many of the most serious diseases, one in seven people died in many smallpox epidemics. Half the children born in Europe during Columbus's life never reached the age of fifteen years. Life expectancy on both sides of the Atlantic averaged thirty-five years as Europeans made sustained contact with the Americas.

Regardless of the number and density of human population in North America before contact, outside a few specific areas (such as Mayan and Aztec cities, as well as Cahokia), population density was not great enough to devastate the environment on a large scale. Instead, early European observers marveled at the natural bounty of America, of Virginia sturgeon six to nine feet long, of Mississippi catfish that weighed more than 100 pounds, and Massachusetts oysters nine inches across, as well as lobsters that weighed 20 pounds. The immigrants gawked at flights of passenger pigeons that sometimes nearly darkened the sky and speculated that a squirrel could travel from Maine to New Orleans without touching the ground. Bison ranged as far east as Virginia—George Washington observed a few of them and wondered whether they could be crossbred with European cattle.

Regardless of the dispute regarding population size and density before the devastation of European diseases, it is rather widely agreed that Native populations in North America bottomed at about half a million in the early twentieth century (using Mooney's figures), and that they have been increasing since. For the United States, statistics contained in the 1990 census indicated that roughly 2 million people listed themselves as Native American, a figure that nearly doubled in the 2000 U.S. census. Such a measure may not be as precise as it sounds because the census allows people to categorize themselves racially. Also, for the first time, the 2000 census was designed to allow people to report more than one ethnicity, a major source of the numerical increase for Native Americans.

THE ECONOMIC CONSEQUENCES OF DISEASE

When English explorer George Vancouver sailed into Puget Sound in 1793, he met Indian people with pockmarked faces and found human bones and skulls scattered along the beach, grim reminders of an earlier epidemic. Such scenes were repeated coast to coast in North America during the surge of European and European American exploration and settlement.

Epidemics of smallpox, measles, bubonic plague, influenza, typhus, scarlet fever, and many other European diseases sharply curtailed Native Americans' economic productivity, generating hunger and famine. Birth rates fell, and many survivors allayed their losses with alcoholic beverages, further reducing Native societies' vibrancy and economic productivity. Societies that had been constructed on kinship ties dissolved as large parts of many families were wiped out. Survivors faced the world without family elders' help, and traditional Native healing practices were useless against European-imported pathogens. The ravages of disease undermined the traditional authority of Native American healers, who found their practices useless.

Historian Colin Calloway described the widespread impact of epidemics on Native American political, economic, and social institutions (1990):

> The devastating impact of disease cannot be measured only in numerical losses. Epidemics left social and economic chaos in their wake and caused immeasurable spiritual and psychological damage. Killer diseases tore holes in the fabric of Indian societies held together by extensive networks of kinship and reciprocity, disrupted time-honored cycles of hunting, planting, and fishing, discouraged social and ceremonial gatherings, and drained confidence in the old certainties of life and the shamans who mediated with the spirit world. (p. 39)

The arrival of European pathogens affected Native American tribes and nations differently, depending on the economic conduct of their lives. Sedentary groups were hit the hardest, and migratory groups (such as the Cheyennes after about 1800) suffered less intensely, at least at first, because they moved from place to place, leaving their wastes (which drew disease-carrying flies and other insects) behind. Migratory peoples also left behind water that they may have contaminated, usually exchanging it for fresh supplies. The Cheyennes were quite conscious of water contamination and always set up camp so that their horses drank and defecated downstream of human occupants. The Cheyennes consciously fought the spread of disease by breaking camp often and scattering into small family groups so that one infected family would not bring disease to an entire band.

Although the worst of the bubonic plague killed one in three Europeans, continuing waves of epidemics nearly obliterated many Native American societies and economies within a few years of the arrival of Europeans in any given area. Plagues of various pathogens—smallpox, influenza, measles, and others—killed nearly all of the Western Abenakis and at least half the Mohawks. A disease frontier spread across North America about a generation, generally, before European American settlers, traders, and miners reached a given area.

The heritage of suffering brought by imported diseases left its mark on Native America well into the twentieth century. As late as 1955, the annual Native American death rate from gastrointestinal illnesses was 15.4 per 100,000, compared with 3.6 in the United States as a whole. The death rate from tuberculosis was 57.9 per 100,000 in 1955, compared to a nationwide average of 8.4. From alcoholism, the rate was at least 60 per 100,000, compared to a national average of 8.1.

During the last half of the twentieth century, some diseases declined dramatically among Native Americans. The death rate from gastrointestinal diseases fell from 15.4 per 100,000 in 1955 to 4.2 in 1983; the national average in 1983 was 2.8. For tuberculosis, the 1983 rate was 3.3 per annual deaths per 100,000, down from 57.9 in 1955; the national rate fell from 8.4 per 100,000 in 1955 to 0.5 in 1983. For alcoholism, the Native American rate of at least 60 per 100,000 in 1955 declined to about 28 in 1983.

FURTHER READING

Adair, James. *History of the American Indians*. Edited by Samuel Cole Williams. Johnson City, TN: Wataugua Press, [1775] 1930.

Ballantine, Betty, and Ian Ballantine. *The Native Americans: An Illustrated History*. Atlanta, GA: Turner, 1994.

Barbeau, C. M. *Huron and Wyandot Mythology with an Appendix Containing Earlier Published Records*. Anthropological Series, no. 11, Memoir 80. Ottawa: Government Printing Bureau, 1915: 35–51.

Borah, Woodrow. The Historical Demography of Aboriginal and Colonial America: An Attempt at Perspective. In William M. Denevan, ed., *The Native American Population of the Americas in 1492*. Madison: University of Wisconsin Press, 1976: 13–34.

Boyd, Julian P., ed. *The Papers of Thomas Jefferson.* Vol. 20. Princeton, NJ: Princeton University Press, 1982.

Calloway, Colin. *The Western Abenakis of Vermont, 1600–1800: War, Migration, and the Survival of an Indian People.* Norman: University of Oklahoma Press, 1990.

Calloway, Colin. *New Worlds for All: Indians, Europeans, and the Remaking of Early America.* Baltimore: Johns Hopkins University Press, 1997.

Colden, Cadwallader. *The History of the Five Nations of Canada.* New York: Amsterdam, [1765] 1902.

Converse, Harriet Maxwell [Ya-ie-wa-noh]. *Myths and Legends of the New York State Iroquois.* Edited by Arthur Caswell Parker. New York State Museum Bulletin 125. Education Department Bulletin no. 437. Albany: University of the State of New York, 1908: 31–36.

Cook, Sherburne F., and Leslie B. Simpson. The Population of Central Mexico in the Sixteenth Century. In *Ibero-Americana* 31. Berkeley and Los Angeles: University of California Press, 1948.

Corkran, David H. *The Cherokee Frontier: Conflict and Survival, 1740–1762.* Norman: University of Oklahoma Press, 1962.

Cornplanter, Jesse J. *Legends of the Longhouse.* Edited by William G. Spittal. Ohsweken, Ontario, Canada: Iroqrafts, [1938] 1992.

Cronon, William. *Changes in the Land: Indians, Colonists, and the Ecology of New England.* New York: Hill and Wang, 1983.

Deloria, Vine, Jr. *God Is Red.* Golden, CO: North American Press, 1992.

Demarest, Arthur A. The Violent Saga of a Mayan Kingdom. *National Geographic* (February 1993):95–111.

Dillehay, Thomas D. *The Settlement of the Americas: A New Prehistory.* New York: Basic Books, 2000.

Dillehay, Thomas D. Palaeoanthropology: Tracking the First Americans. *Nature* 425 (September 4, 2003):23–24.

Dobyns, Henry F. Estimating Aboriginal American Population. *Current Anthropology* 7(October 1966):395–412.

Dobyns, Henry F. *Their Number Became Thinned.* Knoxville: University of Tennessee Press, 1983.

Dobyns, Henry F. More Methodological Perspectives on Historical Demography. *Ethnohistory* 36:3(Summer 1989):286–289.

Dozier, Edward P. *The Pueblo Indians of North America.* New York: Holt, Rinehart and Winston, 1970.

Fenton, William N., and John Gulick, eds. *Symposium on Cherokee and Iroquois Culture.* Smithsonian Institution Bureau of Ethnology Bulletin 180. Washington, DC: U.S. Government Printing Office, 1961.

Frazier, Joseph B. Humans in Oregon 10,000 Years Ago? Associated Press via senior-staff@nativenewsonline.org, November 25, 2002.

Goebel, Ted, Michael R. Waters, and Margarita Dikova. The Archaeology of Ushki Lake, Kamchatka, and the Pleistocene Peopling of the Americas. *Science* 301 (July 25, 2003):501–505.

Gonzalez-José, Rolando, Antonio Gonzalez-Martin, Miquel Hernandez, Hector M. Pucciarelli, Marina Sardi, Alfonso Rosales, and Silvina Van der Molen. Craniometric Evidence for Palaeoamerican Survival in Baja California. *Nature* 425(September 4, 2003):62–65.

Grinde, Donald A., Jr. The Reburial of American Indian Remains and Funerary Objects. *Northeast Indian Quarterly* 8:2(Summer 1991):35–38.

Grinde, Donald A., Jr., and Bruce E. Johansen. *Ecocide of Native America: Environmental Destruction of Indian Lands and Peoples.* Santa Fe, NM: Clear Light, 1995.

Heckenberger, Michael J., Afukaka Kuikuro, Urissap Tabata Kuikuro, J. Christian Russell, Morgan Schmidt, Carlos Fausto, and Bruna Franchetto. Amazonia 1492: Pristine Forest or Cultural Parkland? *Science* 301(September 19, 2003):1710–1714.

Henderson, John F. *The World of the Ancient Maya.* Ithaca, NY: Cornell University Press, 1981.

Hewitt, John Napoleon Brinton, ed. Iroquoian Cosmology, First Part. In *Twenty-First Annual Report of the Bureau of American Ethnology to the Secretary of the Smithsonian Institution, 1899–1900.* Washington, DC: U.S. Government Printing Office, 1903: 127–339.

Hewitt, John Napoleon Brinton, ed. Iroquoian Cosmology, Second Part." In *Forty-Third Annual Report of the Bureau of American Ethnology to the Secretary of the Smithsonian Institution, 1925–1926.* Washington, DC: U.S. Government Printing Office, 1928: 453–819.

Hughes, J. Donald. *American Indian Ecology.* El Paso: Texas Western Press, 1983.

Iverson, Peter. Taking Care of the Earth and Sky. In Alvin Josephy, ed., *America in 1492: The World of the Indian Peoples Before the Arrival of Columbus.* New York: Knopf, 1992, 85–118.

Johansen, Bruce E. Wampum. In D.L. Birchfield, ed., *The Encyclopedia of North American Indians.* Vol. 10. New York: Marshall Cavendish, 1997: 1352–1353.

Johansen, Bruce E. Great White Hope? Kennewick Man: The Facts, the Fantasies, and the Stakes. *Native Americas* 16:1(Spring, 1999):36.

Johansen, Bruce E., and Barbara Alice Mann, eds. *Encyclopedia of the Haudenosaunee (Iroquois Confederacy).* Westport, CT: Greenwood Press, 2000.

Kehoe, Alice Beck. *North American Indians: A Comprehensive Account.* Englewood Cliffs, NJ: Prentice-Hall, 1981.

Kehoe, Alice Beck. *America before the European Invasions.* London: Longman, 2002.

Kroeber, A. L. *Cultural and Natural Areas of Native North America.* University of California Publications in American Archeology and Ethnology 38. Berkeley: University of California, 1939.

Lara, Jesus. *La Poesia Quechua.* Cochabamba, Bolivia: Imprenta Universitaria, N.d., 193–194. Cited in Wright, 1992, 31.

La Republica, Lima, Peru. Reprinted in *World Press Review,* September 1991, 50.

Las Casas, Bartolome de. *The Devastation of the Indies.* New York: Seabury Press, [1542] 1974: 15.

Mann, Barbara A. The Fire at Onondaga: Wampum as Proto-writing. *Akwesasne Notes* New Series 1:1(Spring 1995):40–48.

Mann, Charles C. 1491: America Before Columbus Was More Sophisticated and More Populous than We Have Ever Thought—and a More Livable Place Than Europe. *Atlantic Monthly* March 2002, 41–53.

McDowell, Bart. The Aztecs. *National Geographic* December 1980, 704–752.

McKee, Jesse O., and Jon A. Schlenker. *The Choctaws: Cultural Evolution of a Native American Tribe.* Jackson: University Press of Mississippi, 1980.

Meggers, Betty J., Eduardo S. Brondizio, Michael J. Heckenberger, Carlos Fausto, and Bruna Franchetto. Revisiting Amazonia Circa 1492 [Letter to the Editor]. *Science* 302(December 19, 2003):2067–2070.

Mexican Skull May Explain Indigenous Origins. Reuters, December 5, 2002. Available at http://story.news.yahoo.com/news? tmpl=story&u=/nm/20021205/sc_nm/science_mexico_skull_dc_1.

The Mohawk Creation Story. *Akwesasne Notes* 21.5 (Spring 1989):32–29.

Mooney, J. Population. In F. W. Hodge, ed., *Handbook of American Indians North of Mexico*. Bureau of American Ethnology Bulletin 30(part 2). Washington, DC: U.S. Government Printing Office, 1910: 28–37.

Mooney, James. *The Aboriginal Population of North America North of Mexico*. Edited by J. R. Swanton. Smithsonian Miscellaneous Collections 80(7). Washington, DC: U.S. Government Printing Office,1928.

Moore, John H. *The Cheyennes*. Oxford, U.K.: Blackwell, 1997.

Moore, Oliver. Pre-Mayan Written Language Found in Mexico. *Toronto Globe and Mail*, December 5, 2002. Available at http://www.globeandmail.com/servlet/ArticleNews/front/RTGAM/20021205/w lang1205/Front/homeBN/breakingnews.

Morison, Patricia. Wisdom of the Aztecs, *London Financial Times*. Reprinted in Notes on the Arts, *World Press Review*, January 1993, 54.

Parker, Arthur C. *The Code of Handsome Lake, the Seneca Prophet*. New York State Museum Bulletin 163, Education Department Bulletin No. 530, November 1, 1912. Albany: University of the State of New York, 1913.

Peopling the Americas: A New Site to Debate. *National Geographic* (Geographica), September 1992.

Pitulko, V. V., P. A. Nikolsky, E. Yu. Girya, A. E. Basilyan, V. E. Tumskoy, S. A. Koulakov, S. N. Astakhov, E. Yu. Pavlova, and M. A. Anisimov. The Yana RHS Site: Humans in the Arctic Before the Last Glacial Maximum. *Science* 303(January 2, 2004):52–56.

Pohl, Frederick Julius. *The Viking Settlements of North America*. New York: Potter, 1972.

Pohl, Mary E. D., Kevin O. Pope, and Christopher von Nagy. Olmec Origins of Mesoamerican Writing. *Science* 298(December 6, 2002):1984–1987.

Portilla, Miguel Leon. *The Broken Spears: The Aztec Account of the Conquest of Mexico*. Boston: Beacon Press, 1962.

Ramenofsky, Ann F. *Vectors of Death: The Archeology of European Contact*. Albuquerque: University of New Mexico Press, 1987.

Recer, Paul. Researchers Find Evidence of Sophisticated, Pre-Columbia Civilization in the Amazon Basin." Associated Press, September 19, 2003, in LEXIS.

Recer, Paul. Evidence Found of Arctic Hunters Living in Siberia Near New World 30,000 Years Ago." Associated Press, January 2, 2004, in LEXIS.

Sando, Joe S. *The Pueblo Indians*. San Francisco: Indian Historian Press, 1976.

Schele, Linda. The Owl, Shield, and Flint Blade. *Natural History*, November 1991, 7–11.

Sherzer, Joel. A Richness of Voices. In Alvin Joesphy, ed., *America in 1492: The World of the Indian Peoples Before the Arrival of Columbus*. New York: Knopf, 1992: 251–276.

Slayman, Andrew L. A Battle Over Bones. *Archaeology* 50:1 (January/February 1997):16–23.

Snow, Dean R., and Kim M. Lanphear. European Contact and Indian Depopulation in the Northeast: The Timing of the First Epidemics. *Ethnohistory* 35:1(Winter 1988):16–24.

Snow, Dean R., and Kim M. Lanphear. "More Methodological Perspectives": A Rejoinder to Dobyns. *Ethnohistory* 36:3 (Summer 1989):299–300.

Stannard, David E. *American Holocaust: The Conquest of th* Oxford University Press, 1992.

Stevens, William K. Andean Culture Found to Be as Old as *York Times*, October 3, 1989, C-1.

Stokstad, Erik. Oldest New World Writing Suggests Olme (December 6, 2002):1872–1874.

Stokstad, Erik. Amazon Archaeology: "Pristine" Forest Tee 301(September 19, 2003):1645–1646.

Stone, Richard. Late Date for Siberian Site Challenges 301(July 25, 2003):450–451.

Stone, Richard. A Surprising Survival Story in the Sib (January 2, 2004):33.

Thomas, David Hurst. *Skull Wars: Kennewick Man, Arch Native American Identity*. New York: Basic Books/Peter

Tozzer, Alfred, ed. *Landa's Relacion de las Cosas de Yucat* body Museum of Archaeology and Ethnology Papers, Henderson, 1981, 88.

Trigger, Bruce G. *Children of the Aataentsic: A History of* McGill-Queen's University Press, 1976.

Wallace, Anthony F. C. *The Death and Rebirth of the Senec*

Walton, Marsha, and Michael Coren. Archaeologists Put 50,000 Years Ago. Cable News Network, November 17, 2 cnn.com/2004/TECH/science/11/17/carolina.dig/index.

Weatherford, Jack. *Native Roots: How the Indians Enriched Am*

Wilford, John Noble. Did Warfare Doom the Mayas' Ecc Service. In *Miami Herald*, December 22, 1991, 7-L.

Williams, Stephen. *Fantastic Archaeology: The Wild Side* Philadelphia: University of Pennsylvania Press, 1991.

Wright, Ronald. *Stolen Continents: The Americas Through I* Houghton-Mifflin, 1992.

Stannard, David E. *American Holocaust: The Conquest of the New World.* New York: Oxford University Press, 1992.

Stevens, William K. Andean Culture Found to Be as Old as the Great Pyramids. *New York Times,* October 3, 1989, C-1.

Stokstad, Erik. Oldest New World Writing Suggests Olmec Innovation. *Science* 298 (December 6, 2002):1872–1874.

Stokstad, Erik. Amazon Archaeology: "Pristine" Forest Teemed With People. *Science* 301(September 19, 2003):1645–1646.

Stone, Richard. Late Date for Siberian Site Challenges Bering Pathway. *Science* 301(July 25, 2003):450–451.

Stone, Richard. A Surprising Survival Story in the Siberian Arctic. *Science* 303 (January 2, 2004):33.

Thomas, David Hurst. *Skull Wars: Kennewick Man, Archaeology, and the Battle for Native American Identity.* New York: Basic Books/Peter N. Nevraumont, 2000.

Tozzer, Alfred, ed. *Landa's Relacion de las Cosas de Yucatan.* Harvard University Peabody Museum of Archaeology and Ethnology Papers, Vol. 18, p. 169. Cited in Henderson, 1981, 88.

Trigger, Bruce G. *Children of the Aataentsic: A History of the Huron People.* Montreal: McGill-Queen's University Press, 1976.

Wallace, Anthony F. C. *The Death and Rebirth of the Seneca.* New York: Vintage, 1972.

Walton, Marsha, and Michael Coren. Archaeologists Put Humans In North America 50,000 Years Ago. Cable News Network, November 17, 2004. Available at http://www.cnn.com/2004/TECH/science/11/17/carolina.dig/index.html.

Weatherford, Jack. *Native Roots: How the Indians Enriched America.* New York: Crown, 1991.

Wilford, John Noble. Did Warfare Doom the Mayas' Ecology? *New York Times* News Service. In *Miami Herald,* December 22, 1991, 7-L.

Williams, Stephen. *Fantastic Archaeology: The Wild Side of North American Prehistory.* Philadelphia: University of Pennsylvania Press, 1991.

Wright, Ronald. *Stolen Continents: The Americas Through Indian Eyes Since 1492.* Boston: Houghton-Mifflin, 1992.

CHAPTER 2

~

Mexico and Mesoamerica

BEGINNINGS TO EUROPEAN CONTACT

In present-day Mexico and Central America (*Mesoamerica*, Greek for Middle America), complex civilizations began to organize at about the time that the Roman Empire was expanding across Europe, northern Africa, and Palestine. These civilizations evolved over the centuries in different locations around two centers. One was the highlands of present-day Guatemala into the scrublands of Yucatan, where the Maya flourished. In and around the Valley of Mexico, the second center, a series of city-states had been rising and falling for more than 1,500 years when, in 1519, Cortes met the Aztecs, the last, largest, and grandest civilization of them all.

Both of these centers also formed the nucleus of an agricultural, mercantile, and administrative network, with commercial influence often radiating several hundred miles from the center through a thickly populated agricultural hinterland. The rise of each center was brought about by a well-defined elite purportedly acting under the sponsorship and direction of a pantheon of gods. As archaeologists learn more about the cultures that preceded the Aztecs, a pattern seems to be emerging: More than once, the elites of one center may have escaped popular unrest by moving to other areas and starting the cycle over again. Thus, a similar (but in some ways more technologically advanced) civilization rose in another area as the old city was reclaimed by nature.

URBAN BEGINNINGS IN MESOAMERICA

The Mesoamerican elite tradition probably began with the Olmecs, who constructed towns as centers of politically integrated societies and containing temples, elite residences, stone sculptures, and elaborate tombs. The Olmec civilization, which preceded the Mayan as well as the chain of civilizations that led to the Aztecs in the Valley of Mexico, started organizing complex societies based on the rich wild food resources of the southern Gulf Coast of present-day Mexico shortly after 1500 B.C.E. In the art, rituals, and other lifeways of the Olmecs, one sees the later Mayan, Toltec, and Aztec traditions emerging.

By 1400 B.C.E., the first large Olmec settlement had risen at a site today called San Lorenzo, southwest of the Tuxtla Mountains near Mexico's southern Gulf Coast. The settlement contained large public buildings and stone monuments. Evidence, including the probable number of residential sites, indicates that San Lorenzo was a small city in terms of population but a very large one in terms of economic, political, and religious power across a sizable hinterland (M. D. Coe, 1968).

The elite of San Lorenzo supervised projects involving earth moving of monumental scope, in the hundreds of millions of cubic feet. Thousand of tons of basalt used in construct monuments were quarried in the Tuxtla Mountains. The site also has yielded imported obsidian, mica, and other materials from many hundreds of miles away that were used for jewelry, ritual objects, and other prized possessions. The Olmecs of San Lorenzo also probably imported other items, such as foodstuffs, that left little archaeological evidence. Judging from the number of implements recovered for grinding corn, it was probably the staple food of the common people at San Lorenzo; the people also likely ate turtles and fish; the elite occasionally dined on young puppies raised especially for that purpose.

The Olmecs did not use metal tools, but they did fashion iron ore into shining disks that the elite wore as ornaments. About 1000 B.C.E., San Lorenzo was surpassed in size by another Olmec settlement, La Venta, east of San Lorenzo, near the Gulf Coast. Although La Venta's public and ceremonial areas were larger, its culture was similar to that of San Lorenzo. La Venta reached its peak between 1000 and 750 B.C.E. Other Olmec sites have been identified but, as of this writing, not widely excavated.

The Olmecs did not occupy Mesoamerica alone; other peoples also were establishing organized societies with agricultural bases at about the same time. In the Valley of Oaxaca, for example, a dozen settlements began between 1300 and 1600 B.C.E. Later, at about 750 B.C.E., as La Venta declined, the Oaxacan capitol of Monte Alban included a civic center with large pyramids and surrounded by rich agricultural land. Olmec sculptures also may contain the earliest hints of hieroglyphic writing of a form that later was adopted by the Mayas and Aztecs. (See details on writing systems in chapter 1.)

As the Olmecs' civilization declined after 600 B.C.E., other groups rose and fell at other sites, each enjoying brief authority over an agricultural hinterland. Each in turn organized its society under a religious and military elite, with social classes, rituals, and art forms that continued the tradition that began with the Olmecs and ended with the Aztecs.

More than a century before the birth of Christ, the first true sizable urban areas in North America arose in the Valley of Mexico, at Teotihuacan, northeast of the vast lake on which the Aztecs would later build Tenochtitlan (which translates to place of the prickly-pear cactus). Another urban area arose at Cuicuilco, in the southwestern part of the Valley of Mexico, near the Mexico National University's present-day campus, on the southern side of Mexico City. Cuicuilco probably was the larger city in the beginning, before a volcanic eruption and lava flow ruined its site (and hinterland) and sent much of its population to Teotihuacan, which swelled in size from 20,000 to 30,000 people by about 100 C.E. to as many as 200,000 by 700 C.E. (Maxwell, 1978, 52).

With an estimated population of 200,000, Teotihuacan (meaning place of the gods in Nahuatl, the Aztec language) was one of the largest—if not the largest— urban areas on earth at that time, nearly equal in population to the Aztec capital of Tenochtitlan 700 years later. Cities such as London and Paris did not reach that size until after Europe's Age of Exploration began. Teotihuacan covered twenty square kilometers (or eight square miles) and was thick with ceremonial buildings and more than 2,000 large apartment blocks, some of which functioned as workplaces as well as homes. Some of them specialized in the manufacture of obsidian blades; others manufactured pottery. About 150 ceramic shops have been identified in Teotihuacan, which produced sturdy cooking ware for common people as well as intricately designed vessels for the well-to-do. In other shops, artisans fashioned the elaborate feathered costumes worn by the elite during ceremonial occasions. Artisans carved hundreds of large monuments from basalt blocks, ranging in size up to 40 tons each; these portrayed secular and supernatural rulers and events.

Archaeological evidence indicates well-developed societies with military and religious elites supported by intensive agriculture in an area that was probably much more lush than the capital city of Mexico appears today. During the last 500 years, vegetation has been stripped by overgrazing sheep imported from Europe. In the twentieth century, urban air pollution also has stunted the growth of vegetation in the Valley of Mexico.

Teotihuacan cast a trading net as far as the region today occupied by Guatemala City, where in about 500 C.E. colonists from the Valley of Mexico transformed the Mayan town of Kaminaljuyu into an outpost. The rulers of Teotihuacan had practical motives: The Mayan town lay on the route to their main sources of cocoa and jade. The town also was situated near routes that controlled access to one of North America's richest obsidian mines. No ruler of the time could field an effective army without access to obsidian for weaponry. At about this time, 350 obsidian workshops in Teotihuacan employed thousands of people. Obsidian tools and weapons had become the city's main export.

The Aztecs worked earlier civilizations into their own mythologized history, which maintained that theirs was the last of five epochs during which the universe had been destroyed and reborn. One of the prior epochs was said to have occurred in Teotihuacan; its influence passed to the Aztecs through Tula, the capital of the Toltecs, which reached its height shortly after 1000 C.E. although the Aztecs did not originate in the Valley of Mexico, they were in effect absorbed by the 1,500-year-old urban tradition of the area after they arrived and conquered the descendants of Teotihuacan and other cities. The Aztecs' Great Temple contained an area (two so-called red temples) that affected Teotihuacan-style symbols, including architecture.

According to Aztec myth, the gods met at Teotihuacan to recreate the sun, the moon, and the rest of the universe:

> When it was still night,
> When there was no day,
> When there was no light,
> They met,
> The gods convened,
> There at Teotihuacan
> They said
> They spoke among themselves:
> "Come here, oh Gods!
> Who will take upon himself,
> Who will take charge
> of making days,
> of making light?
>   —Leon-Portillo, 1972, 23-24

Richard A. Diehl described Teotihuacan as follows:

A truly cosmopolitan center whose inhabitants included farmers, craftsmen, priests, merchants, warriors, government officials, architects, laborers, and enclaves of resident foreigners. Most of the people lived in single-story rectangular masonry apartment houses sheltering more than 100 residents [each]. (1981, 24)

Teotihuacan was divided into four quadrants by two major causeways, on which fronted most of the important secular and religious buildings of the city. One of these causeways, called the Street of the Dead, ran roughly north to south and was the site of most of these larger buildings. The two avenues intersected at an array of temples, including one dedicated to Quetzalcoatl, the Feathered Serpent who also became an Aztec god. This area also included temples to the sun and the moon (also similar to Aztec cosmology), which were two of the largest pyramidal mounds erected anywhere in the world to that time. The Sun Pyramid measured 200 meters on its sides and 60 meters high. The plazas, parks, and causeways of the ceremonial center comprised a paved area roughly three miles long and two miles wide.

The city of Teotihuacan reached the height of its power about 500 C.E. and declined by roughly 800 C.E., after which other cities competed for power. At about 800 C.E., or just a century before the widespread decline of Mayan culture to the south (see the section "The Maya: Mystery and Speculation" below), Teotihuacan was destroyed by enemies from the outside who set fires in the city. Teotihuacan's sizable population fled in large numbers, leaving only small agricultural communities. One of these, Cholula, was located near modern Puebla, east of the Valley of Mexico. It had been a satellite city of Teotihuacan but survived long after the larger city's demise, well into the Spanish conquest. Xochicalco, in the lowlands near present-day Morelos, collapsed two centuries after Teotihuacan. The best-known urban successor to Teotihuacan was Tula, north of present-day Mexico City and the capital of the Toltecs, whose culture the Aztecs both ransacked and mythologized with tales of how the Toltecs had grown multihued cotton and giant ears of corn.

Tula later was sacked by the invading Aztecs, whose popular history held that the Toltecs had become decadent, drunken into a stupor on *pulque*, a Mexican alcoholic beverage. Before the Toltecs' Tula reached its height in the Valley of Mexico, the Maya spread a diffuse array of city-states to the south. They shared several cultural attributes with their northern neighbors, which indicated copious trade and travel between the two areas.

THE MAYA: MYSTERY AND SPECULATION

To many of the scholars who have studied them, the Maya remain a subject of mystery and speculation. Scholars who had not deciphered their written language once speculated that the Maya at their height had been relatively peaceful—perhaps playing, in imagination, Greeks to the Aztecs' Rome. History displayed in the Maya's own writing now portrays them as very warlike (Demarest, 1993, 95–111).

At the height of their civilization, about 600 to 900 C.E., the Maya dominated most of what is today southern Mexico, Guatemala, and Belize. Their civilization was not an organized empire in the Inca, Roman, or Aztec sense but a collection of independent city-states. The ramparts of fortresslike Tulum looked out over the ragged surf of the Yucatan shore, gateway to a network of trading routes that connected such Mayan cities as Copan, Tikal, Chichen Itza, and Palenque. Maya cities thrived in natural surroundings of great contrast, from the flat, hot, and humid lowlands of Yucatan, to rain forests further inland, to highland valleys that can be as arid as northern Mexico, and to higher mountains, many volcanic, that are thick with forests.

For fifteen centuries, the Maya made some of the most inhospitable jungles in the world bloom with "the sunbeams of the gods." Corn was the dietary staple of a civilization of substantial monuments that in many respects was a match for any in the Eastern Hemisphere. In more than 100 cities, Mayan artists produced some of the most exquisite art in the world of their time, and Mayan scientists calculated solar and lunar eclipses with an accuracy that would not be exceeded until modern times. The Mayan calendar is a few minutes a year more accurate than the Roman calendar used today but was vastly more complex, requiring a priest trained in its use to establish the date. The Maya also calculated the path of Venus and were the first to develop a

Chichen Itza scene. (Courtesy of the Library of Congress.)

concept of negative numbers in mathematics. Yet, by the time the first Spanish explorers reached Mesoamerica, Mayan civilization was crumbling, probably from incessant warfare and ecological exhaustion.

Origins of the Maya

The origins of the Maya are not known to contemporary scholars, aside from speculation that aspects of their culture may have been borrowed from the Olmecs, who may have spoken a language related to one or more of the Mayan dialects. Some evidence exists that the Maya may have begun the building of their civilization in Kaminaljuya, which is today part of Guatemala City, before 1100 B.C.E. by the European calendar. In 1936, the Carnegie Institution began excavating the largest "preclassic" Mayan site discovered to that time. These discoveries (and later ones) showed that the Maya were predominantly urban with a complex agricultural infrastructure supporting their cities. These early ruins (dating to roughly 800 to 300 B.C.E.) also showed evidence of hiero-glyphic writing that would later open even more detail of the Mayan worldview and daily life. Scholars unraveling the Maya's writing are discovering that their efforts have been complicated by the fact that Maya scribes apparently liked to play tricks with words: puns, homonyms (two words with the same sound but different meanings), verbal allusions, metaphors, and other wordplay.

From the highlands of Guatemala, the Maya may have moved into the lowlands of Peten and Yucatan (in present-day Mexico) at about the time Christ was born in the Old World. In the Mexican state of Chiapas, Mayan monuments have been found that date to 36 B.C.E.; the precision of this date, and others, is made possible by the Maya's own calendar, which can be matched with ours. The earliest such monuments at Tikal date to about 300 C.E.

A Mayan city known as Dzibilchaltun, excavated by E. Wyllys Andrews IV of Tulane University (New Orleans, LA) beginning in 1956, was occupied con-tinuously between 500 B.C.E. and the time of the Spanish conquest. At its height, this city was probably home to at least 40,000 people, a population roughly equal to that of Alexandria, Egypt, at about the same time (La Fay, 1975, 733–734). Scholars also found evidence of intensive agriculture prac-ticed on terraced fields and platforms raised to escape seasonal flooding. "These features indicate that the Maya practiced permanent and intensive agricul-ture capable of supporting a large population," said Professor B. L. Turner II of the University of Oklahoma (Norman, OK). "If you could have flown over the Peten at the height of the [Mayan] Classic Period, you would have found something akin to central Ohio today" (La Fay, 1975, 733).

The major Mayan urban areas often battled with each other for dominance, even developing their own language dialects and art forms. Slowly, scholars are building a history of Mayan civilization that may someday rival that of Egypt and other Old World civilizations. The description of this history has faced hazards since the first contact; some of the Spanish friars knew how to

A Mayan temple in Tikal. (Courtesy of the Library of Congress.)

read Mayan hieroglyphs but left no guides to later generations. The Spaniard Avendano produced a dictionary and grammar of Mayan language while living among the Yucatec during the eighteenth century, but all copies of it have been lost.

The Maya built a civilization on an epic scale. Tikal, the largest of the Maya's many cities, housing about 100,000 people, rambled over 23 square miles at about the same time that imperial Rome, which was more densely populated, covered only a third as much area. Depictions of early rulers in Uaxactun and Tikal indicate that before the birth of Christ in the Old World, Mayan city-states were raiding each other for captives. Later depictions show warriors holding obsidian-edged clubs and spear throwers. In one depiction, Great Jaguar Paw, a ruler at Tikal, is shown celebrating a military victory with a bloodletting from his genitals. Some of the stellae (rock carvings used to depict historical events) were erected on top of human skeletons. The stellae also contain indications that some of the Mayan cities traded with Teotihuacan in the Valley of Mexico; it is likely that the residents of Mexico traded high-land products (such as obsidian blades) with the lowland Maya for cotton, tropical bird feathers, shells, and other lowland items.

Archaeologists have excavated only a fraction of what the Maya built during their classic period. In the Mexican state of Chiapas, for example, by 1990 archaeologists had unearthed between two and three dozen structures from the thickly wooded hills at Palenque. This collection of buildings make a distinctive site, but they are only a fraction of the structures that stretch for seven miles.

After its founding about 1000 B.C.E., Copan grew into "the most artistically embellished of all the great Maya sites" (Fash and Fash, 1990, 28). To archaeologists, the inscriptions on stellae and altars as well as temple panels, stairways, and portable objects used in everyday life comprise an open history book that allows the life of Copan to emerge. From them, contemporary scholars are reconstructing dynastic lineages as well as the lives of ordinary Maya.

During the height of their civilization, the Maya surrounded themselves with decoration, on their buildings as well as their bodies. The Maya etched tattoos into their bodies and painted them a variety of colors. Priests were painted blue, warriors in black and red, and prisoners in black and white stripes. Some Maya filed their teeth and distended their pierced earlobes, hanging earplugs in them. Many also pierced the septum of their noses and inserted carved jewelry. They flattened their foreheads and worked to make themselves cross-eyed, a standard of beauty. Feathers also conveyed beauty; the Maya wore the plumage of birds bred in aviaries for their most gorgeous plumes. According to William Brandon, "men wore brilliant little obsidian mirrors hanging in their long hair" (1961, 32).

Bishop Diego de Landa's *Relacion de Las Cosas de Yucatan* was written in 1556 during the first years of the Spanish conquest with a sense of awe at the civilization of the Maya, remarking on the large number and grand nature of their buildings, at a civilization so exotic that Spaniards at home would think he was fabricating a tall tale.

Today, scholars often find that looters have ransacked newly discovered Mayan sites. The scholars are pursuing knowledge as the looters seek high prices paid in illicit art markets the world over. One such site, uncovered at Rio Usumacinta during 1946, contained multicolored frescoes that described a battle in the middle of the eighth century in detail, from the armed conflict itself to the ritual sacrifice of prisoners afterward. A chronicler described warriors in animal pelts and feathers:

> They came over the hill with the first rays of the rising sun, filling the air with their shouts and war cries, displaying their banners.... It was terrible, this descent of the Quiche. They advanced rapidly in columns, down to the edge of the river. The clash was horrible, the screams and shouts. The din of flutes, drums and conch-shell trumpets resounded as the Quiche chiefs vainly sought to save themselves by divine magic. Soon they were hurled back, and many died. A great number were taken prisoner, along with their chiefs. (La Fay, 1975, 735–736)

The Numerical Precision of the Maya

The Maya developed remarkable precision in timekeeping and astronomy because it served their theology; unlike the development of secular science in Europe (which often conflicted with religious beliefs), religion and science were one and the same among the Maya. Their numeric system utilized a

Gregoria Pat, a Maya Indian. (Courtesy of the Library of Congress.)

system of dots and bars and was based on 20 (the sum of fingers and toes) rather than 10 (the sum of fingers), which was used in Europe.

Also, unlike European practice, the Maya generally did not distinguish among past, present, and future; the same word, *kin*, described all three concepts in their language. Time was said to be circular. Events experienced in the past were expected to happen again, in a cycle. A person who knew the past was believed to be able to predict the future. Success in predicting such natural phenomena as eclipses was said to be divine proof of this. Time was seen as one immutable stream, stretching back to a date corresponding to August 11, 3114 B.C.E., the first date on the Maya's "Long count" calendar. After 5,200 years, the Maya's Long Count calendar comes to a close on the winter solstice in 2012. This is not the end of time, however; the Maya tradition has counted three Long Counts before this one and will begin counting again after it.

Mayan religious beliefs and rituals seem similar to those of the Valley of Mexico, which is more than circumstantial. The headdresses of priests and other high officials sometimes included symbols similar to those used in Teotihuacan; traders from the Valley of Mexico ranged into Mayan country very early, and culture traveled with them. As with the Aztecs, Mayan religious life was dominated by a pantheon of gods serving various purposes: Itzamna, the Lord of Life; Ah Kin, the sun god; Ah Puch, who ruled the land of the dead, and Chac, god of rain, among many others. The Maya also worshipped a feathered serpent, Kukulcan, which resembled the Aztecs' Quetzalcoatl.

As with the Aztecs, the Maya believed that their gods required sacrifices of human blood on a regular schedule. Most of this blood was collected from prisoners of war (a motivating factor for many of the intercity raids). Some members of the lower classes were forced to die for the gods, and people of all economic levels sometimes volunteered to feed the gods' appetites with offerings of their blood. Early Spanish records contain accounts of priests drawing thorny ropes through their tongues to draw blood with which to appease the gods; others took blood from their genitals. The sacrifices were accompanied by complex ceremonies, during which priests sometimes slit the chest of a person being sacrificed, emerging with the heart, which often still beat. The Spanish, who seemed to have little qualm with Mayan bloodshed in the name of Christianity's conquest, recoiled in horror at the sight of sacrifices to gods they regarded as pagan; Bernal Diaz del Castillo, the soldier-historian who accompanied Cortes and other explorers during the sixteenth century, described in *Conquest of New Spain, 1517–1521* Mayan priests whose hair was so matted with blood that it could never be combed out.

The Maya pantheon of gods was complex not only because of their large number, but also because their identities were not static; most Mayan deities had four distinct persona, one for each of the four cardinal directions. These multiple persona often embodied contradictions, such as male and female, old and young, good and evil. Sometimes, gods' attributes (and even names) changed from city to city. All of this, along with difficulty in matching gods named in Mayan glyphs with those in postconquest documents, has frustrated experts seeking to assemble a single, definitive inventory of Mayan theological symbols.

Mayan Class Structure

Mayan religion also prescribed a rather strict class structure in which the common people, most of whom were farmers, worked to sustain a small elite that understood astronomy, language, and religious rites. The class structure was so ingrained that when members of the elite traveled, common people often shouldered their litters for miles at a time. In this way, the common people were enlisted in a social structure in which they produced the necessities of life so that the elite could appease the gods and maintain the universe according to Mayan theology. When a baby came into the world, for example, Mayan priests predicted its future using star charts and other records; every moment in time was thought to be governed by the various deities; a child's future was believed to be predetermined.

Mayan custom dictated that people marry within their classes, but outside their families. This was as true for commoners as for the nobility; people in all classes of Mayan society maintained family lineages and married outside them. Between the common farmers and the aristocracy, merchants, artisans, military men, and others occupied the Mayan middle class. Below them were a class of landless serfs who sharecropped the lands of the elite; many of these serfs were freed prisoners of war who had not been sacrificed to the gods. Convicted criminals and people who had failed to pay their debts formed the lowest class of society. The poorest of the poor could be sold into slavery by their relatives; slavery often was the last stop before sacrifice.

Although Mayan society was constructed along well-defined class lines, limited social mobility did exist. Occasionally, a person could ascend in status by marriage or fall because of indiscretions such as chronic indebtedness. The elite seemed to have encouraged the infusion of some new blood into its ranks. For example, several high political offices were designated for commoners who distinguished themselves in battle. A degree of social mobility also was evident in Mayan burial customs, which could be similar for people of all classes. During 1992, archaeologists Arlene and Diane Chase of the University of Central Florida (Orlando), unearthed tombs showing similarities across classes at Caracol, in present-day Belize. The ruins of Caracol cover 55 square miles, and the Chases estimated that its population during the classic Mayan period reached 180,000. In 562 C.E., Caracol defeated Tikal, which had been the preeminent city in the region, in one of an intensifying series of wars that may have been one of many factors, including environmental degradation, that led to the Maya's eventual collapse as a civilization.

Each person in Mayan society was born into a family lineage, which included individuals related through the male side of the family. Inheritance of land, jewelry, and other items of material value also usually was governed by the male line. After marriage, however, a man by custom moved into the home of his bride's family, where he was destined for a period of service of six years or more. Women sometimes owned land in their own right, however, and passed it to their daughters; they also sometimes held high office in civil Mayan society, which was organized into municipal wards, each of which had an administrative officer. The municipal officers of all the wards in a town formed a governing council.

Although the society was fashioned to cater to them, nobles' lives were not without challenge or danger. They often led the intercity wars and often competed in a ritual ball game that also seems to have been tied into Mayan theology. The game shares some attributes of present-day basketball and soccer. Members of two teams tried to put a rubber ball through an elevated stone ring at each end of a ceremonial court. Players were not permitted to touch the ball with their hands (as in soccer). Penalties may have been assessed if the ball touched the ground. Losers at this game sometimes were sacrificed to the gods.

The Unearthing of Tikal and Other Sites

Archaeologists began to unearth a large metropolis at Tikal (in northern Guatemala) during 1956, yielding the tallest group of temple-pyramids in the New World (W. R. Coe, 1975). At Tikal, the Maya built large temples linked by causeways the width of modern freeways, as well as ball courts, a covered marketplace, and thousands of residences. Tikal was well developed by the time of Christ's birth. By its height, 800 years later, Tikal's population was between 30,000 and 60,000. The city's 3,000 structures included six pyramids, seven temple palaces, and several man-made reservoirs, all covering an area at least one mile square. The city is still an impressive sight, even in its decayed state, with remains of the pyramids towering 200 feet into the air and connected by wide causeways. Tikal's location took advantage of a nearby portage between rivers leading to the Gulf of Mexico and Caribbean Sea.

Like most of the other Mayan cities, Tikal declined about 890 C.E. according to the history recorded in its monuments. The religious and scientific elite collapsed, and squatters moved onto the ceremonial plazas amid the temples, living among piles of their own refuse, as the jungle reclaimed the city's outskirts.

The actual spadework at such sites takes large amounts of money and often trails speculation about what the forest still may hold. Like the ancient Egyptians, the rulers of the Maya were very good at immortalizing themselves in stone sculptures and other artifacts with a life of thousands of years. From these inscriptions and monuments, scholars are building a genealogy of rulers at Palenque, the Maya's westernmost major city, which lasted from 500 to nearly 800 C.E. Surprisingly, given the male dominance in most Mesoamerican cultures, at least two of the rulers in this city were women.

The Decline of the Maya

Palenque, like most other Mayan cities, declined abruptly in the ninth century C.E. The Spanish found the Aztecs in their full flower, but the Maya, with a few exceptions, were past their prime. Tulum, for example, still hosted an active trading culture along the Yucatan coast long after much of Mayan civilization had declined. The reasons for this eclipse are not known precisely; various arguments advance a case for the breakdown of trading relations, wars, environmental exhaustion of agriculture near the largest urban centers, earthquakes, hurricanes, and invasions by other peoples.

Disease may have played a role in the Maya's decline even before the Spanish conquest. Medical evidence indicates that the Maya shrunk in stature at the end of the classic period, probably because of malnutrition (La Fay, 1975, 762). The religious and scientific elites may have become overbearing in their demands on the common people, only to have them rise up and destroy the social structure that maintained the elites, according to a theory advanced by Eric Thompson (cited in Gann, 1925), a British scholar. Thompson has speculated that some of the Maya's former rulers may have escaped, joined the Toltecs, then later returned with them to reconquer parts of their former fiefdoms. The history of the Toltecs supports this idea. After most of the Mayan cities fell, the Toltecs are said to have established colonies in the area.

The final glory of Mayan civilization probably played itself out at Uxmal, forty-five miles southwest of present-day Merida, on the Yucatan peninsula. The Xiu family, which had originated elsewhere, became Mayanized and ruled the city from roughly 1000 C.E. until shortly before the Spanish conquest. Tulum may have been a trading outlet for Uxmal, which means "thrice built," a name that suggests the city had suffered a collapse twice before and then been rebuilt (Williams, 1991, 22).

As scholars learned more about Mayan society, they have discovered that, although a marked general decline occurred in Mayan society at about 900 C.E., it was not uniform. From time to time, new cultural infusions (mainly from the north, including the Valley of Mexico) seemed to cause some centers to rise again. For example, Chichen Itza saw the rise of a new dynasty that included both Mayan and Toltec elements for roughly two centuries after 1000 C.E. This dynasty dominated most of northern Yucatan at that time. The monumental architecture of Chichen Itza during this period shows Toltecs and their Mayan allies winning battles and their Mayan adversaries being led to the altar of the gods. After Chichen Itza declined about 1200 C.E., another center, Mayapan, dominated northern Yucatan. Further inland, the Quiche capital of Utatlan, in the highlands, began to dominate its hinterland at about 1400 C.E., and was in full flower at the time of the Spanish conquest a century and a quarter later.

In some locations, murals that are richly descriptive of the Maya's daily lives were buried under successive renovations of ceremonial centers with great care to ensure that they would survive intact for centuries. The best example of such intentional history comes from Cacaxtla, east of Mexico City, which apparently was a Mayan traders' center between 650 and about 1000 C.E. Spurred by treasure hunters' discoveries in 1975, archaeologists have been uncovering sets of huge murals that still retain much of their original coloration and detail.

The city was renovated eight times, and rebuilt atop its earlier site, which contained the richly hued murals, careful buried against layers of sand that preserved them (Stuart, 1992, 120–136).

The Role of War in the Mayan Decline

By the beginning of the twenty-first century, details of civilization-destroying wars among the Maya became evident as an important cause of their decline. A hurricane during the summer of 2001 uncovered carvings at Dos Pilas indicating that what previously had been described as a series of local wars during the seventh and eighth centuries C.E. really was a "world war" among the Maya between two blocs of allies, centered in Tikal and Calakmul. This picture emerged from explorations made public during 2002 by Arthur Demarest of Vanderbilt University's Institute of Mesoamerican Archeology (Nashville, TN) ("Scholars Rewrite," 2002, 12-A). According to Howard La Fay (1975):

> Gone forever is the image of the Maya as peaceful, rather primitive farmers practicing esoteric religious rites in their jungle fastness. What emerges is a portrait of a vivid, warlike race, numerous beyond any previous estimate, employing sophisticated agricultural techniques. And, like the Vikings half a world away, they traded and raided with zest. (p. 732)

Continual warfare probably also played a role in the environmental destruction of the Copan Valley; the monuments of the ceremonial center provide a chronicle of conflict lasting centuries. At one point, the thirteenth ruler of Copan, a man known to us as 18-Rabbit, was captured by the ruler of another Mayan city and decapitated. The historical evidence contained in inscriptions scattered all around Copan is so detailed that archaeologists can reconstruct not only the names and ruling dates of kings, but also the names or titles of the nine men who usually acted as advisors to the ruler.

According to Jared Diamond, more and more people fought over fewer resources. Maya warfare, already endemic, peaked just before the collapse. That is not surprising when one reflects that at least 5 million people, most of them farmers, were crammed into an area smaller than the state of Colorado. That's a high population by the standards of ancient farming societies, even if it wouldn't strike modern Manhattan-dwellers as crowded (Diamond, 2003, 49; Webster, 2002).

Climate Change and Mayan Decline

In addition to intercity violence, the Maya's final years as a high civilization also were afflicted by three intense droughts that crippled their corn-based agriculture. Recent research indicates that a population in the millions also degraded the environment. "This reinforces the tenuous nature of human civilizations in the face of a capricious Mother Nature," said Tom Pedersen, a University of Victoria (British Colombia) professor who is a recognized world authority on ancient climates (Calamai, 2003).

A research team led by Gerald Haug (who did postdoctoral studies with Pedersen) reconstructed Yucatan rainfall year by year using improved techniques to extract climate information preserved in ocean floor sediments. The scientists were able to read the sediments as if they were tree rings, said Haug, who is now researching ancient climates at a geosciences institute in Potsdam, Germany (Calamai, 2003). The researchers identified three decade-long droughts (around 810, 860, and 910 C.E.) that devastated Mayan society. According to this research, rainfall already had been declining slowly for a century because of changes in large-scale atmospheric circulation patterns. Haug and colleagues (2003) concluded that "a century-scale decline in rainfall put a general strain on resources in the region, which was then exacerbated by abrupt drought events, contributing to the social stresses that led to the Maya demise" (p. 1731).

Intensive harvesting of wood, along with agriculture (which depleted fragile tropical soils), also seems to have caused the abandonment of some Mayan urban centers during the general collapse of Mayan society about 900 C.E. One example of this decline may be found in Copan, once a major Mayan ceremonial center in present-day Honduras. Scholars have discovered that the Copan Valley became overpopulated and overdeveloped. The destruction of the valley's forests (mainly to open new farming fields and to provide cooking fuel) ultimately destroyed the ecological balance of the area, forcing the abandonment of the ceremonial center. Researchers from Pennsylvania State University (University Park) "have demonstrated that that at the end of the [Mayan] Classic Period there was extensive soil loss, massive erosion, a long-term decline in rainfall, and probably a number of highly communicable diseases" (Fash and Fash, 1990, 28).

THE TOLTECS

North of the Valley of Mexico, in the southern reaches of present-day Hidalgo, the Toltecs' capital of Tula emerged as the premier Mesoamerican urban center as most of the Maya centers to the south declined. The urban area and ceremonial center of Tula was situated in a highland river valley that supplied water necessary for the irrigation to support intensive agriculture. Farmers began to occupy the area a few centuries before the birth of Christ; shortly afterward, Chingu, a regional center, rose a few miles north of the site that would later host Tula, probably as part of Teotihuacan's network of commerce. By 600 C.E., however, Chingu was declining as the trade network collapsed.

Documentary and archaeological records indicate that between 800 and 900 C.E., members of elites (as well as some people from the lower classes)

A Toltec princess. (Courtesy of the Library of Congress.)

moved from other cities toward Tula in large numbers, building a new urban center. These records combine history with myth. Some sources indicate that the majority of the Toltecs came from the Gulf Coast or even from northern Mexico. Tula reached a peak population of about 40,000 before the invading Aztecs arrived about 1170 C.E.

One class of priests, craftspeople, and merchants (called the *Nonoalca*) played a particularly pivotal role in making Tula the most influential urban center in Mesoamerica between roughly 900 and 1170 C.E. Various sources indicate that the Nonoalca were multiethnic, and that they spoke several languages (including Nahuatl, the language later used by the Aztecs, Popoloca, Mixtec, Mazatec, and even Maya). Such population movements tend to support the belief that some members of the urban elites and people who provided services for them moved from city to city over the generations and centuries.

At its height, Tula covered 5.4 square miles (Diehl, 1981, 58), including nearly half a square mile of uninhabited swamp (El Salitre), which was used mainly as a source of materials for baskets. This area may have provided Tula its original Toltec name, *Tollan*, which means place of the reeds.

Mesoamerican Urban Population Estimates

Because the number of people who occupied any given prehistoric urban site cannot be counted with a high degree of precision, archeologists have developed systems for obtaining educated guesses. They recognize the imprecision of estimates, so population figures are usually expressed in a range.

Tenochtitlan, the Aztecs' capital, has been estimated (Diehl, 1981, 58) to have had between 175,000 and 300,000 inhabitants at the beginning of the Spanish conquest. David Stannard, a historian of holocausts, wrote in 1992 that an estimate of 350,000 could be regarded as "conventional" (p. 3). Other estimates of the city's population range up to a million people. The range of estimates illustrates two things: first, that demographic history and archeology are not exact sciences; second, even at a consensus estimate of about 300,000, the Aztec capital was at least four times the size of any European urban area when the Spanish arrived in the Valley of Mexico (Gibson, 1964, 337–338).

One common method used to estimate urban populations in Mesoamerica has been to multiply the total occupied area by a density factor of 5,000 people per square kilometer, a figure derived from ethnographic studies of modern rural villages in the same area. This method assumes (perhaps in error) that modern people in that area utilize space in the same ways (vis-à-vis density) as their ancestors. Another method, according to Diehl (1981), is to determine the total number of housing units in an urban area and then multiply that number by the average population that each was believed to have housed. To get an accurate estimate using this method, one must know the total number of housing units, which is not always available. This figure is not known for Tula. Using various methods, the population of Tula, for example, has been estimated at between 18,000 and 55,000, with a compromise figure at 30,000 to 40,000. Because the methodology is not precise and because there are several ways to estimate populations, estimates cited by different authorities often vary widely.

The Design of Tula

The main focus of Toltec archeology has been the urban area's largest buildings, in which ceremonies and affairs of religion and state were carried out: temples, large, colonnaded halls, ball courts, and, most recently, palaces, marketplaces, and storehouses. During the late 1970s and early 1980s, research teams from the University of Missouri at Columbia also made an intensive study of Toltec urban residences. To date, however, archeology has focused almost entirely on the capital, Tula, so very little is known about the network of agricultural villages that surrounded the city and fed its elite. A similar bias is evident in the archeology of other Mesoamerican civilizations, so the concrete results that we see often accentuate the grandeur of the cities and underplay the day-to-day business of feeding a civilization, which leaves fewer artifacts.

The center of Tula featured the usual array of temples and other pyramidlike structures that frequently closely resemble their predecessors in other cities around the valley of Mexico as well as the Maya's cities. Tula was much smaller than Teotihuacan (perhaps one-fifth or fewer population), and its artistic development often pales beside that of the earlier city. Although the Aztecs mythologized the Toltecs in many ways, the capital onto which Cortes' eyes fell in 1519 made Tula look like a provincial outpost. The archeological landscape of Tula is relatively barren in large part because the Aztecs stripped Tula bare of luxuries as they conquered the city. Many artifacts that originated in Tula have been found among the ruins of Tenochtitlan, under contemporary Mexico City. Nevertheless, the Toltecs were capable of producing elaborate friezes (which also often served as a form of written communication), as well as elaborately carved sculptures that served as roof supports for the major temples of Tula.

Private homes at Tula nearly always have been found in groups of three to five, each containing several rooms, all facing into a common interior courtyard. This pattern indicates the presence of extended families who lived together and acted as economic and family units. Each group of houses often was fenced off from other clusters, indicating an interest in privacy. Entrances often were built into halls that turned ninety degrees to ensure the privacy of occupants. The house clusters usually were constructed of stone and earth, with flat roofs resembling those of the later Aztecs. The houses often were used as tombs as well as to attend to the daily needs of the living. Instead of burying their dead in separate tombs or cemeteries, Toltec families often buried the deceased in a pit under the floor of their homes. High-status individuals sometimes were buried under altars in family courtyards. Many of those tombs were looted by the Aztecs.

The houses were well adapted to their highland environment, with thick adobe walls that retained cool air during hot summer afternoons. The same structures also held warmth during cold winter mornings. Drainage pipes were constructed to siphon occasional heavy rains that fell on Tula, and stone foundations helped prevent moisture from leaking into homes through the floors (Diehl, 1981, 90–96).

Like many other major Mesoamerican urban areas, Tula was surrounded by a network of agricultural villages. Although little is known about these villages (compared to knowledge of the urban areas), the Spanish chronicler Bernardino de Sahagún left descriptions of agricultural superlatives attributed to the Toltecs that were probably embellished by Aztec mythology. The Toltecs, for example, were said to have grown cotton in many colors. This is improbable because cotton does not grow well in the highlands.

Toltec Agriculture and City Life

The Spanish chronicler Sahagún wrote that that Toltec ears of corn (their basic food) were of a size that (in Diehl's words) "would have been the talk of the annual Missouri State Fair" (1981, 98), another superlative that probably stretches the truth because early corn was quite small compared to today's varieties. Aside from corn, the people of Tula ate chili sauces, beans, several varieties of squashes, amaranth seeds, wild seeds, fruits, and magueys, sap from the hearts of which could be fermented into the alcoholic brew called *pulque* that the Aztecs said caused the city's drunken downfall. Meat (usually small dogs and turkeys) was rare and usually eaten by most people only on ceremonial occasions.

Agriculture around Tula was made possible by extensive irrigation from a nearby river. The area is laced with ditches and canals, which indicate that water was moved from place to place in large quantities. Some farm fields also were terraced, and many private home clusters also contained intensively cultivated domestic gardens in which people raised vegetables, herbs, and medicinal plants (Diehl, 1981, 98–100). Farmers usually traded their surplus for goods and services in the city; they also had no choice but to pay tax levies utilized to support the urban elite who offered them its protection. Perhaps the heavy hand of tribute played a role in popular uprisings that ended each Mesoamerican empire's era of technological achievement and hierarchical social organization; Cortes could certainly attest to the eagerness with which people who had been subjugated by the Aztecs forged alliances with him. If the Aztecs had been kinder to their subject peoples, Cortes might never have reached Tenohtitlan.

Most of the Valley of Mexico's urban areas (like many Mayan cities) contained ball courts with large spectator areas, indicating the popularity of a ritual game that was played on an enclosed court shaped most often like the capital letter *I*. Although the game was probably first played by the Olmecs, formalized play (indicated by the well-developed courts) came to the Valley of Mexico after the fall of Teotihuacan. Early Spanish chroniclers described the game as being played by two teams; the aim was to get a hard rubber ball into the court of the other team and through stone hoops mounted on the walls of the enclosed court. Players were allowed to move the ball in any way as long as they did not use hands or feet. Spectators at Tula probably engaged in avid betting matches based on the outcome of the game (some were reduced to poverty by their gambling). As with the Maya, the losers sometimes found themselves sacrificed to the gods. In Tula, the skulls of the losers were sometimes displayed on specially made racks, like trophies. As an added attraction at Tula, evidence indicates that the winners were sometimes encouraged to rob losing spectators of their clothing and jewelry.

As with empires of more recent vintage, political power often followed commerce among the Toltecs, as it would with the Aztecs. Traders, who ranged far beyond the areas within which tribute was collected, often traveled in the employ of their home city's military elite, acting as spies, sometimes as double agents. Traders from Tula covered an area that included the entire Yucatan Peninsula and most of the northern reaches of Mayan highland country. In the north, traders sought precious materials, such as turquoise, copper, gold, and silver, in the arid steppes of what is now northern Mexico. Tula seems to have been a manufacturing center for such objects as obsidian cutting tools and other crafts.

A lively debate has arisen among archeologists concerning the quality and quantity of Toltec crafts. Sahagún wrote (probably borrowing from an Aztec account) of the Toltecs' mastery:

> Many of them were scribes, lapidarians, carpenters, stone cutters, masons, feather workers, feather gluers, potters, spinners, weavers. They were very learned. They ... knew of green stones, fine turquoise, common turquoise. ... They went on to learn of, to seek out, the mines of silver, gold, copper, tin, mica, lead. ... They performed works of art, they performed works of skill, [creating] all the wonderful, precious, marvelous things they made. (1950–1969, 10:167)

Some Toltec art portrays men wearing large amounts of jewelry (which may have been copper or gold) around their wrists and upper arms. Tula also bears widespread evidence of having been a center of manufacture for obsidian blades.

Skilled craftspeople gathered in urban centers that had a need for their skills and the means to pay for them; they usually were members of hereditary guilds, distinct ethnically from the cities in which they lived. Often, the craftspeople moved from city to city with the traveling elites. Like craft production, trade in many Mesoamerican civilizations was conducted by a specialized class. Wealth accumulated in trade could improve one's social status to a certain degree in the home city, but if a trader became overly greedy or ostentatious, the envy of fellow residents could cause problems.

Regarding the Toltecs' crafts and commerce, much remains to be discovered. The marketplace at Tula awaits exploration, for example. Some Toltec crafts have been found, including intriguing children's toys with axles and wheels, a discovery that contradicts a former belief that indigenous Americans were ignorant of the wheel. The Toltecs knew of the device but never adapted it to transportation because they had no draft animals. Without large animals, a wheeled conveyance would have been practically useless unless humans pulled it.

At the height of the Toltec culture, continuing into the Aztec period, trade flourished between Mesoamerica and Native nations to the north. Live parrots from the Valley of Mexico were traded with the Pueblos 1,200 miles to the north; other bearers of wares crossed the Gulf of Mexico northward, into eastern North America, spreading goods from as far south as Mayan country through "a grand alliance of prosperous little nations, stretching from the Gulf Coast to Wisconsin, from New York to Kansas and Nebraska" (Brandon, 1961, 50). Many of the people with whom the Mesoamericans traded also sometimes built large earthworks, including temple mounds.

As each major culture rose, expanded, then fell, several smaller cultures sharing some of the same attributes also existed along the fringes of the major administrative states. This was especially true during times of instability, such as those that followed the fall of Teotihuacan. The major center at this time (around 1000 C.E.) was Tula, but other major sites have been found east of the mountains that separate the Valley of Mexico from the Puebla Valley (Cholula), as well as along the Gulf Coast. Tula also competed with Xochicalco, an urban center built on several hilltops near the border of Morelos and Guerrero. This city features well-developed ramparts, indicating warfare in the vicinity, possibly with Toltec forces. Xochicalco controlled access to deposits of jade and other minerals that may have been a source of conflict.

By about 1170 C.E., Tula succumbed to invaders from the north whom they called Chichimecs (Dog People). Lean, hungry, and barbarous, they arrived behind a barrage of bows and arrows and stayed to absorb the culture of the Valley of Mexico. Sources disagree whether the Aztecs, one of the groups of migrants flowing southward, were the first on the scene to pillage Tula. Some of them may have arrived as late as around 1325 C.E. A number of peoples came south, jostling with each other for power, transforming themselves from primitive hunters to "grand patrons of the arts, swooning esthetically over bouquets and manipulating feather fans with a fine aristocratic grace" (Brandon, 1961, 66). Those who did not speak the Aztecs' Nahua language learned it as they began to build a collection of city-states around the lake that would host the crowning glory of the Aztecs.

THE AZTECS (MEXICAS)

The Spanish conquistadors encountered the Aztecs' remarkable civilization in its full flower. A few of them described the Aztec Empire in detail before Spanish guns, avarice, and disease destroyed it. The architectural center of the Aztecs, Tenochtitlan, occupied the contemporary site of another great metropolis, Mexico City.

Much of our archeological knowledge of the Aztecs comes by way of Mexico City public works projects, such as the city's subway, which involved digging into the earth. The most significant remains of the Aztecs' 200-foot high Templo Mayor (Great Temple) were not found until 1978. The first traces of the Great Temple were unearthed during excavations for a sewer line in 1900. In 1913, another public works project uncovered the southwest corner of the temple; in 1967, construction of the Mexico City subway began to unearth sizable numbers of Aztec artifacts. Without such intense (if unintentional) spadework, we would know much less about the capstone civilization that followed more than a millennium of remarkable cities in Mesoamerica.

Archeologists and others, some of whom have deciphered pre-Columbian texts in the Valley of Mexico, are piecing together a fascinating story. Many modern scholars in this area, especially in present-day Mexico, are not using the name "Aztec" as a generalized name for the people who lived in the valley when Cortes arrived. Instead, they refer to "Mexicas," as they called themselves, speakers of the Nahuatl language, a rich quilt of peoples living in cities that rose and fell after the decline of Tula. Several peoples lived in the Valley of Mexico only a few miles from the island that became the Aztecs' "City of the Gods." The people who moved into the valley in the fourteenth century called the place where they lived "Mexica," from which "Mexico" is derived.

As in the Old World, the seat of civilization had passed from people to people over the centuries: from the fertile crescent to Egypt to Greece and Rome in Europe and nearby Africa and Asia; from the Olmec and Maya, to the Toltecs, and to the Mexicas. While Europe endured its Dark Ages, the world of the Mexica flourished. The Aztecs reached their peak as Europe emerged from its own Dark Age during a burst of overseas exploration that began with the voyages of Columbus.

The first Spaniards to witness Tenochtitlan described a city more splendid, and more mysterious, than any their well-traveled eyes ever had seen. While some Spanish conquistadors and priests warmed their hands over fires built from valuable artifacts and records that would have been of immense use to archeologists today, the Franciscan friar Bernadino de Sahagún, born in Spain during 1499, traveled to Mexico and mastered Nahuatl as he began a Franciscan school for sons of surviving Aztec nobles. At the same time, Sahagún prepared a dozen hand-embellished manuscripts (called codices) describing Mexica (Aztec) history, cosmology, legends, and daily life. King Philip II of

Spain refused to permit publication of the codices, which were finally published two and a half centuries later (Sahagún, 1950–1969).

The Mexicas or Aztecs were only the last, largest, and (because of Spanish historians) the best known of many peoples who built civilizations in the Valley of Mexico. Today, archeologists agree that the prehistoric and protohistoric periods of Mexico cover at least 20,000 years. The comparison of this long period with the 300 years of colonial life and the fewer than two centuries of the modern independent (Mexican) nation makes it appropriate to identify the pre-Columbian millennia as "the substratum and root of present-day Mexico" (Leon-Portilla, 1972, 3).

Origins of the Aztecs

The Aztecs probably moved to the Valley of Mexico from the present-day Mexican state of Nayarit, about 450 miles northwest of the site on which they later established Tenochtitlan (Smith, 1984, 153–186). The marshes of the Pacific Coast, not far from Mexicaltitan, fit ancient descriptions of the Aztecs' origin place, Aztlan, "place of the herons," from which they derived "Aztec," meaning "people of the heron place." Professor Wigberto Jimenez-Moreno (1970) believes that the first Aztec village may have been located at Mexicaltitan, on an island in the San Pedro River in Nayarit State. This site has been called the "Venice of Mexico" because during the rainy season its streets flood, and people often convey themselves mainly by boat. Aztec history relates that the people wandered for centuries after leaving Nayarit in search of a permanent home, passing through Tula for a century or longer.

Imagine the amazement of the Aztecs when they found a vast lake in the mountains of central Mexico. On an island in that lake, they built the grandest of early American cities. In its heyday, after their travels returning members of Tenochtitlan's ruling elite were welcomed back into the city with a chant that welcomed them to the court-city, Mexico-Tenochtitlan, in the still water, where the eagle cried, and the serpent hissed, where fish leaped.

Following the decline of the Toltecs, a number of city-states contended for power in the Valley of Mexico before the Aztecs became dominant. Azcapotzalkco, to the west of Lake Texcoco, rose early, followed by the Acolhuas, who ruled the city of Texcoco, to the east of the lake. At one point, they collected tribute from seventy surrounding towns. The Culhuacan also grew in power to the south of Lake Texcoco where it joined Lake Xochimilco. When the Mexicas first came to the valley of Mexico, the Culhuas probably employed them as mercenaries. At one point, the Mexicas decided to "honor" the Culhuan king by slaying his daughter. They asked the king to attend a ceremony "celebrating" the slaying. The king did not appreciate the Aztecs' concept of honor. He enslaved or killed the leaders of the "ceremony" and drove the rest of the Mexicas into exile.

The history of the Aztecs indicates that they were not greeted warmly by peoples who had resided in the Valley of Mexico before them:

> Upon arriving
> when they were following their path
> they were not received anywhere.
> Everywhere, they were reprehended.
> No one knew their face.
> Everywhere they were told:
> "Who are you?
> "Where did you come from?"
> Thus they were unable to settle anywhere;
> they were only cast out,
> everywhere they were persecuted...
> —Sahagún, 1992, 30

According to the Aztecs' chroniclers, their people settled in the Valley of Mexico in a year corresponding to 1325 C.E. on the Christian calendar. From their capital city, the Aztec Empire eventually reached the Gulf of Mexico and into Guatemala, which is a Nahuatl name.

Growth of the Aztec Empire

Eventually, the Aztecs settled on the marshy island where some of their enemies figured that the abundant snake population would torture them. Instead, the Aztecs roasted the snakes and ate them. In the century between 1325 and the early 1400s, the Mexicas negotiated a number of alliances and subjugated other city-states. In the end, they even came to dominate peoples who once had looked down on them. The residents of Texcoco, perhaps the most powerful of these, were besieged, then overwhelmed during 1416. Legend has it that the Aztecs killed Texcoco's king, Ixtlilxochitl, as his son, Nezahualcyotl (Hungry Coyote), escaped to become one of Mexico's most famous legendary figures. Nezahualcyotl hid in the mountains writing poetry, developing a philosophy that centered around the Unknown God, who demanded only prayers instead of human blood. It is said that Hungry Coyote sometimes visited the Aztec-dominated cities in disguise, rallying followers to his faith, as the Aztec minions tried to capture him. At one point he was captured, but a guard released him and was put to death in Hungry Coyote's place.

The rituals of blood sacrifice were so engrained in the culture of the Mexicas and other residents of the valley that Nezahualcoytl, who ruled Texcoco shortly before Columbus' voyages, could not persuade the people to give them up. The priests forcefully talked Nezahualcoytl out of his campaign to stop blood sacrifice, and Nezahualcoytl had to be content with building a new temple, ten stories high, capped by an ornate chapel dedicated to "the

Aztec priest performing a sacrificial offering. (Courtesy of the Library of Congress.)

Cause of All Causes, the Unknown God," in which offerings were made in flowers and scented gums instead of blood.

As the Aztecs' empire spread, Tenochtitlan grew on land reclaimed from surrounding swamps. Two aqueducts three miles long were built to carry freshwater from the mainland; each had two sluices so one could be closed for cleaning without interrupting the water supply. Tribute and captives flowed into the city after conquests that spread from the Gulf of Mexico to the Pacific Ocean. West of the Valley of Mexico, however, the Aztecs' armies were stopped by the bowmen of the Tarascans. The Aztecs never completely conquered the Tlaxcalans to the east, although they did surround their city and cut off its commerce. The Aztecs' hegemony was only rarely administrative; after they pillaged another people's city, the conquered people usually were left alone to manage their own affairs until the next call for tribute and captives to satisfy the blood hunger of the Aztecs' gods.

Aztec Warfare and the Power of Ritual

Aztec warfare was as much a pageant as a battle. Wars were fought hand to hand. Aztecs disarmed their opponents and forced them to surrender or beat them unconscious. Soldiers made fashion statements as much as war, wearing headdresses and shirts of yellow parrot feathers and quetzal feathers set off with gold. Soldiers wore jaguar skins and hoods of gold with feather horn adornments. Their shields were decorated with golden disks displaying butterflies and serpents. The armies of the Aztec Empire went to battle with "two-toned drums, conch-shell trumpets, shrill clay whistles, screams full-voiced (. . . to shock and terrify the enemy) calling to the heavens for help and witness" (Brandon, 1961, 67). Priests led the soldiers into battle with trumpet blasts calling on the gods to witness. The priests then waited in the rear with razor-sharp obsidian blades, ready to feed the gods with the still-warm blood of captives' beating hearts.

Like few other peoples in the Americas, the Aztecs were mobilized for war, for expansion, and for expropriation of tribute from less-militaristic peoples. Every Mexica man over the age of 15 years was considered a potential member of the army except those in training for the priesthood or as civil officials. The entire male population was never mobilized at once, however. All young boys were taught the use of basic weapons, such as the spear thrower and bow and arrow. At 15 years of age, most young men in Tenochtitlan were sent to live for a number of months in "houses of youth," where they were taught arts of war, as well as academic subjects. The capital city had 20 "houses of youth," each affiliated with a different *calpulli*, an administrative district.

The Aztecs usually initiated a confrontation with another group of people by sending an emissary to its leaders to exact a set tribute. If the group agreed to submit, the Mexica foreign minister returned with gifts and a schedule of payment, and a peace was established. If no tribute was pledged, the Aztec delegate (or delegates) applied white paint to the prospective enemy's commanding officer, placed feathers on his head, then handed him a sword and shield as a formal declaration of war. The Aztecs did not always follow their own customs, however. Sometimes, they engaged in surprise attacks and pillaging.

After a battle, members of the ruling class often hired musicians to memorialize the occasion in song. A small orchestra usually played for Mochtezuma (the Mexicas' supreme leader at the time of Cortes' arrival) at mealtimes as well. Most Aztec music had overtones not only of war and power, but also of divine rite. All ritual music was performed by members of a specially trained professional caste. A single error, one small departure from established ritual, could result in death because an erring musician was said to have disturbed the gods. The rituals required very well-developed memories, as well as a sense of creative showmanship. The best ritual singers were said to have enjoyed high social prestige (Driver, 1969, 205).

The Aztecs were acutely aware of the power that their capital symbolized in the Mesoamerica of their day. They were not accidental imperialists, as the following Aztec narrative indicates:

> Proud of itself
> Is the city of Mexico—Tenochtitlan

Here no one fears to die in war
This is our glory
This is Your Command
Oh Giver of Life
Have this mind, oh princes
Who would conquer Tenochtitlan?
Who would shake the foundation of heaven?
—Leon-Portilla, 1969, 87

Symbols played a very important role in the Mexica mind. Their capital was believed to be the center of the universe, and the Great Temple of Tenochtitlan was the center of Aztec spiritual and secular power. Tenochtitlan's two main temples were dedicated to the two gods who influenced the most important events and values in Mexica life: the god of agriculture, rain, and water (*Tlaloc*) and the god of war, tribute, and conquest (*Huitzilopochtli*). The temples dedicated to these two gods displayed an Aztec attitude of dominance over the peoples around them—an attitude that the Spanish replicated when they built their own religious center, a major cathedral, on top of the Great Temple. Eduardo Matos Mochtezuma, a descendant of the Aztec ruler who first met Cortes and general coordinator of the Mexican project that is unearthing the Great Temple, wrote that the great temple was a symbol of the Aztecs' way of thinking, living, and sometimes dying (1988, 15–60).

During the century and a half that the Aztecs dominated Mesoamerica, the Aztecs' Templo Mayor was rebuilt seven times. It became so complex that after the Spanish thought it had been destroyed, several levels still remained to be discovered under the Catholic cathedral that the Spanish built on the same site. The full complexity of the temple was not discovered until the unintentional excavations of twentieth century public works, notably Mexico City's subway, uncovered subterranean levels that had been bypassed by the colonists.

The Blood Sacrifice

The Aztecs were not benign rulers; they dragged thousands of subject peoples back to Tenochtitlan for forced labor and religious sacrifice. The Great Temple was not substantially completed until 1487, a little more than three decades before Cortes' Spanish forces invaded the area. During those three decades, estimates of the number of people sacrificed for religious purposes ranged from 10,000 to 80,000 (McDowell, 1980, 726–727). Bernal Diaz de Castillo wrote that he counted 100,000 skulls of sacrificial victims in the plazas of Tenochtitlan (Wilkerson, 1984, 445–446).

During the periods of ritual killing, four people at a time were sacrificed at the Great Temple from dawn to dusk. The entire city—otherwise a place of magnificent architecture and brilliant colors where fierce warriors often walked the streets celebrating the virtues of flowers in poetry—stank of burning flesh.

At times, the stench was sealed into the valley by the same atmospheric inversions that today capture some of the world's worst air pollution. When the number of prisoners of war available for sacrifice ran low, the Aztecs and neighboring city-states engaged in ritual Wars of the Flowers simply to harvest candidates for sacrifice.

Even as they sacrificed human beings to their gods en masse, the Aztecs seemed to have had no concept of torture solely for the sake of cruelty. Their gods were not conceived as angry as much as they were thought to be hungry. Some of the priests stationed at the foot of the Great Temple even prayed for sacrificial victims: "May he savor the fragrance, the sweetness of death by the obsidian blade" (McDowell, 1980, 729–730). The Aztecs exacted tribute, as well as lives, from vassal peoples; they built a commercial network that brought to the Valley of Mexico all manner of food, rare feathers, precious metals, and other commodities, many of which were traded at a great market at Tlatelolco. Cortes reported having seen up to 60,000 people at a time bartering in this grand bazaar, where disputes were settled on the spot by judges. Among the items for sale in the market were turkeys, which the Aztecs were the first to domesticate. The Spanish took some of the birds home. Turkeys reached England before the first voyages of settlement from Britain. The Pilgrims had turkeys aboard their ships when they arrived in the New World and found similar wild fowl being hunted by Native people.

The imagery of the Aztecs' volatile cosmology resembled the mountainous, volcano-studded land that surrounded them. They believed that the world had been destroyed four times. To create the sun and moon for the fifth epoch, two gods committed suicide by immolating themselves in fire. The Aztec god representing darkness was not a kind personage. The spirit of darkness was described in a poem that survived the conquest:

> He mocks us.
> As he wishes, so he wills.
> He places us in the palm of his hand,
> He rolls us about;
> Like pebbles we roll, we spin . . .
> We make him laugh.
> He mocks us.
> —McDowell, 1980, 729–730

The Mexicas built all their temples, monuments, and homes without using bronze tools. They did use the wheel, but only on children's toys. Instead of using wheeled conveyances to transport building materials, the vassals of the Aztecs carried them or rolled them on beds of logs. All of this also was accomplished without beasts of burden. Scholars have speculated on what the Aztecs might have accomplished had their civilization not been put to the torch by the Spanish. No one really knows; it is known, however, that the rapid growth of the large city was already using up nearby resources of firewood. In 1454, a debilitating famine had swept the area.

Aztec Socioeconomic and Governmental Structures

In Aztec society, each person was born into a social class. At the head of this socioeconomic pyramid was the king (*tlatoani* or *tlacatecuhtli*), a descendant of the Toltec prince Acamapichtli, who in turn was believed to have been descended from Quetzacoatl, an important god of the Toltecs and Aztecs. Aztec history described how the prince had come to Tenochtitlam to found the city's royal line, from unions with 20 wives, probably one from each *calpulli*, or local governing unit.

The Nobles (*pipiltin*) were distinguished by the legal permission afforded them to own land in their own names on reaching adulthood. They also were taught to use glyphs (a form of Mexica writing) along with knowledge of cultural arts and religion. They held the highest judicial, military, civil, and religious posts, but membership in this class did not guarantee a prestigious office. Office also required leadership skills. Nobles who did not have such skills might end up being palace servants or even enduring unemployment. Below the Nobles stood a class of Knights (*caballeros pardos*), who had been raised to their standing, usually from the lower classes, because of valor in warfare.

The commoners or working class (*macehualtin*) were educated to farm communal lands or to practice trades. They could not own land (farms were the common property of the *calpulli*), but they could consume, sell, or exchange what they produced from their labor on the land. A talented member of this class could rise to the higher offices of his *calpulli* and thereby, in practice, outrank a Noble who had no official position. A separate class, a proletariat, owned no land, but also had no masters. Typically, members of this class might work as craftspeople or day laborers. Below the working class, the serfs (*mayeques*) sometimes worked their way upward.

Aztec class structure was sometimes fluid; people could rise and fall on merit or luck. Serfs were assigned to certain plots of land and were paid with a portion of their produce from it. If land was sold, the serfs assigned to it were considered part of the transaction. Besides agricultural work, serfs were expected to render menial services to their masters. Men might haul water or build a house; women might prepare meals. A large number of Mexica serfs had been commoners from conquered nations; some native Aztec commoners even tried to pass as serfs to avoid paying taxes.

The slaves were at the bottom of the hierarchy; they could be assigned to any job by their masters. The master owned only the labor of the slave, not his or her life. A slave could own a residence and could not be traded or sold to another master without consent. The status often was temporary; a slave also was allowed to own the services of another slave.

The Aztecs governed themselves according to a clan-based system that included aspects of consensus and hierarchy. This system did not fit any European category of government. The 20 *calpulli* of the state each elected officials similar to county clerks or aldermen. Each clan also elected a speaker (*tlatoani*), who sat on a supreme state council. From these leaders, four were appointed to executive posts. In Tenochtitlan, one of these four, called *tlacatecuhtli* (chief of men) or *hueytlatoani* (revered speaker), was chosen to be chief executive, a lifetime appointment.

The dual nature of the system considers that some Spanish accounts refer to the government as a "republic," and others called Aztec leaders kings. Elected along kin lines, Aztec leaders enjoyed total authority once they were elevated to office. Ownership of most land (except that owned by members of the elite) rested with the clans. This concept often confused the Spanish, who were accustomed to individual or royal ownership.

Another concept that sometimes confused the Spanish, who came from a male-dominated society, was the influence of Mexica women. The Mexica language referred to a woman as "the owner of a man" (McDowell, 1980, 730–731).

Aztec Cosmology

Mexica cosmology placed the people at the mercy of an array of gods; some researchers have counted as many as 1,600. Most Aztecs believed that the gods could not keep the sun and moon moving (and by implication, continue the cycle of life on earth) without a steady diet of human flesh and blood. The Aztecs waged war to procure prisoners for sacrifice to their gods.

The appetites of the Mexica gods were interpreted according to the so-called Calendar Stone, which is not a calendar at all. The calendar weighs 24 metric tons (of basalt) and measures 3.6 meters (about 12 feet) in diameter with a thickness of 72 centimeters. The stone, which was uncovered in 1790 in Mexico City's Zocalo district, site of Tenochtitlan's main square, is sometimes thought of as a calendar because of the day signs that surround its center. The significance of this enormously complex sculpture was not to mark the passage of time, however, but to help the Aztecs interpret the demands of their gods, whose satisfaction they believed crucial to the continuance of life on earth.

The Stone of the Fifth Sun (so called because the Aztecs believed that they were living in the fifth, and last, epoch of life on earth) detailed how the Aztecs believed the cosmos had begun and would end. According to Aztec cosmology, the fifth epoch had begun in the year they called 13-Reed, or 1011 C.E. Aztec belief held that the fifth epoch would end if the Aztecs' deities were not satiated with an abundant supply of human blood, which required the sacrifices. The history of the Mexica provided precedents in four preceding failed foundings. Earlier generations were said to have been dispersed in the mountains, cross-bred with monkeys, or returned to the earth as turkeys after they refused to please the gods.

The Aztec cosmos was filled with gods for every human activity, from fertility to death. Each community and craft had its deity; some of them were believed to change their characteristics to confuse their enemies. Some of the gods required more than blood to maintain the sun's compass across the sky. They also demanded homage—lavish ritual processions with music, cakes, and costumes. The coming of a vengeful bearded people from the east (the direction of the rising sun) fit the Aztecs' own worldview. Initially, many Mexicas believed the Spanish to be emissaries of their own gods. Some of the gods fused history and myth. Quetzalcoatl, for example, combined the memories of a man who had ruled the Toltecs at Tula with an earlier serpent god; tradition held that he created civilization (agriculture and writing). Quetzalcoatl had been forced out of Tula in disgrace because of public drunkenness, but that he would someday return from the east.

Premonitions of Change

Throughout the decade before the bearded, armor-clothed Europeans whom the Aztecs sometimes called "the people from heaven" arrived, the Aztecs had premonitions that they were about to meet a terrible power greater than their own. The 5,000 priests of Tenochtitlan, who heretofore had been concerned mainly with garnering enough blood to satisfy the appetites of the gods, had religious premonitions that the life of their city was about to be permanently altered. In 1507, a dozen years before Cortes arrived, the New Fire ceremonies were held for the last time. These rituals came at the end of the 52 years that comprised the Aztec temporal cycle. Temples were enlarged or rebuilt, old animosities forgiven, and debts paid.

At about the same time, the people of Tenochitlan witnessed a number of supernatural events that indicated trouble ahead. The history of the Aztecs says that a temple burst into flame for no apparent reason. At a musicians' school, a ceiling beam sang of impending doom. Lightning struck another temple from a cloudless sky. A sudden flood washed away a number of homes. A terrifying column of flame rose by night in the east, causing a terror-filled populace to panic: "All were frightened; all waited in dread" (Brandon, 1961, 76). The Serpent Woman and Earth Goddess *Cihuacoatl*, who haunted the streets at night telling mothers when their children would die, was said to be heard weeping, night after night, "My beloved sons, whither shall I take you?" (ibid., 76).

The Spanish Marvel at Tenochtitlan

The Spanish soldier Bernal Diaz del Castillo described Tenochtitlan as one of the greatest cities in the world. Although Tenochtitlan's solid temples, residences, and storehouses lent an air of permanence, the city was not old by

Mesoamerican urban standards. Less than two centuries before Diaz saw it, the site had been little more than a small temple surrounded by a few mud-and-thatch huts.

By 1519, however, Diaz found a city of unexpected splendor. He described Tenochtitlan from the top of the Great Temple:

> Here we had a clear prospect of the three causeways by which Mexico [Tenoch-titlan] communicated with land, and of the aqueduct of Chapultepec, which sup-plied the city with the finest water. We were struck with the numbers of canoes, passing to and from the mainland, loaded with provisions and merchandise, and we could now perceive that...the houses stood separate from each other, communicating only by small drawbridges, and by boats, and that they were built with terraced tops. We observed also the temples...of the adjacent cities, built in the form of towers...wonderfully brilliant...and those [Spanish soldiers] who had been at Rome and Constantinople said, that for convenience, regularity, and population, they had never seen the like. (Molina Montes, 1980, 753)

The Spanish compiled a careful chronicle of this amazing new world as their soldiers and pathogens laid waste to it. Friar Sahagún enlisted Aztec eyewitnesses and trained observers (in some ways similar to English bards). He also utilized the Aztecs' hieroglyphic codices. Sahagún himself was fluent in Nahuatl, the Mexicas' language.

Aztec prisoners did the muscle work of building Tenochtitlan's majestic tem-ples and causeways, along which eight horsemen could ride abreast. According to Cortes' accounts, the "excellence" and "grandeur" of the Aztecs' capital outshone anything he had ever seen. "In Spain, there is nothing to compare," he wrote, continuing:

> During the morning, we arrived at a broad causeway, and continued our march from Ixtapalapa, and when we saw so many cities and villages built into the water and other great towns on dry land and that straight and level causeway going towards Mexico [Tenochtitlan], we were amazed, and said that it was like the enchant-ments they tell of in the legends of Amadis, on account of the great towers and cues [temples], great towers that stood in the water, and all of masonry...[T]here were even some of our soldiers who asked if what they saw was in a dream. It is not to be wondered at that I here write it down in this manner, for there is so much to think over that I do not know how to describe it, seeing things as we did that had never been heard of or seen before. (Del Castillo, 1958, 190–191)

The Aztecs' capital was a cavalcade of color—the architecture was painted turquoise, yellow, red, and green—often annotated with visual history in murals. An observer could have seen the eagle, snake, and cactus that com-prise Mexico's modern national symbols on some of the buildings. The Aztecs' history maintained that they had been led to this spot by divine prophecy, to a place where an eagle perched on a cactus extended its wings toward the rays of the sun. The fact that such a city was built in less than two centuries is awesome enough even in modern times. When one reflects on the Aztecs' lack of construction machinery (even the wheel), the scope of the metropolis that grew here becomes even more astonishing. The island on which Tenochtitlan was built contained no construction materials, so virtually everything used to construct it had to be ferried aboard canoes at first. Later, supplies were carried, or rolled on logs using ropes and pulleys, along the causeways that connected the city with the mainland.

Diaz del Castillo marveled at the Mexicas' armaments, and he did not stop at their design. The Aztecs' flint blades cut better than the Spaniards' swords, he admitted:

> Many of them [blades] were richly adorned with gold and precious stones. There were large and small shields, and some *macanas* [clubs], and others like two-handed swords set with some flint blades that cut better than our swords, and lances longer than ours, with a five-foot knife set with many blades. (del Castillo in Leon-Portilla, 1972, 122)

If Tenochtitlan's population was about 300,000, which seems likely, it was the largest Native American city in the hemisphere and the largest urban area of any type in North or South America until after 1800. At the time the United States became independent, its largest cities (Boston, New York, and Philadelphia) housed no more than 50,000 people each. The architects of the Aztec capital faced some problems apart from scarcity of materials and labor. The subsoil of the area was very soft, and buildings, once constructed, tended to sink into it, with some parts of them sinking more quickly than others. Aztec architects tried to combat this problem by building large sections of their temples with light, porous volcanic stone called *tezontle*, which could be quarried in abundance nearby. Slabs of *tezontle* often were cut (with stone, not metal tools) and then assembled so precisely that structures required no mortar. Early Spanish architecture in the Valley of Mexico sometimes utilized the same methods of construction; several of these buildings (such as the National Palace) still stand today in Mexico City (Molina Montes, 1980, 760–761).

The Spanish Conquest of the Aztecs

Cortes and his roughly 400 men forged alliances with many Native peoples, who were more than ready to turn on the domineering Mexicas. Through the adroit use of informants (such as the legendary Malinche) and an uncanny sense of timing that Aztec leaders sometimes thought was supernatural, Cortes's small band of Spanish conquistadors reduced a state that had subjugated millions to ashes within two bloody years. The Spanish also were aided by European diseases (the foremost of which was smallpox) and the Aztecs' own fear of a troublesome future.

The Spaniards' technology was superior but not by enough to swing the balance of power on its own. The Spanish recognized early, for example, that some of the Aztecs' weapons were sharper than theirs. Aztec cotton-padded armor was good enough that some Spanish troops adopted it. Very quickly, the conquistadors set about to turn the Native peoples into their own work-force, usually by compulsion. The rigors of labor, along with conquistador terror and disease, caused the Native population to decline rapidly. Henry Dobyns estimated that the population of Mexico declined from between 30 and 37.5 million people in 1520 to 1.5 million in 1650, a holocaust of a severity unknown in the Old World (1966, 395–449). Even if one argues that Dobyns' figures are too high, cutting them almost in half to 20 million in 1520 would produce a mortality rate in 130 years of 92.5 percent (Driver, 1969, 457).

Cortes began recruiting Indian allies against the Aztecs in Cempoalla, near the Gulf Coast, home to about 30,000 people of the Totonac nation, the first city he visited on his way to Tenochtitlan. The leaders of this city met Cortes on friendly terms and told him of how intensely many of the Aztecs' tributary tribes hated their oppressors. Despite the intensity of this hatred, the people of Cempoalla dared not revolt. However, Cempoalla supplied Cortes with about 400 *tamanes*, or equipment carriers, for the next leg of his journey, to nearby Chiahuitztla.

In that city, Cortes and his men met five Aztec tribute collectors, dressed in finery, whose assistants walked behind them shooing away flies with fans. The Aztecs upbraided the Totonacs for aiding Cortes and demanded twenty young men and women for sacrifice as punishment. Cortes made an emotive speech demanding that the Totonacs throw the tribute collectors into prison. After some frenzied discussion, they did. The following night, Cortes arranged for the escape of two of the tribute collectors, then convinced the Totonacs to transfer the other three to his "care" as well.

With the five captive Aztec tribute collectors in tow, Cortes and his men continued to climb the mountains bordering the Mexican plateau, toward Tenochtitlan. Along the way, Cortes encountered the Tlascalan nation, also en-emies of the Aztecs, whose warriors engaged his men in a round of inconclusive fighting before they joined Cortes in his war on the Aztecs. Allied with the Tlascalan warriors, Cortes entered the Valley of Mexico with enough manpower to initiate serious combat.

Cortes then stopped at Cholula, where he was welcomed with open arms. Cortes took advantage of the hospitality to invite leaders of the Cholulan nation to the public square of the city, which the Spanish said contained at least 20,000 buildings within its walls. Once most of the important people in Cholula had assembled to parlay with Cortes, his soldiers and their Tlascalan allies carried out prearranged orders to slaughter the Cholulans. The massacre left thousands of dead. Racing among the carcasses littering the streets, the Spanish then looted Cholula.

The Spanish asserted after the fact that the Mexica ruler Mochtezuma had conspired with a number of Cholulan headmen to exterminate the Spaniards before they reached the capital of the Aztecs. The veracity of this alibi was doubtful because the Spanish used it several times again in Mexico and against the last of the Incan emperors, among others. It was more likely that Cortes sought to paralyze the Aztecs into inaction with a swift and brutal massacre at Cholula. The strategy worked.

Cortes and his allies were received in Tenochtitlan as ambassadors of a mighty foreign country. Mochtezuma housed, fed, and entertained the conquistadors and gave them free access to the city, a period during which Bernal Diaz produced the descriptions that today provide a glimpse through European eyes of the Aztec capital in its full flower. As he had at Cholula, Cortes repaid hospitality with violence: At first, he took Mochtezuma prisoner, then slowly, ruthlessly, undermined his power among the Mexicas. The imprisonment included physical and psychological torture.

Matthew Restall, a professor at Pennsylvania State University, argues that the Aztecs did not perceive the Spaniards as gods (as often has been asserted); he writes that this account was invented decades after the fact by the Catholic Church and its Native allies. The first Native scribes to write the history of the conquest were tutored by Franciscan monks who hoped, in retrospect, to make the Spanish arrival seem providential. Because the scribes hailed from a group unfriendly to the Aztecs, they did not hesitate in their chronicles to disparage their rivals as weak and indecisive (Restall, 2004; Burnham, 2004).

One such incident was described by Benjamin Franklin. In November 1774, following the Boston Tea Party, Franklin scoffed at proposals that Boston ought to negotiate a treaty with Britain while its port was closed and the city itself was occupied by British Army Redcoats. "They will plead at ease, but we must plead in pain," Franklin argued, comparing Boston's position to that of Mochtezuma in the hands of the conquistador Cortes, who demanded "a surrender of his cash." Franklin wrote that the Aztec "Made some objections and desired A TREATY on the reasonableness of the demand.... Cortes heated a gridiron red hot, and seated poor Montezuma on it, and consented to TREAT with him as long as he pleased" (Labaree, 1978–, 21:354).

The Spaniards held Mochtezuma captive for several months, while rumors regarding his health spread through the capital. At one point, quite accidentally, Cortes's men discovered a massive amount of gold and silver that belonged to Mochtezuma's father—in effect, the state treasury. While subjugating the ruler personally, the Spanish extracted 162,000 *pesos de oro* (or 19,600 troy ounces) of gold from this cache. At 2002 gold prices, this hoard would have been worth about $8 million (Wright, 1992, 38). Much of what the Spanish purloined comprised many large pieces of intricate artwork that they melted into bullion for convenient shipment back to Spain. Cortes preserved a few of the art pieces intact to impress his sponsors.

Reception of Hernando Cortez by Emperor Mochtezuma. (Courtesy of the Library of Congress.)

After six months in Mexico City, Cortes marched back to the Gulf Coast to meet a new Spanish expedition headed by Panfilo de Narvaez; the expedition had reached Vera Cruz from Cuba, drawn like a bee to honey by reports of Mexican gold. Cortes appointed Pedro de Alvarado, a personal friend, to command the Spanish forces that remained in the Aztec capital.

A few days after Cortes and a contingent of men marched out of Tenochtitlan, the Aztecs prepared to celebrate their annual feast to Huitzilopochtli, the god of war. The festival of song, dance, and human sacrifice was held on the grounds of a monument to Huitzilopochtli, within eyeshot of the Spaniards' quarters, as well as the chambers in which Mochtezuma was held prisoner. Nearly all the royalty of Tenochtitlan gathered, resplendent in their best costumes, decked with gold and silver ornaments, including ceremonial gold and silver swords and other implements of war. Otherwise, the Aztec nobility was unarmed and ready prey for yet another Spanish ambush in the style of Cholula. Alvarado and his cohorts prepared just such a surprise as they surrounded the ceremonial court. Aztecs who tried to escape the massacre were impaled on pikes thrust by Spanish soldiers stationed at the exits. The Spanish then stripped the dead of their gold and silver.

The Florentine Codex described the scene:

> The blood . . . ran like water, like slimy water; the stench of blood filled the air, and the entrails seemed to slither along by themselves. And the Spanish went everywhere, searching the public buildings, thrusting with their weapons. (Sahagún, 1956, 116–117, cited in Wright, 1992, 40)

The Spanish said they feared the Aztecs had secreted their weapons on the ceremonial grounds, requiring that they be killed. The Spaniards' real motive probably was to score an easy hit on the cream of the Aztec nobility and thus collect material rewards.

After months of Spanish torment, Mochtezuma also was killed. The Spanish did their best to argue that he was struck in the head by a rock thrown by an outraged Aztec during a public speech. Diaz even asserted that the Spanish offered to feed Mochtezuma and dress his wounds, but he refused. The ambivalence of his account indicates that Diaz was probably not an eyewitness to the murder. Cortes rather lamely excused himself by asserting that the murder occurred while he was away from Tenochtitlan, on his way back to the capital from the Gulf Coast. The historical record rather irrefutably indicates otherwise. Aztec sources, such as Chimalpahin, a native historian who based his work on the glyphic codices, argued that the Spaniards "throttled him." The Aztecs who relayed their history to Friar Sahagún agreed (Wright, 1992, 42).

Cortes and his comrades soon found the Mexica capital in full revolt against the Spanish, its residents angered by their leader's murder. Publicly, Cortes upbraided Alvarado, but the Aztecs were not consoled. The Spanish then departed Tenochtitlan by night, along one of the causeways that connected the city with the mainland. Seven thousand Spanish and Tlascalan allies surged onto the causeway as the Aztecs attacked them from boats. The battle of Noche Triste became an Aztec folktale, a special comeuppance for many of the Spaniards who drowned because they had tied so much gold to their bodies (Collier, 1947, 64). Having retreated to the mainland, Cortes and his allies awaited reinforcements from Cuba. When they arrived, Cortes began his final march of conquest to Tenochtitlan. In the meantime, most of the Mexicas' former allies had abandoned them.

THE SPANISH SUBJUGATION OF THE MAYA

To the south, Spanish subjugation proceeded much more slowly against the Maya. Generally, when the Spanish won a clear and quick victory over Native peoples in Mesoamerica, they did so with Native allies attacking a centralized authority. Such a situation vis-à-vis the Aztecs and Incas made for a relatively quick conquest. Against the Maya, however, the Spanish had neither allies nor a single head to decapitate. Thus, they stumbled for decades around the hot coastal plains of Yucatan. One ill-fated Spanish expedition after another was repulsed from Maya country. In 1511, a Spanish ship en route from Panama to Santo Domingo sank off the eastern coast of Yucatan, and its entire ragged, starving crew was captured by Natives along the coast. Some of them were eaten in ceremonies; others died in slavery. Only two men, Aguilar and Guerrero, survived, both enslaved to Mayan chiefs. In 1516, an intense epidemic of smallpox hit the Mayan territories, killing people with "great pustules that rotted the body" (Brandon, 1961, 81).

Shortly after he subjugated the Aztecs, Cortes turned his attention to the Maya. At one point, he ransomed Aguilar, but Guerrero refused to leave his Mayan captors, telling Aguilar, according to the chronicler Diaz, who traveled with Cortes:

> I am married and have three children, and the Indians look upon me as a Cacique [chief] and a leader in wartime. You go and God be with you, but I have my face tattooed and my ears pierced, and what would the Spaniards say should they see me in this guise? (Brandon, 1961, 82)

Following destructive wars with each other, the Mayan city-states had been declining for hundreds of years before the Spanish tried to conquer the area. The Maya's slow decline continued long after the Spanish subjugation of the Valley of Mexico. European diseases accelerated the Maya's decline. Mayan intellectuals and their descendants created "living books, copied, recopied and expanded" generation after generation. The pre-Columbian history of the Maya was preserved in these books from memory after the original texts flared on Spanish bonfires (Wright, 1992, 165). From one such book of *Chilam Balam* (meaning spokesman of God, the Jaguar Prophet), written in the

Mayan language using the Spanish alphabet, comes this ironic critique of Christianity:

> With the true God, the true Dios.
> came the beginning of our misery.
> It was the beginning of tribute,
> the beginning of church dues...
> the beginning of strife by trampling on people,
> the beginning of robbery with violence,
> the beginning of forced debts,
> the beginning of debts enforced by false testimony,
> the beginning of individual strife
> —Roys, 1967, 77–79, cited in Wright, 1992, 165–166

The Spanish conquest of the Quiche and the Cakchiquel, the most prominent Maya peoples during the sixteenth century, proceeded quickly, with a brutality that also had marked the Spanish subjugation of the Aztecs. The Cakchiquel's own history, transcribed by the Spanish practically before the conquest had ended, reveals just how brutal it was:

> On the day 1 Ganel [February 20, 1524], the Quiches were destroyed by the Spaniards. Their chief, he was called Tunatiuh Avilantaro, conquered all the people.... [The Spaniards] went forward to the city of Gumarcaah [capital of the Quiche, also called Utatlan], where they were received by the kings.... The Quiches paid [The Spanish] tribute. Soon the kings were tortured by Tunatiuh. On the day 4 Qat [March 7, 1524] the kings Ahpop and Ahpop Quamahay were burned by Tunatiuh. The heart of Tunatiuh was without compassion for the people. (Recinos and Goetz, 1953, 119–125)

In another city, the Spanish commander "asked for one of the daughters of the king," who was furnished to him; he followed that demand with another, for money. "He wished for them to give him piles of metal, their vessels and crowns." When the kings did not comply immediately, Tunatiuh was said to have become very angry. He threatened them with death by burning and hanging. Finally, Tunatiuh forced the Maya to flee their own city, and then he chased them: "Ten days after we fled from the city, Tunatiuh began to make war upon us. On the day 4 Camey [September 5, 1524], they began to make us suffer. We scattered ourselves under the trees, under the vines, oh, my sons" (Stannard, 1992, 82).

As the Spanish struggled to subdue the decentralized Maya, the conquest also rolled over Native peoples to the south. In Panama, between 1514 and 1530 as many as 2 million Native people were killed, many after having been taken into slavery. As many as half a million people were taken out of

Nicaragua in chains (most later died); 150,000 were taken from Honduras. Historian David E. Stannard commented:

> Since numbers such as these are so overwhelming, sometimes it is the smaller incident that best tells what it was like—such as the expedition to Nicaragua in 1527 of Lopez de Salcedo, the colonial governor of Honduras. At the start of his trip, Salcedo took with him more than 300 slaves to carry his personal effects. Along the way he killed two-thirds of them, but he also captured 2,000 more from villages that were in his path. By the time he reached his destination in Leon only 100 of the more than 2,300 Indian slaves he had begun with were still alive. All this was necessary to "pacify" the natives. (Stannard, 1992, 82)

During the first half-century of the conquest, the Maya's population fell by 82 percent in the Cuchumatan highlands of Guatemala. On Cozumel Island, off the eastern coast of Mexico's Yucatan Peninsula, 96 percent of the people perished in seventy years. Within sixty years, the Native population of present-day Nicaragua declined by 99 percent, from about 1 million to fewer than 10,000. These are representative figures for the devastation that occurred throughout Mesoamerica during the bloody sixteenth century (Stannard, 1992, 86). The Maya's *Chilam Balam* described it as follows:

> [W]hat the white lords did when they came to our land: "They taught fear and they withered the flowers. So that their flower should live, the maimed and destroyed the flower of others.... Marauders by day, offenders by night, murderers of the world." (Ibid., 86)

Smallpox (as well as other imported diseases) and repeated attempts at Spanish invasion and colonization broke the Maya only slowly. Pedro de Alvarado marched from the Valley of Mexico to Guatemala with 400 Spanish soldiers and as many as 20,000 Native allies, blazing a path of terror through Mayan country, catching women and hanging them. The Spaniards hung babies from their dying mothers' feet. Alvarado, who had recently married a native woman from compliant Tlaxcala, threw unmarried Mayan women to packs of hunting dogs, which tore them to pieces.

Many Maya fought a determined guerilla war that drove the Spanish from Yucatan during 1536. In 1541, after the Spanish forged alliances with some of the Maya and after famine, pestilence, and the ravages of civil war, the Maya finally fell to yet another Spanish invasion. Scattered bands held out for decades longer. The Itza of Lake Peten resisted Spanish domination for more than 100 years after that. For most Maya, however, a way of life ended by 1550 as Spanish priests burned their cherished books. Remarked Bishop Landa of Yucatan: "As they contained nothing but superstition and lies of the devil, we burned them all, which the Indians regretted to an amazing degree" (Recinos and Goetz,

1953, 105). An unnamed Mayan poet wrote: "With rivers of tears we mourned our sacred writings among the delicate flowers of sorrow" (ibid., 105).

The Spanish invented all manner of exotic methods to inflict pain and death—the more excruciating the better. They built a long gibbet, low enough for the toes to touch the ground and prevent strangling, and hanged thirteen Natives at a time in honor of Christ and the twelve Apostles. The Spaniards then tested their blades against the dangling *Indios*, ripping chests open with one blow and exposing entrails. Straw was wrapped around their torn bodies, and they were burned alive. One man caught two children about two years old, pierced their throats with a dagger, then hurled them down a precipice.

One conquistador pastime was indicative of their disregard for Native life. It was called "dogging"—the hunting and maiming of Native people by canines specifically trained to relish the taste of human flesh. According to David E. Stannard, some of the dogs were kept as pets by the conquistadors. Vasco Nunez de Balboa's favorite was named Leoncico, or Little Lion, a cross between a greyhound and a mastiff. On one occasion, Balboa ordered 40 Indians dogged at once. "Just as the Spanish soldiers seem to have particularly enjoyed testing the sharpness of their yard-long blades on the bodies of Indian children, so their dogs seemed to find the soft bodies of infants especially tasty," wrote Stannard (1992, 83).

Las Casas thundered against the practice of "commending" Indians to *encomenderos*, which resulted in virtual slavery. He was rebuffed by Spanish authorities, who had a financial interest in this system of legalized slavery. Las Casas, the first priest ordained in the New World, called down a formal curse on the main agent of the bloody terror that eliminated Native people from Cuba, Panfilo de Narvaez. One of the gentle Tainos, offered baptism as he was about to be burned at the stake, refused because he thought he might find himself in the Christians' heaven, populated by even more of the light-skinned people who were torturing him (Las Casas, 1971, 121).

Mayan resistance continued for more than three centuries. In 1848, continuing through 1850, remnants of the Maya launched the Caste War, a coordinated attack on Spanish settlements in Yucatan, the nucleus of the old lowland Mayan cultures. This revolt has been called "without question the most successful Indian revolt in New World history" (Bricker, 1981, 87, cited in Wright, 1992, 255). For a time, the Maya nearly drove the Spanish into the sea, only to see their army dissolve as soldier-farmers returned to their fields for the crucial corn-planting season. The revolt in Quintana Roo was not completely crushed by Mexican troops until 1901.

Five centuries after the Spanish conquest, more than 2 million Maya still live in the homelands that their cities once dominated. Some have become partially assimilated into Western culture; others, such as the Lacandon in the remote forests west of the Rio Usumacinta, still live in relative isolation. In recent years, the population of the Lacandon Maya has dropped to a few hundred people as they have moved deeper and deeper into the lowland forests to escape the pressures of Mexico's twenty-first century society (Duby and Blom, 1969, 7:276–297).

In Guatemala, which had been the Maya's highland nucleus, subjugation that now approaches 500 years goes on in the guise of a bloody and intractable civil war that has been killing an average of 10 people a day for political reasons for more than 30 years. The death toll of 138,000 people includes 100,000 murdered for political reasons and 38,000 more "disappeared." This figure is political murders only; other civilian and military casualties of the war are not included. The war, in a country that is still 60 percent Maya, follows the race and class lines of the original *conquista*—a *meztiso* (or Ladino) landed class brutally holding down a poverty-stricken Mayan majority by every means at its disposal, sometimes (as in 1954) with the political and economic muscle of the United States behind it (Wright, 1992, 266).

FURTHER READING

Borah, Woodrow, and Sherburne Cook. *The Aboriginal Population of Mexico on the Eve of the Spanish Conquest.* Ibero-Americana No. 45. Berkeley: University of California Press, 1963.

Brandon, William. *The American Heritage Book of Indians.* New York: Dell, 1961.

Bricker, Victoria R. *The Indian Christ, the Indian King.* Austin: University of Texas Press, 1981.

Burnham, Philip. Review *Seven Myths of the Spanish Conquest*, by Matthew Restall. *Indian Country Today*, August 5, 2004. Available at http://www.indiancountry.com/?1091714398.

Calamai, Peter. Demise of Maya Tied to Droughts: Study Points to Climate Change Culture Depended on Growing Maize. *Toronto Star*, March 14, 2003. Available at http://www.thestar.ca/NASApp/cs/ContentServer?pagename=thestar/Layout/Article_Type1&c=Article&cid=1035779188042&call_page=TS_Canada&call_pageid=968332188774&call_pagepath=News/Canada&pubid=968163964505&StarSource=email.

Coe, Michael D. *America's First Civilization.* New York: American Heritage, 1968.

Coe, William R. Resurrecting the Grandeur of Tikal, *National Geographic*, December 1975, 792–799.

Collier, John. *Indians of the Americas.* New York: New American Library, 1947.

Cook, Sherburne F., and Woodrow Borah. *The Indian Population of Central Mexico, 1521–1610.* Ibero-Americana No. 44. Berkeley: University of California Press, 1960.

del Castillo, Bernardino Diaz. *Conquest of New Spain.* New York, 1958.

del Castillo, Bernal Diaz. *Historia Verdadera de la Conquista de la Nueva Espana*, edited by Joaquin Ramirez Cabanas. Mexico City: Editorial Purrua, 1968, 2:273, cited in Leon-Portilla, 1972, 122.

Demarest, Arthur A. The Violent Saga of a Mayan Kingdom. *National Geographic*, February 1993, 95–111.

Diamond, Jared. The Last Americans: Environmental Collapse and the End of Civilization. *Harper's*, June 2003, 43–51.

Diehl, Richard A. *Tula: The Toltec Capital of Ancient Mexico*. London: Thames and Hudson, 1981.

Dobyns, Henry F. Estimating Aboriginal American Population. *Current Anthropology* 7(1966): 395–449.

Driver, Harold E. *Indians of North America*. 2nd ed. Chicago: University of Chicago Press, 1969.

Duby, Gertrude, and Frans Blom. The Lacandon. In Robert Wauchope, ed., *Handbook of Middle-American Indians*. Vol. 7. Austin: University of Texas Press, 1969.

Fash, William L., Jr., and Barbara W. Fash, Scribes, Warriors and Kings: the Lives of the Copan Maya. *Archaeology*, May–June 1990, 28.

Gann, Thomas. *Mystery Cities: Exploration and Adverture in Lubaantun*. London: Duckworth, 1925.

Gerhard, Peter. *A Guide to the Historical Geography of New Spain*. Princeton, NJ: Princeton University Press, 1972.

Gerhard, Peter. *The North Frontier of New Spain*. Princeton, NJ: Princeton University Press, 1982.

Gibson, Charles. *The Aztecs Under Spanish Rule: A History of the Indians of the Valley of Mexico, 1519–1810*. Palo Alto, CA: Stanford University Press, 1964.

Hassler, Peter. Cutting Through the Myth of Human Sacrifice: The Lies of the Conquistadors. *World Press Review* (reprinted from *Die Zeit*, Hamburg), December 1992, 28–29.

Haug, Gerald H., Detlef Gunter, Larry C. Peterson, Daniel M. Sigman, Konrad A. Hughen, and Beat Aeschlimann. Climate and the Collapse of Maya Civilization. *Science* 299(March 14, 2003):1731–1735.

Henderson, John S. *The World of the Ancient Maya*. Ithaca, NY: Cornell University Press, 1981.

Jimenez-Moreno, Wigberto and Alfonso Garcia-Ruiz. *Historia de Mexico: Una Sintesis*. Mexico City, D. F.: INAH, 1970.

Kelley, David H. *Deciphering the Maya Script*. Austin: University of Texas Press, 1976.

Labaree, Leonard, ed. *The Papers of Benjamin Franklin*. New Haven, CT: Yale University Press, 1950–.

La Fay, Howard. The Maya, The Children of Time. *National Geographic*, December 1975, 729–766.

Las Casas, Bartolome de. *History of the Indies*. Translated and edited by Andree Collard. New York: Harper and Row, 1971.

Leon-Portilla, M. *Los Antiguos Mexicanos a Traves de sus Cronicas y Cantares*. Mexico City: Fondo de Cultura Economica, 1972.

Leon-Portilla, Miguel. *Pre-Columbian Literature of Mexico*. Norman: University of Oklahoma Press, 1969.

Lovell, W. George. *Conquest and Survival in Colonial Guatemala: A Historical Geography of the Cuchumatan Highlands, 1500–1821*. Montreal: McGill-Queen's University Press, 1985.

Maxwell, James A., ed. *America's Fascinating Indian Heritage*. Pleasantville, NY: Reader's Digest, 1978.

McDowell, Bart. The Aztecs. *National Geographic*, December 1980, 704–752.

Mochtezuma, Eduardo Matos. Templo Mayor: History and Interpretation. In Johanna Broda, David Carrasco, and Mochtezuma, eds., *The Great Temple of Tenochtitlan: Center and Periphery in the Aztec World*. Berkeley: University of California Press, 1988, 15–60.

Molina Montes, Augusto F. The Building of Tenochtitlan. *National Geographic*, December 1980, 753–766.

Radell, Davis R. The Indian Slave Trade and Population of Nicaragua During the Sixteenth Century. In William E. Denevan, ed., *The Native Population of the Americas.* Madison: University of Wisconsin Press, 1976, 67–76.

Recinos, Adrian, and Delia Goetz, trans. *The Annals of the Cakchiquels.* Norman: University of Oklahoma Press, 1953.

Restall, Matthew. *Seven Myths of the Spanish Conquest.* New York: Oxford University Press, 2004.

Roys, Ralph L. *The Book of Chilam Balam of Chumayel.* Norman: University of Oklahoma Press, 1967, cited in Wright, 1992, 165–166.

Sahagún, Bernardino de. *Historia General de las Cosas de Nueva Espana.* 4 vols. Edited and translated by Angel Maria Garibay. Mexico City, DF: Porrua, [ca. 1555] 1956.

Sahagún, Bernardino de. Historia de las Cosas de la Nueva Espana (1905–1907). Cited in Miguel Leon Portilla, *The Aztec Image of Self and Society: An Introduction to Nahua Culture.* Salt Lake City: University of Utah Press, 1992.

Sahagún, Friar Bernardino de. *Florentine Codex: General History of the Things of New Spain.* Vol. 10. Translated by Arthur J. O. Anderson and Charles Dibble. Santa Fe, NM: School of American Research, 1950–1969.

Scholars Rewrite Mayan History after Hieroglyphics Found. *Omaha World-Herald*, September 20, 2002, 12-A.

Smith, Michael E. The Aztec Migrations of the Nahuatl Chronicles: Myth or History? *Ethnohistory* 31:3(1984):153–186.

Stannard, David E. *American Holocaust: Columbus and the Conquest of the New World.* New York: Oxford University Press, 1992.

Stuart, George E. Riddle of the Glyphs. *National Geographic*, December 1975, 768–791.

Stuart, George E. Etowah: A Southeast Village in 1491. *National Geographic*, October 1991, 54–67.

Stuart, George E. Mural Masterpieces of Ancient Cacaxtla. *National Geographic*, September 1992, 120–136.

Webster, David. *The Fall of the Ancient Maya.* London: Thames and Hudson, 2002.

Wilkerson, Jeffery K. Following the Route of Cortes. *National Geographic*, October 1984, 420–459.

Williams, Stephen. *Fantastic Archaeology: The Wild Side of American Prehistory.* Philadelphia: University of Pennsylvania Press, 1991.

Wright, Ronald. *Stolen Continents: America through Indian Eyes Since 1492.* Boston: Houghton Mifflin, 1992.

CHAPTER 3

Native America Meets Europe

THE COLONIAL ERA

European immigrants who flowed across North America in successive waves encountered a very large array of Native American peoples. A great variety of Native languages existed in North America at contact, an estimated 500 to 1,000. An even wider variety of languages was spoken in South America (Brandon, 1961, 106). Estimates of the total number of languages at contact on both continents range from 1,000 to 2,000 (Driver, 1969, 25; Beals and Hoijer, 1965, 613). This variety of languages was a result of cultural development spanning many thousands of years that was ended, or arrested, with the advent of immigrating European people and their pathogenic diseases. This chapter briefly sketches the evolution of cultures in parts of the present-day United States, from the Southwest to Southeast. This description is followed by a narrative of contact, first among the Spanish, then the English and French.

THE RISE OF COMPLEX CULTURES

About 5,000 years ago, at the beginning of the epoch that geologists call the Holocene, complex cultures with stable agricultural and trading bases began to form in the area now occupied by the continental United States of America. Although Clovis and Folsom styles of weapons diffused rapidly across North America (indicating trade and other forms of communication), we know little about these cultures other than that they hunted now-extinct forms of large wildlife. We are only beginning to learn from the scanty trail of evidence they left behind how the people of North America's various cultures conducted other aspects of their lives (such as religions). At a half-dozen sites across the United States west of the Rocky Mountains, underground chambers have been found housing caches of items that many believe Clovis era people found valuable, such as their distinctive projectile points. Were these places burial sites? We do not yet know.

At about 3000 B.C.E., not so long after the trail of a complex history begins for the Old World, organized societies began to develop in North America. Perhaps not coincidentally, the Mayan calendar, the most precise measure of time developed in prehistoric America, dates to 3114 B.C.E. North of the Rio Grande, peoples who earlier had subsisted mainly by hunting and gathering began to develop agriculture around 500 B.C.E. Settled societies evolved earliest in two geographic areas: the Southeast (including the Mississippi Valley) and the Southwest. The Southwestern cultures evolved a few hundred years earlier, planting the seeds of the Anasazi (Navajo for ancient ones), who by 1000 C.E. had built communal structures containing up to 650 rooms each across the arid landscape of contemporary Arizona, New Mexico, Colorado, and Utah. In the Southeast, agriculture-based societies evolved into the mound builders of the Mississippian culture. The first Spanish explorers found only the last remnants of both.

CAUTIONS

When surveying the prehistory of North America, one must recognize the fluidity of scholarship and how quickly new knowledge and conjecture may turn recent veracity to dross. Civilization in the Americas is ancient, but much of our knowledge of these civilizations is relatively recent. When studying the condition of societies in the Americas before persistent contact with Europeans, realize that most of our knowledge of these cultures dates from the twentieth century, and that we are still by and large discovering America. Who knows what still waits to be unearthed, deciphered, connected, and revealed.

More good advice comes from Duane Champagne, former editor of the University of California at Los Angeles' *American Indian Culture and Research Journal* and a professor of sociology at the university. Champagne commented on the nature of political consensus and leadership among Native peoples that often confused Europeans, who were accustomed to top-down, command-and-control hierarchies. Although some Native peoples (such as the Aztecs) conformed to this model, many others did not.

When examining Native cultures, both in prehistory and after contact with European colonialism, it is important to distinguish between the types of disagreement between individuals and groups that are routine parts of decision making and change and those that rend the social fabric and make consensus impossible. Champagne, who is a Turtle Mountain Chippewa, wrote the following:

> The literature on Native North Americans tends to regard Indian societies as endemic with internal factionalism. However, what many observers have recorded is largely routine conflict. Since many Indian societies are politically decentralized, with segmentary bands, villages or kinship groups having considerable local political,

social, and economic autonomy, they have considerable difficulty organizing sustained collective action.... While such absence of concerted action may look like factionalism [to an outside observer] the major subgroups are merely exercising their prerogative to make their own political decisions. (1989, 4–5)

"Factionalism," according to Champagne (1989, 4), "should be reserved for conflicts over the rules of social order." The rapid and uncontrolled exposure of a society to outside influences—as occurred across the Americas at the onset of European colonialism—may cause such society-destroying factional splits, most often between those people within the culture who assert that the invasion should be resisted and those who wish to accommodate it. Societal factionalism also may be introduced from within or because of environmental changes. This was the most common cause of major changes in Native North American societies before contact with Europeans.

On contact, historical accounts often display just how ignorant the immigrants were of this consensus model of politics. Leaders of colonial expeditions often asked Natives they met to take them to a clearly identifiable leader with whom they could negotiate for an entire nation. Just as often, the immigrants assumed that Native people they met were leaders who could speak for others, when they could not.

Another problem with much contemporary commentary on Native societies, according to Champagne, is that when change in them is described, it is usually analyzed solely in terms of colonial influence (Champagne, 1989, 4–5). Observers (who usually have been educated within the context of European American society) do not begin their studies with descriptions of the complex indigenous societies that formed and re-formed before contact, but rather as "a mere reflection or reaction to the powerful forces of colonial societies" (ibid., 4–5). Although it is true that European peoples and their cultures have wrought great changes in Native American ways of living during the five-plus centuries since persistent contact began, the Native societies that have absorbed these changes did not adopt them without modification. At the other end of the spectrum, many traditionally trained scholars do not study the ways in which American Indian ways of living, thinking, and organizing societies influenced the many peoples who immigrated to North America from overseas.

Societies indigenous to North America also influenced each other for many thousands of years before continuing contact with Europeans began. The Maya, for example, developed the concept of negative numbers and passed it to the Aztecs, in ways in some ways similar to the Greeks' shaping of Roman knowledge. Native people traded in a wide net across the continent; cultural traits and other types of knowledge were transmitted as well. Because so little of this trade was recorded and because many of the peoples who carried it on do not survive, reconstructing an accurate "prehistory" of North America is one of historical scholarship's greatest challenges. The fact that our interpretations of this period have changed so fundamentally during this century is reflective of how little we still do not know.

AGRICULTURE COMES TO THE SOUTHWEST

A people archeologists call the Mogollon became the first in the present-day United States to adopt agriculture and pottery, around 300 B.C.E. Their pit dwellings and kivas resembled those of other peoples in the present-day U.S. Southwest as well as the early Anasazi. The Mogollon people were a branch of the broader Cochise culture, from which the Anasazi also evolved a few centuries later. They lived in western New Mexico and eastern Arizona (roughly the area occupied by the Navajos today), weaving fine blankets out of cotton, feathers, and wool made from the fur of animals. Some of the modern Hopis and Zunis are descended from the Mogollon peoples.

Another branch of the Cochise, the Hohokam, adopted agriculture as their predominant way of life about 100 C.E. in the Salt and Gila River areas of present-day southern Arizona. To cope with the dry conditions of the area, the Hohokam built massive irrigation works, some of which were still in use when the first Spaniards arrived. The people diverted river water into canals six feet deep and up to thirty feet wide, some of which extended up to ten miles, to nourish the crops that fed the population of their principal settlement, now called Snaketown. This site, close to present-day Phoenix, was occupied for 1,200 consecutive years. The Hohokam also developed a process for etching almost 300 years before it was used in Europe. Hohokam craftspeople worked the surface to be etched with pitch, as they transferred the design with a stylus. They then laced the design with an acid created from the fruit of the saguaro cactus. The Pimas and Papagos, who occupied southern Arizona during early Spanish contact, were descended from the Hohokam people.

THE ANASAZI

Roughly 1000 C.E., the Anasazi, ancestors of today's Hopis and Pueblos, built a network of large stone dwellings atop and into the sides of mesas in the present-day southwestern United States. Their network of villages, centered in Chaco Canyon, covered an area extending from west of Albuquerque (on contemporary maps) westward to Las Vegas, Nevada. Dwellings in these villages housed tens of thousands of people in preplanned complexes as large as 300 rooms each. The settlements were connected by roads as wide as some of today's interstate highways; these roads may have been used to transport food quickly from settlement to settlement to address shortages in a land where rainfall could be scarce and harvests could easily fail. The Anasazi ingeniously utilized what little water they had, but in the end their civilization, which flourished for a little more than a century, collapsed in the face of a severe drought that began about 1150 C.E.

Anglo-American explorers discovered the remains of the Anasazi in 1877, when photographer William Henry Jackson found spectacular ruins of a people who were first called the Basketmakers because their earliest generations used intricately woven baskets even to carry water, while most others used pottery. Only slowly did scholars realize that Chaco Canyon had been the center of a very large civilization. By 2,000 years ago, the people who would build these large settlements were discovering how to grow corn, the basis of a sedentary existence. When the Navajo (Dine) arrived from the north, they called the people they met ancient ones, Anasazi in their language.

Anasazi settlements covered the landscape, giving the area they occupied a population density greater than today, outside of major urban areas. At least 25,000 Anasazi sites have been found in New Mexico, a similar number in Arizona, and thousands more in Utah and Colorado. Archeologists believe that many thousands more will be discovered in the future (Canby, 1982, 563). Many of the canyon walls in an area that European settlers regarded as inhospitable became peppered with cliff dwellings after the Anasazi imported the bow and arrow and discovered the hefted axe about 500 C.E. because they also refined their cultivation of corn, beans, and squash. Even the walls of the Grand Canyon became home to some of the cliff-dwelling Anasazi.

Coaxing food out of the often-dry soil required some ingenuity. The Anasazi learned to mulch soil with gravel to help it retain moisture as they fashioned an irrigation system that took advantage of runoff from drenching summer thunderstorms. As a thunderstorm gathered strength, the Anasazi would leave their other work and rush to the north-facing walls of nearby canyons to channel the runoff into canals leading into their farming fields. In this way, they designed irrigation without access to rivers. Some of these canals were as long as four miles. They required constant, cooperative labor, especially during the summer growing season, when sudden thunderstorms often were the only form of precipitation.

By roughly 700 C.E., Anasazi dwellings began to increase in size and complexity; 300 years later, they built dwellings that could enclose an entire village in one structure, the largest residential housing blocks built in North America until about 1870. These dwellings housed a society in which women usually owned family property, and men oversaw the ceremonial side of life, centered in underground kivas.

Life in this area could be precarious. Crops could fail, and game could disappear for months on end, bringing to the Anasazi haunting memories of droughts and famines past. Archeological reports indicate that many Anasazi died in infancy, and that in old age (by 45 years, on average) many were nearly crippled by arthritis. The Anasazi prospered despite their harsh environment. At 919 C.E., the ceiling beams were cut for Pueblo Bonito, the grandest of all the cliff settlements. Such precision in dating is made possible by measuring the growth rings of the trees used as beams.

By roughly the year 1150, the Anasazi reached their height. When it was completed, Pueblo Bonito contained 650 rooms. Eleven other smaller pueblos surrounded it, many of them connected by roads. Seventy other similar communities lay outside Chaco Canyon; others spread across an area 500 miles east to west and up to 300 miles north to south (Canby, 1982, 564–565, 578). The Anasazis also devised a communication system to complement their roads. One school of thought has it that the various pueblos communicated with fires or mica mirrors reflecting sunlight in coded signals from the tops of mesas (ibid., 585).

After 1150, the Anasazis' civilization quickly collapsed because of severe drought coupled with cooling temperatures. This drought was a drastic, wrenching climatic change that lasted more than a century, reaching its peak between 1276 and 1299, when practically no rain or snow fell in the area. The Chaco River dried up. Agriculture always had been risky in this region, anywhere above 7,000 feet or below 5,500 feet in elevation; the higher elevations were too cold, and lower locations too were hot and dry. With the change in climate, farming became nearly impossible in many locations.

A few Anasazi settlements survived the drought, such as Mesa Verde, one of the latest and most spectacular, but the majority of the pueblos lay in ruins by the time the Spanish arrived. The cliff dwellers at Mesa Verde left a magnificent masonry temple that indicated a massive attempt to appease the gods after the great drought. The construction of religious structures also may have indicated cultural influence from trading with the civilizations of the Valley of Mexico, several hundred miles to the south. The Anasazi also traded buffalo meat with Native peoples of the plains to the east and north. Before the great drought, Pueblo Bonito hosted a large market that may have been a crossroads for traders ranging over thousands of miles. Most of this network died in the dust before 1200 C.E. Scattered remnants are still occupied today. Acoma, for example, is still a functioning community, as is the Hopis' Orabi, which is the oldest continuously occupied community in the present-day United States.

SPANISH EXPLORATION AMONG THE PUEBLOS

The Spanish, who sent several expeditions northward from Mexico beginning in 1540, were the first Europeans to meet Native peoples in the present-day land area comprising the United States of America. Very quickly, learning of the Anasazi, the Spanish explorers realized that Native cultures had been evolving in the area for many centuries before their arrival. The Pueblos, their descendants, built a remarkably intricate culture in their cliff dwellings. Their pottery and jewelry turned Spanish heads. Some of their turquoise necklaces contained thousands of worked stones.

The Pueblos' government was a democratic theocracy; nearly all houses were of roughly equal size. The highest-ranking theocrats were farmers, like the people they led. In some towns, two groups of residents (the Summer

Acoma water carriers. (Courtesy of the Edward S. Curtis Collection, Library of Congress.)

People and the Winter People) took six-month turns at governing. Ruth Benedict's *Patterns of Culture* (1934, 100) extolled the democratic nature of government among the Zuni Pueblos. They, and the rest of the Pueblos, seemed to have operated their political system with an innate sense of egalitarianism; the passage of wealth and power by heredity was almost unknown; a man or

Terraced houses, Acoma Pueblo. (Courtesy of the Library of Congress.)

woman distinguished him- or herself through real achievements in daily life. Although the Pueblos and other southwestern people seem to have borrowed liberally from Mesoamerica in their material cultures, their political system was much more egalitarian than those of the Aztecs and Maya (Driver, 1969, 338–339).

Although archeologists agree that the Acoma Pueblo has been continuously inhabited since at least 1200 C.E., Native elders in the area assert that the site has been occupied for about 2,000 years. Acoma (historically also spelled Akome, Acu, Acuo, Acuco, and Ako) is taken by many elders to mean "a place that always was," as a home, or as an eternal resting place. The Spanish were drawn to the area by rumors of gold (such as the Seven Cities of Cibola and Quivera). Hernando de Alvarado and his companion Fray Juan Padilla, traveling with a small body of soldiers (as part of the Coronado expedition), were the first Europeans to see the Acoma Pueblo.

The Coronado expedition, Spain's initial foray north of the Rio Grande, returned to Mexico in 1542, bereft of gold or other precious cargo. Coronado's failure to find tangible treasure kept Spanish gold seekers out of the area for more than a half century. Spanish missionaries visited the area during 1581 and 1582. The first, led by Fray Agustin Rodriguez, visited Acoma briefly; the account of Hernan Gallegos (1966), a soldier on the expedition, says only that the pueblo was built on a high mesa and contained about 500 houses, each three or four stories high. A second expedition, led by Bernaldino Beltran, brought back reports that Acoma was home to about 6,000 people whose pueblo rose about 250 to 300 feet in the air and who possessed plentiful food stores and enough cotton blankets (called *mantas*) to share with the Spanish. The Spanish noted farm fields two leagues from the pueblo, as well as irrigation works fed from a local river. The members of the expedition also hungrily eyed the mountains, believing that their presence guaranteed riches of gold and silver. Initial contact with the Pueblo people at Acoma was friendly. Many of them juggled and danced to celebrate the Spaniards' arrival; some of the dances were performed with live snakes.

Sustained immigration into New Mexico by the Spanish began in 1598 as about 400 men, women, and children marched northward along the slopes of the Sierra Madre with 7,000 head of stock and 80 wagons. Only at the pueblo of Acoma, on the summit of a steep mesa, did the Spanish meet active resistance. After a short battle, the Spanish invaded the pueblo and imprisoned its men, women, and children. Men who resisted lost one foot and twenty years of their lives to slavery. Women and children older than twelve also were enslaved for twenty years, and children under that age were handed over to the Catholic Church's missionaries for indenture. Two Hopis who were visiting Acoma were sent home missing their right hands as a warning. Fifteen years later, Juan de Oñate, the provincial governor who had been the leader of and chief investor in the original colonization, was stripped of his honors by a Spanish tribunal and was fined for torture and mass enslavement of the Natives. Thus ended the governorship of Oñate, son of one of the richest mine owners in Mexico who had married a great-granddaughter of Mochtezuma. (Four hundred years after his troops chopped off the limbs of their ancestors, Native people in New Mexico removed a foot from a statue of Oñate to memorialize his cruelty.)

Bartolome de las Casas Decries Spanish Cruelty

Oñate had the miserable fortunate of having gone colonizing with illegal zeal during the late stages of Spanish expansion. The charges levied against Oñate reflected the growing muscle within Spanish government circles, as well as the Catholic Church, of people who sought to check the cruelty and avarice of the conquistadors, several of whom were hauled in front of inquiries into their conduct. In the Americas, the Catholic priest Bartolome de las Casas avidly encouraged inquiries into the Spanish conquest's many cruelties. Las Casas chronicled Spanish brutality against the Native peoples in excruciating detail. It was Las Casas who laid on Spanish desks and Catholic consciences the history of Latin America's bloody depopulation at the hands of the Spanish. He described how Native people choked to death on mercury fumes in the silver mines as conquistadors bet Native lives in games of cards (Las Casas, 1974).

In large part because of Las Casas's work, a movement arose in Spain for more humane treatment of indigenous peoples. Some of the conquistadors made public statements repudiating their past cruelties. In his will, Hernan Cortes raised the slavery issue. A sharp debate followed within the Catholic Church regarding whether the Natives possessed the spiritual nature (e.g., whether they had souls) suitable to absorb Christian doctrine. Europeans who thought of the Indians as subhuman laughed, asserting that their intelligence was "no more than parrots" (Minge, 1991, 7). During 1552, Lopez de Gomara (1556), known in contemporary Spain as a biographer of Cortes, described Indians as barbarous heathens who fornicated in public (specializing in sodomy), liars, and cannibals who cursed the Old World with syphilis. Gomara asserted that Indians were by nature inferior to Europeans, thereby fit only for slavery in the Spanish New World order.

In the papal bull *Sublimis Deus* (1537), Pope Paul III declared that Indians were to be regarded as fully human, and that their souls were as immortal as those of Europeans. This edict also outlawed slavery of Indians in any form several decades before Oñate sold the Pueblos he had captured. Las Casas's *New Laws for the Indies* (1544) called for gradual elimination of forced labor for Native Americans under Catholic Church sponsorship.

To counter criticism that the conquest had been brutal and cruel, the laws of Spain required a conquistador, at the moment of first contact, to read Native peoples a long statement that explained the story of Adam and Eve, the supremacy of the Pope, and reasons why they should embrace the Catholic faith. This statement was phrased as a contract by which the Native peoples agreed to submit peacefully to the authority of the king of Spain as well as the Church of Rome. If Native people decided not to submit to the Spanish at this point, armed force was brought to bear. By the middle 1500s, the semantics of this statement were refined into a genial proclamation of greeting from the king of Spain to the kings and republics of the "mid-way and western lands." By 1573, the revised New Laws outlawed any mention of conquest. Instead, the role of the explorers was said to be "pacification."

After Oñate's inglorious fall, later governors of New Mexico tried to recoup their investments in the colony, surveying a landscape that was utterly lacking deposits of gold and silver. Unable to wrest wealth from the land themselves, the colonists squeezed the Pueblos more harshly for food and labor. The priests railed against the Indians' devil worship and from time to time whipped some of the Pueblos' most respected elders (sometimes to death) in public displays for their practice of non-Catholic rituals.

The Pueblo Revolt (1680)

Spanish arrogance and cruelty provoked considerable resentment among Native peoples. Fifty years after their first colonization, the Pueblos joined with their ancient enemies the Apaches in an effort to drive the Spanish out. This initial revolt failed, but thirty years later, in 1680, a coalition of Pueblos knit by the war captain Pope raised a furious revolt that killed a quarter of the Spanish immigrants, trashed the hated churches, and sent the surviving Spanish down the trail to El Paso Notre, leaving behind almost everything they owned. The governor summed up the situation: "Today they [the Pueblos] are very happy without religious [missionaries], or Spaniards" (Brandon, 1961, 129).

Pope's policies after the rout of the Spanish proved too zealous for most Pueblos. He took on the airs of a petty tyrant and forbade his people from using anything that the Spanish had imported, including new crops. Most of Pope's edicts regarding crops were ignored. Pope even ordered the execution of some of his reputed enemies, after which the Pueblo Confederacy that had expelled the Spanish broke into two camps, one favoring Pope, the other opposing him. Pope was deposed but was restored to power in 1688, shortly before he died. Four Spanish attempts at reconquest in eight years combined with a plague of European diseases, as well as the Pueblos' existing internal dissension, led to depopulation of the Pueblos' villages after Pope's death. In 1692, the Spanish returned.

THE EASTERN MOUND BUILDERS

The pyramidlike mounds of Cahokia (described in chapter 1) are now known to have been one relatively spectacular and recent example of mound-building cultures that occupied the southeastern quadrant of North America during roughly 4,500 years before Columbus first made landfall.

At Poverty Point, Louisiana, people living in about 1000 B.C.E. constructed earthen mounds on a scale smaller than those of Cahokia 2,000 years later. One such pyramid, at Bayou Macon, fifteen miles west of the Mississippi River, measures 70 feet high and contains 200,000 cubic yards of earth. (The largest pyramid mound at Cahokia fills ten times as much space and rises 100 feet high.) The mounds at Poverty Point are the earliest construction of such size thus far found anywhere in North America. This culture flourished at about the time the Olmecs were becoming organized along the Gulf Coast of Mexico; relationships between the two (possibly via trade across the Gulf of Mexico or by land around it) have been proposed, but not proven. The earthworks at Poverty Point rival those of Mexico's Teotihuacan in size but not in artistic detail. The presence of these and other, smaller mounds indicates a fair-size settlement, as do the thousands of tools left behind. Other remains include small carvings of owls done in great detail and an abundance of goods that were probably imported, some of them from great distances, such as iron, lead ore, and copper.

The Adena culture (named after an estate near Chillicothe, Ohio, where a large mound was excavated in 1902) occupied portions of the Ohio Valley located in contemporary Ohio, Kentucky, and West Virginia. The Adena did not develop organized agriculture but lived in large towns characteristic of later agricultural peoples, supporting themselves by harvesting the rich game of the surrounding forests and by gathering food plants. The Adena did use pottery and copper tools from metal probably imported from the Lake Superior areas. They were the first to construct large earthen mounds in the Mississippi Valley, a custom that continued with the Hopewell and Mississippian cultures for more than a thousand years.

The mounds were symbols of a highly developed religion that probably embraced the Adenans' entire social order. The mounds could not have been constructed without considerable labor organized by a central authority. Most of the mounds served as burial chambers, and considerable time and effort were invested to provide materials to be buried with the dead. One such artifact depicts a man who seems to be dancing and singing, styled into a smoking pipe. He wears a breach cloth with a stylized snake cut across its front and spool-shaped earrings which make him look rather Mesoamerican. Most of the mounds were built in rectangular shapes similar to those of temples in Mesoamerica, but one, the Great Serpent Mound, snaked its way for a quarter mile along a hillside near present-day Cincinnati, Ohio.

THE HOPEWELL CULTURE

In the Hopewell culture, mounds were used as burial sites beginning about 500 B.C.E. According to one estimate, 30 million cubic yards of earth were moved to form all of the Hopewell culture burial mounds, some of which approached the size of Poverty Point's earthworks (Stuart, 1991, 61). Although the precision of this estimate is open to question, it is obvious that a large number of people spent many years building them. They also were highly organized by some sort of central authority, at least at the village level. Artifacts found in the burial mounds indicate a complex, well-developed network of Native settlements centering in present-day Ohio. Archeology in the area indicates that, by 2,000 years ago, the Hopewell peoples were importing obsidian from the Black Hills and alligator teeth from Florida. These and other commodities indicate that a well-developed trading network extended across much of the eastern continent very early.

Unlike the Adena peoples, the Hopewell culture adapted agriculture, principally of maize (Indian corn). Studies of prehistoric climate indicate that warming temperatures allowed the cultivation of corn over larger areas of the Mississippi Valley as the Hopewell Culture reached its height between 200 B.C.E. and 500 C.E. Hopewell people continued to hunt and gather as well; they often located their villages on or near river floodplains to take advantage of mussels, fish, and other aquatic life. The rivers also formed a trading network.

Like many of the Native peoples that Europeans encountered later (such as the League of the Iroquois), the Hopewell peoples may have governed themselves through multiple chieftainships, in some sort of confederation, unlike the more centralized Aztecs. The Hopewell peoples had a trade network large enough to bring them gold, silver, and copper from hundreds of miles away. From these and other materials, they fashioned intricate objects of art. Some of their materials, such as volcanic rock, came from as far away as Wyoming; sheets of mica also found their way to the Hopewell settlements from North Carolina.

The Hopewell was one variant of the Mississippian mound-building cultures that flourished in the southeastern United States shortly after the Anasazi rose in the Southwest. Both show some indications (such as objects of trade, some religious customs, and artistic styles) of contact with the peoples of Meso-america. The Hopewell mounds themselves may have been an imitation of Mayan or Aztec architecture. Mound-building cultures developed across much of the Southeast, from portions of Virginia (Thomas Jefferson found a small mound at Monticello, in Virginia) to the Ohio Valley and the area that today comprises the U.S. Deep South. The Spanish explorer de Soto encountered some of the last mound builders in the vicinity of Natchez. As a whole, however, the people who built the mounds had taken up other pursuits by the time immigrants from Europe found them. In the absence of verifiable history, the earliest trans-Appalachian immigrants from Europe attributed the mounds to visitors from Israel, Egypt, or other Old World locales.

About 450 C.E., the climate cooled again, and archeological evidence indicates that the Hopewellian people were forced to spend less time pursuing art and other aspects of high culture and more time gathering enough food to survive longer, snowier winters. Over two centuries, the residents of the towns dominated by giant mounds tried to maintain their cultures in the face of climatic change as raiding neighbors preyed on their fields and food stores. The trading network collapsed because the culture could no longer afford to support large numbers of people who did not directly participate in the production of food. The number of artists and craftspeople who produced trade articles also declined. Chiefs of the villages also may have sustained a loss of authority associated with their inability to command material tribute. The next focus for developing culture in the Southeast would form further south, where corn could still be grown in abundance, even in a relatively cooler, wetter climate.

A LEGACY OF THEOCRACIES

The oral history and mythology of the Cherokees indicate that they (like several other people in the region) once were governed by a theocracy, possibly a remnant of the Temple Mound cultures that had flourished in the area. One version of the Cherokee creation myth holds that their lives originated in seven clans. Each clan appointed a headman, who was subordinate to a head priest and a council of seven, who aided the priest with ceremonies. Villages also included political councils as well as warriors' societies, but both were subordinate to the priests. The people of the villages came to resent the priests' heavy-handed control of their lives and rebelled. After the religious hierarchy was dismantled, the Cherokees maintained their affairs through a network of roughly sixty highly autonomous villages. The principal loyalty of the

Cherokee in precontact times seems to have been to the village, not to a national council.

Like the Cherokees, the Choctaws' oral history indicates that they overthrew a priesthood during the end of the mound builder era, roughly between 900 and 1600 C.E. Following the fall of their theocracy, the Choctaws abandoned the town of Nanih Waiya, a Mississippi culture town with rampart-style defenses surrounding a large mound. Following the collapse of the Choctaw theocracy, the nation was divided into six politico-social divisions called *iksa*, a term that combined kindred group, political chiefdom, and identification with a specific locality. Each *iksa* claimed its own territory. Members of many *iksa* spoke distinct dialects and shared attributes of culture that was theirs alone. Each *iksa* also maintained communal lands for farming. Although men helped clear the fields, women customarily tended them while men hunted and fished. Precontact Choctaw society was probably organized more strongly along kinship lines than the Cherokee. Villages sometimes sent delegations to regional or even national councils as well, but little is known of their powers or how they functioned.

The Chickasaws maintained vestiges of the mound builder culture after the Cherokee and Choctaw abandoned their theocracies. Records from the de Soto expedition, which crossed their homelands in present-day Louisiana and western Tennessee, indicate that the Chickasaw maintained a well-organized agricultural society headed by a chief, who was carried about in a litter and shown great deference. By the time the Chickasaws experienced sustained contact with the British (during the early 1700s) reports indicate that the society had become less hierarchical. Chiefs were regarded as equals of other people unless they showed special talents. A decline in the prestige of leaders may have been a result of the general decline of the mound-building cultures during the first years of steady European contact.

Like the Choctaws, the Chickasaws maintained an integrated kinship system (*iksas*). The nation was divided into two primary kinship groups (called phratries), which also were subdivided into smaller kinship groups down to the family level. Some leading political titles were hereditary, and political organization was to some degree divorced from the kinship system. A national council included civil and military leaders as well as representatives of the various *iksas*. The Chickasaws also utilized more definite notions of social rank than most of the other peoples in the region. At the Green Corn Ceremony, their primary annual meeting and social event, various bands camped in a prescribed pattern indicating each person's rank.

Although Chickasaw political life was more centralized than that of the other peoples in the area, decisions of the national council required unanimous consent. Leaders had little coercive authority. Priests held a special position in this political organization. They could read and interpret signs and omens and pass these messages on to the people, but they did not control the whole system (Champagne, 1989, 38–39).

The Creeks had no myth of an ancient theocracy, indicating that they perhaps migrated to central Georgia and Alabama from the west and did not originate with the Mississippi mound-building peoples. One Creek myth describes how the people migrated from the west searching for "the house of the sun." Reaching the Atlantic, they settled because they could go no farther east.

The Creek world revolved around four principal villages, which later organized into two groups that the English called the red and white towns. This division reflected the cosmology of the Creeks, which they shared with other peoples in the area. The white world was said to be the vault of heaven, the residence of a supreme diety, the home of peace, order, harmony, cleanliness, purity, and wisdom. The red sphere, under the earth, was said to be occupied by monsters and demons that could emerge through caves, rivers, and other breaches in the earth to do harm to human beings who had acted improperly. Red symbolized fertility, change, strife, danger, growth, disorder, and war. The Creeks saw life as the realm between the red and the white in which human beings struggled to achieve a balance between the competing forces. In times of war, red towns governed the Creek Confederacy. In times of peace, governance passed to the white towns. The four major Creek settlements were divided into two red and two white sections (Champagne, 1989, 52).

Primary loyalties among the Creek (as among the Cherokees) were established through the village; each settlement that was large enough to have a ceremonial center also had a myth of having received its ceremonies, laws, and sacred objects from the white world. If people in the village followed these ceremonies, they believed that they would be protected from the evil spirits of the red world, which could bring crop failure, natural calamities, death, and disease. Each village also contained kinship groups divided along red and white lines. As would be expected, the two divisions were delegated authority for civil and military functions; the red groups governed warfare, and the white performed civil government and religious ceremonies (Champagne, 1989, 59).

Like many Mesoamerican peoples, many indigenous Americans who lived in what is now the southeastern United States made an artistic canvas of their bodies. The most esteemed warriors were tattooed with graphic displays of their deeds, until some of them were covered head to foot. In addition, most men donned geometric designs of paint for war, ball games, and other public occasions. In addition to their tattoos and paint, men often wore layers of wooden, shell, copper, stone, or pearl bracelets, necklaces, armbands, and other jewelry.

ETOWAH: A TYPICAL VILLAGE

Etowah, a typical Mississippian village, housed about 3,000 people at a site west of contemporary Atlanta, Georgia, later Cherokee territory. Etowah's principal mound, rather average sized by Mississippian standards, was the height of a six-story building and contained about a million buckets of earth (Stuart, 1991, 60). Thatched-roofed dwellings surrounded the mound, and the whole village was ringed by palisades of spiked logs, indicating a high probability of warfare.

Archeologists have unearthed remains of an Etowahan war chief they called Eagle Warrior. Eagle Warrior wore a heavy necklace of solid shell beads the size of golf balls. From it hung a slender, foot-long pendant crafted from a whole conch shell. Wide bands of shell beadwork encircled his wrists and upper arms. Around his head lay more insignia of the highest status, among them copper-covered wooden coils fastened to a plate of sheet copper cut and embossed in the image of an open bird's wing to form an imposing headdress. Across his chest lay a splendid ceremonial axe, its blade and handle carefully wrought from a single piece of greenstone. The weapon, much too delicate for practical use, served as an emblem of power.

Such chiefs led warriors into battle against other towns, often in the spring. They went into battle almost naked, having painted their faces and upper bodies with red and black ochers that the people of Etowah found nearby. Each warrior carried a club, knife, bow, and arrows. The earliest Spanish explorers found the people of the area exceptionally well trained for war. One of them observed that the warriors he met were "warlike and nimble. . . . Before a Christian can make a single shot [with crossbow or harquebus] . . . an Indian will discharge three or four arrows; and he seldom misses his object" (Stuart, 1991, 64).

Estimates place the occupation of Etowah at about 1200 C.E., with its height of population and cultural development about two centuries later, about 100 to 150 years before the first Spanish explorers traversed the area. The native inhabitants, whose oral history says migrated from the west, found sandy loam soil that was ideal for farming, with a climate with a long growing season, abundant rainfall, and forests jumping with game, including white-tailed deer and many smaller animals. The shoals of rivers near Etowah abounded with mussels, turtles, and fish.

THE NATCHEZ: A LONG-LIVED MOUND PEOPLE

The Natchez are an atypical example of a temple mound people who survived into the period of sustained contact with Europeans. The Natchez were ruled by a man called the Great Sun, whose decisions regarding individuals were absolute and despotic. In decisions regarding the nation, however, he was subject to the consensus of a council of respected elders. Unlike the Pueblos, whose houses were egalitarian, the Natchez gave their ruler a palace. The Great Sun lived in a large house, twenty-five by forty-five feet, built atop a flat-topped earthen mound eight to ten feet high. The Great Sun was an absolute ruler in every sense. A French observer said that when the Great Sun

Gives the leavings [of his meal] to his brothers or any of his relatives, his pushes the dishes to them with his feet. . . . The submissiveness of the savages to their chief, who commands them with the most despotic power, is extreme.... If he demands the life of any one of them he comes himself to present his head. (Champagne, 1989, 59–60)

Nearby, on another mound, stood a large building, with two carved birds at either end of its roof: the temple in which reposed the bones of earlier Great Suns. Only the Great Sun (who was also head priest as well as king) and a few assistants could enter the temple.

The sons and daughters of the Great Sun, the younger members of the royal family, were called Little Suns. Below the royal family in status was a class of nobles, and below them was a class of Honored Men. The rest of the people occupied the lower orders, the Stinkards. The term was not used in the presence of Stinkards themselves because they considered it offensive. Into this hierarchical society, the Natchez introduced marriage customs that introduced some (usually downward) class mobility. A Great Sun had to marry from among the Stinkards. The male children of Great Suns became Nobles, who were also obliged to marry Stinkards. The male children of Honored Men became Stinkards. Descent followed the female line, and children of female Suns became Suns themselves. The system was matrilineal, but in the household the man's word was law.

By the time the first English colonists established themselves on the eastern seaboard of North America, Spanish explorers had crossed the Mississippi Valley and regions southeast and southwest of it, fruitlessly seeking gold and other riches. They traveled as far into the Plains as present-day Nebraska, ruining their welcome among a number of Native peoples with their penchant for arrogant plunder. The French also were using the Mississippi River as an aquatic highway, seeking furs. Outside of a few small settlements and a scattering of tiny forts, the Europeans had not become established before the year 1600 C.E. They left trade goods, missionaries, and liquor, as well as disease, the first fingers of the demographic rush that later would swirl across North America during the westward expansion of the United States.

FIRST ENGLISH CONTACT: THE POWHATAN CONFEDERACY

As Shakespeare began staging his most notable plays and England delivered its first colonists to America, the tidewater area of Virginia was home to the numerous and powerful Powhatan Confederacy, which refers to the name the indigenous people gave to the falls of the river that the English named after their King James and that dissects the urban area they later named Richmond. Powhatan, derived from the Algonquian words *pau't-hanne* or *pauwau-atan*, was the name that the English affixed to the leader of the area's Native people. The immigrants believed him to be a king, in the English style, although Powhatan probably was not an absolute ruler.

Powhatan's name among his own people was Wahunsonacock (ca. 1547–1618). He was a remarkable figure who probably had assembled most of the

Powhatan Confederacy during his tenure as leader of one of its bands. The confederacy included about 200 villages organized into several small nation-states when the English encountered it for the first time. Wahunsonacock was about 60 years of age when Jamestown was founded in 1607. Wahunsonacock and other Native people in the area may have met with other Europeans before the Jamestown colonists. The Spanish had established a mission on the York River during 1570 that was destroyed by indigenous warriors. Gangs of pirates also occasionally sought shelter along the Carolina Outer Banks as they waited for the passage of Spanish galleons flush with booty from Mexico, Meso-america, and Peru.

Wahunsonacock's father had been forced northward with his people by the Spanish invasion of Florida. He began the political work that forged an alliance of more than 100 Algonquian-speaking villages containing 9,000 people in Virginia's tidewater country. Wahunsonacock himself strengthened this alliance into a confederacy that included the Pamunkey (his people), Mattaponi, Chickahominy, Nansemond, Potomac, and Rhappahanock. This confederacy stretched from the Potomac River in northern Virginia to Albemarle Sound in North Carolina. Wahunsonacock's main village was located on the York River. He probably had eleven wives, twenty sons, and at least eleven daughters. Pocahontas, who would figure in the founding mythology of the Jamestown Colony, was reputed to have been Wahunsonacock's favorite child.

The Powhatan Confederacy was one example of many Native confederacies that had been assembling and dissolving in eastern North America, perhaps for thousands of years. Most of the villages in the Powhatan Confederacy enjoyed considerable autonomy, although tribute was sometimes paid to the central authority. Individual villages sometimes decided to make war on the English without consulting other members of the confederacy.

In the beginning, as Wahunsonacock sought peace with the English, the colonists were in no demographic position to compete with the Natives. Within the first few years after Jamestown was founded, the peoples of the Powhatan Confederacy could have eradicated the English settlement with ease. Jamestown, in fact, would not have survived in its early years without their help. Of 900 colonists who landed during the first three years (1607–1610), only 150 were alive in 1610. Most of the colonists were not ready for the rugged life of founding a colony; many died of disease, exposure to unanticipated cold weather, and starvation. At one point within a year of their landfall in America, the Jamestown colonists became so hungry that some of them engaged in cannibalism. According to the journals of John Smith, the leader of the colony, one colonist killed his wife and "powdered" (salted) her "and had eaten part of her before it was known; for which he was executed, as he well deserved" (Page, 2003, 159).

General peace persisted during those years, however, because Wahunsonacock as well as the new Virginians wanted it. The owners of the Virginia colony in London decided to treat Wahunsonacock as an independent sovereign and to accept his aid. They even sent him a copper crown. The Powhatans seem to have valued English copper as avidly as the hungry colonists valued the Natives' corn during the early years.

Although Wahunsonacock was deeply suspicious of the English, he fostered an awkward peace between the Jamestown colonists and his people so that they could establish the first permanent English colony in North America. Following the colony's early hardships, some of Wahunsonacock's people, including his son Namontack, provided the English colonists with food and taught them to plant maize (Indian corn).

When John Smith was captured by Wahunsonacock's people during the fall of 1608, he was released unharmed—as legend has it, at the request of Pocahontas. The name *Pocahontas* actually was a nickname that meant frisky or something similar. The name by which the Native woman who befriended the Virginia colonists called herself was Matowake. Captain John Smith wrote of "blessed Pocahontes, the great King's daughter of Virginia, [who] oft saved my life. . . . She, under God, was the instrument to preserve this colony from death, famine, and utter confusion" (Maxwell, 1978, 76).

In 1610, the Virginians tried unsuccessfully to capture and imprison Wahunsonacock. Reacting to such hostility, Wahunsonacock moved his people farther inland. In spite of this precaution, in 1613 the Virginians took Pocahontas as a hostage. As a result, Wahunsonacock had to ransom her with some English captives. During her captivity, Pocahontas and a young widower, John Rolfe (one of the colony's most prominent men), developed a romantic interest in each other. Pocahontas was about 18 years of age in 1614 when she married Rolfe. The marriage was a political move to ally the colony with Wahunsonacock. On one occasion, Rolfe took Pocahontas to London, where she created a sensation and met the queen. She later contracted a deadly disease, possibly smallpox, and died at about age 21, leaving a son.

During the years following Pocahontas's death, tobacco became the Virginia colony's only export to England, bringing prosperity. The crop exhausted the soil in which it grew after two or three years, so the owners of expanding tobacco plantations expanded onto Native lands. This expansion, along with the death of Wahunsonacock in 1618, caused friction to increase between colonists and Native peoples.

At the time of Powhatan's death (and elevation to the chief's role of Opechancanough, who hated the English), the population of the colony was only 350, but by 1622, with tobacco-induced prosperity, it had grown to four times that. The Native peoples exploded in fury, killing 350 colonists and destroying many homes within a few hours. The colonists then responded in kind, swearing to exterminate the Powhatans and nearly succeeding. Natives were eliminated from the lower James and York Rivers; villages were burned and their inhabitants killed during several expeditions over the next three years. Hostilities continued on and off for several years; in 1641, a surprise attack cost the English hundreds of lives in one day. The attack was coordinated by Opechancanough, who was then more than 90 years of age. He was carried about his official business on a litter. The elderly chief was captured and shot, thus ending the Powhatan Confederacy. The English made peace with its constituent tribes one by one on English terms and assigned them to reservations, which were steadily reduced in size during subsequent years as tobacco farms expanded rapidly, catering to the rapid spread of tobacco addiction in Europe.

THE PILGRIMS' LANDFALL IN NEW ENGLAND

Squanto, who met the Pilgrims on a Plymouth Rock beach speaking English, was kidnapped from his native land (the immigrants later called it New England) about 1605 by English merchants. After Captain George Weymouth anchored off the coast of Massachusetts, he and his sailors captured Squanto and four other New England natives and took them back to England as slaves to impress his financial backers (Richard B. Williams, 2002). Squanto was taken to live with Sir Ferdinando Gorges, owner of the Plymouth Company, who quickly realized Squanto's value to his company's exploits in the New World. Gorges taught Squanto to speak English so that his colonists could trade with the Indians. In 1614, Squanto was returned to America to act as a guide and interpreter and to assist in the mapping of the New England coast. He was kidnapped along with twenty-seven other Indians and taken to Malaga, Spain, to be sold as slaves (ibid.). When local priests learned the fate of the Indians, they took them from the slave traders, Christianized them, and eventually sent them back to America in 1618.

Squanto's travels had not ended. He was recognized by one of Gorges's captains, captured a third time, and sent back to England as a slave. Squanto was later sent to New England once again with Thomas Dermer to finish mapping the coast, after which he was promised his freedom. During 1619, Squanto returned to his homeland once again to find that a large proportion of his people had been wiped out by smallpox. A year later, the Pilgrims met him on the beach, speaking English.

The English immigrants needed help. Half of the 102 people who had arrived on the Mayflower six weeks before the onset of winter (with no provisions for food or shelter) died before the immigrants' first growing season began in America. Those who survived did so by plundering the corn stores of Native American villages emptied by the diseases that had arrived before them. Fishermen from Europe, who occasionally made landfall in the area, probably brought pathogens ashore long before the immigrants' arrival. The English trader Thomas Morton wrote that all along the coast Indians had "died in heapes, as they lay in their houses" (Mann, 2002, 42). Most had died of viral hepatitis, according to research by Bruce D. Spiess, director of clinical research at the Medical College of Virginia (Richmond) (ibid., 43). Roughly 90 percent of the Native peoples in the area had died of disease, but William Bradford, who had no understanding of how disease spread among peoples with no immunity, credited "The good hand of God," which had "favored our beginnings by sweeping away great multitudes of the natives . . . that he might make room for us" (ibid., 43).

As the Plymouth Colony was established, Squanto became an invaluable interpreter. He promoted peace between Native peoples and the Pilgrims as he taught the settlers the skills required to survive their second winter. Among other things, Squanto showed the immigrants how to plant corn in hillocks using dead herring as fertilizer. Imported seeds of English wheat, barley, and peas did not grow in American soil. Squanto also taught the immigrants how to design traps to catch fish; he acted as a guide and interpreter.

ROGER WILLIAMS'S ERRAND IN THE WILDERNESS

Like many another Puritan, the preacher Roger Williams originally came to America "longing after the natives' soules" (Chupack, 1969, 63). Within a few months of Williams's arrival in Boston during 1631, he was learning the Algonquian language. He would master the dialects of the Showatuck, Nipmuck, Narragansett, and others. Williams's oratorical flourish and compassion won him esteem with congregations at Plymouth and Salem, as well as among native peoples of the area, all of whom sought his "love and counsel" (Ernst, 1932, 179).

Williams's quick mastery of Native languages did not alarm the soul soldiers of Puritania. What landed him in hot ecclesiastical water was what he learned from the Native peoples as he picked up their languages. Asked by William Bradford (governor of the Plymouth Colony) to compose a paper on the compact that established the Puritan colony in America, Williams declared it invalid. How, he asked, could the Puritans claim the land by "right of discovery" when it was already inhabited? Furthermore, Williams argued that the Puritans had no right to deny the Indians their own religions. Soon, the authorities were fretting over how easily Williams won friends not only among colonists, but also among the Native peoples of the area.

Those friendships would be used to advantage a few years later when Williams founded Providence Plantations, later called Rhode Island. Williams became friendly with Massasoit, a sachem among the Wampanoags (also called Pokanokets), a man described by Bradford in 1621 as "lustie . . . in his best years, an able body grave of countenance, spare of speech, strong [and] tall" (Covey, 1966, 125). Williams met Massasoit when the latter was about 30 years of age and, in Williams's words, became "great friends" with the sachem (Brockunier, 1940, 47).

Massasoit (ca. 1580–1661) was among the first Native American leaders to greet English settlers in what would become Puritan New England. Like Powhatan, Massasoit (father of Metacom) initially favored friendly relations with the English colonists when he became the Wampanoags' most influential leader in about 1632. The Wampanoags assisted the Puritans during their first hard winters in the new land and took part in the first Thanksgiving. Massasoit allied with the Pilgrims out of practical necessity; many of his people had died in an epidemic shortly before the whites arrived, and he

Roger Williams. (Courtesy of the Library of Congress.)

sought to forge an alliance with them against the more numerous Narragansetts.

Williams also became close to Canonicus (ca. 1560–1647), an elderly leader of
the Narragansetts. With Canonicus and Massasoit, Williams traveled in the forest
for days at a time, learning what he could of their languages, societies, and

Massasoit on his way to meet the Pilgrims, 1621. (Courtesy of the
Library of Congress.)

opinions, absorbing experiences that, along with his knowledge of European ways, would provide the intellectual groundwork for the model commonwealth Williams sought to establish in Providence Plantations. Canonicus regarded Williams nearly as a son.

At their height, the Narragansetts, with Canonicus as their leader, held sway over the area from Narragansett Bay on the east to the Pawcatuck River on the west. The Narragansetts were rarely warlike, and their large numbers (about 4,000 men of warrior age in the early seventeenth century) usually prevented other native nations from attacking them.

William Wood, writing in *New England's Prospect*, characterized the Narragansetts as "the most numerous people in those parts, and the most rich also, and the most industrious, being a storehouse of all kinds . . . of merchandise" (1977, 80–81). The Narragansetts fashioned wampum in bracelets and pendants for many other Indian nations. They also made smoking pipes "much desired by our English tobacconists for their rarity, strength, handsomeness, and coolness" (ibid., 80–81). According to Wood's account, the Narragansetts had never desired "to take part in any martial enterprise. But being incapable of a jeer, they rest secure under the conceit of their popularity, and seek rather to grow rich by industry than famous by deeds of chivalry" (ibid., 80–81). In this fashion, the Narragansetts built a confederacy in which they supervised the affairs of Indian peoples throughout most of present-day Rhode Island and eastern Long Island, about 30,000 Native people in the early seventeenth century (Chapin, 1931, 7).

By 1635, Williams was arguing that the church had no right to compel membership, or contributions, by force of law, the central concept of church-state separation. "Natural men," as Williams called the Native peoples, should not, and could not, be forced "to the exercise of those holy Ordinances of Prayers, Oathes, &c." (Giddings, 1957, 21). By January 1635, the Puritans' more orthodox magistrates had decided to exile Williams to England, jailed if possible, and shut up. They opposed exiling Williams in the American wilderness, fearing that he would begin his own settlement, from which his "infections" would leak back into Puritania. A summons was issued for Williams's arrest, but he stalled the authorities by contending he was too ill to withstand an ocean voyage.

At the same time, Williams and his associates were rushing ahead with plans for their new colony, from which the worst fears of the orthodox magistrates would be realized. Williams already had arranged with Canonicus for a tract of land large enough to support a colony. Canonicus would not accept money in payment for the land. "It was not price or money that could have purchased Rhode Island," Williams wrote later. "Rhode Island was purchased by love" (Winslow, 1957, 133). Williams was allowed to remain in Salem until the spring of 1636, provided he refrained from preaching.

About January 15, 1636, a Captain Underhill was dispatched from Boston to arrest Williams and place him on board a ship bound for England. Arriving at Williams's home, Underhill and his deputies found that Williams had escaped. No one in the neighborhood would admit to having seen him leave.

Aware of his impending arrest, Williams had set out three days earlier during a blinding blizzard, walking south by west to the lodge of Massasoit at Mount Hope. Walking eighty to ninety miles during the worst of a New England winter, Williams suffered immensely and likely would have died without Indian aid. Nearly half a century later, nearing death, Williams wrote: "I bear to this day in my body the effects of that winter's exposure" (Guild, 1886, 20).

Near the end of his trek, Williams lodged with Canonicus and his family. He then scouted the land that had been set aide for the new colony. Williams's trek took place during a smallpox epidemic that was ravaging native populations in the area. The Plymouth Colony's Governor Bradford described its toll:

> For want of bedding and linen and other helps they [Natives] fall into a lamentable condition as they lie on their hard mats, the pox breaking and mattering and running one into another, their skin cleaving by reason thereof to the mats they lie on. When they turn them, a whole side will flay off at once . . . and they will be all of a gore blood, most fearful to behold. (Stannard, 1992, 108)

Week by week, month by month, Williams's family and friends filtered south from Plymouth and Salem. By spring, they were erecting houses, and fields were being turned. The growing group of immigrants also began to create an experimental government very novel by European (or Puritan) standards of the time. For the first time among English-speaking people in America, they were establishing a political order based on liberty of conscience and other natural rights.

Very quickly, Williams's house became a transcultural meeting place. He lodged as many as fifty Indians at a time—travelers, traders, sachems on their way to or from treaty conferences. If a Puritan needed to contact an Indian or vice versa he more than likely did so with Williams's aid. Among Indian nations at odds with each other, Williams became "a quencher of . . . fires" (Ernst, 1932, 252). When citizens of Portsmouth needed an Indian agent, they approached Williams. The Dutch did the same after 1636. The Narragansetts' council sometimes used Williams's house for its meetings.

When word reached Boston that the Pequots were rallying a Native alliance to drive the Massachusetts Bay settlements into the sea, the Massachusetts Council sent urgent pleas to Williams to use his "utmost and speediest Endeavors" to keep the Narragansetts out of it. Within hours after the appeal arrived in the hands of an Indian runner "scarce acquainting my wife," Williams boarded "a poor Canow & . . . cut through a stormie Wind and with great seas, euery [sic] minute in hazard of life to the Sachim's [Canonicus's] howse" (Ernst, 1932, 252). After traveling thirty miles in the storm, Williams arrived at a Narragansett town larger than most of the English settlements of his day, knowing that the success or failure of the Pequot initiative might rest on whether he could dissuade his friends from joining in the uprising.

Canonicus listened to Williams with his son Mixanno at his side. The younger sachem was assuming the duties of leadership piecemeal as his father aged. The three men decided to seal an alliance, and within a few days, officials from Boston were double-timing through the forest to complete the necessary paperwork. Later, Williams also won alliances with the Mohegan and Massachusetts nations, swinging the balance of power against the Pequots and their allies. The Indians welcomed the Puritan deputies with a feast of white chestnuts and cornmeal with blackberries ("hasty pudding," later a New England tradition); Williams translated for both sides, sealing the alliance.

The Puritan deputies were awed at the size of the Narragansett town, as well as the size of the hall in which they negotiated the alliance. The structure, about fifty feet wide, was likened to a statehouse by the men from Boston. Canonicus, so old that he had to lay on his side during the proceedings, surprised the Puritans with his direct questions and shrewd answers. The treaty was finally sealed much to the relief of the Puritans, who thought the Narragansetts capable of fielding 30,000 fighting men. Although they had only a sixth that number, the Narragansetts still were capable of swinging the balance of power for or against the immigrants, who had been in America only sixteen years at the time.

The outcome of the Pequot War during the summer of 1636 radically altered the demographic balance in New England. Before it, the English colonists were a tiny minority. After it, they were unquestionably dominant. The atrocities of the war stunned Williams's conscience. He had been able to prevent a rout of the English, but at a profound moral cost. He could not prevent the war itself or the cruel retribution the Puritans took on the Pequots and their allies. Williams had put himself in the position of aiding those with whom he shared a birthright, although he disagreed with the rationale of their conquest. All during the war, Williams gleaned intelligence from Narragansett runners and traders, who knew far more about Pequot movements than any European. He was doubtless deeply grieved by their deaths.

Williams was revolted by the Puritans' slaughter of the Pequots. The war reached its climax with the burning of a thatch fort in the Pequot village at Mystic, trapping as many as 600 Indian men, women, and children in a raging inferno. The few who managed to crawl out of this roaring furnace jumped back into it when they faced a wall of Puritan swords. Puritan soldiers and their Indian allies waded through pools of Pequot blood, holding their noses against the stench of burning flesh. The wind-driven fire consumed the entire structure in half an hour. A few Pequot bowmen stood their ground amid the flames until their bows singed; they fell backward into the fire, sizzling to death. Bradford recalled:

> Those that escaped the fire were slain with the sword, some hewed to pieces, others run through with their rapiers, so that they were quickly dispatched and very few escaped. It was conceived that they thus destroyed about 400 at this time. It was a fearful sight to see them thus frying in the fire, and the streams of blood quenching the same, and horrible was the stink and scent thereof. (1967, 296)

Having described the massacre, Bradford then indicated how little guilt the Puritans felt about it. "The victory seemed a sweet sacrifice, and they gave the praise thereof to God, who had wrought so wonderfully for them, thus to enclose their enemies in their hands and give them so speedy a victory" (1967, 296). Although a few Puritans remonstrated, many put the war in the category of God's necessary business, along with all sorts of other things, from smallpox epidemics to late frosts and early freezes.

Williams had collected material for an Indian grammar much of his adult life, but the press of events left him little time to write. However, during a solitary sea voyage in 1643 to England, Williams composed his *Key into the Languages of America* (1643), the first Indian grammar in English, as well as a small collection of Williams's observations among Native Americans. In the *Key*, Williams also began to formulate a critique of European religion and politics that would be a subject of intense debate on both sides of the Atlantic for decades to come.

In the *Key*, Williams makes it obvious that "barbarian" had a more positive connotation to him than the same word would carry three centuries later. Like Peter Martyr before him and Benjamin Franklin after him (among many other observers), Williams used the Indian as counterpoint to European conventions in words very similar to those of Montaigne:

They [Indians] were hospitable to everybody, whomsoever cometh in when they are eating, they offer them to eat of what they have, though but little enough [is] prepared for themselves. If any provision of fish or flesh comes in, they presently give . . . to eat of what they have. . . . It is a strange truth that a man can generally find more free entertainment and refreshing amongst these Barbarians than amongst the thousands that call themselves Christians. (Rider, 1904, 22)

Some of Williams's American lessons were offered in verse:

> I've known them to leave their house and mat
> To lodge a friend or stranger
> When Jews and Christians oft have sent
>   Jesus Christ to the Manger
> Oft have I heard these Indians say
>   These English will deliver us
> Of all that's ours, our lands and lives
>   In the end, they'll bereave us
> —Rider, 1904, 44

Williams disputed notions that Europeans were intellectually superior to Native Americans:

For the temper of the braine [*sic*] in quick apprehensions and accurate judgements . . . the most high and sovereign God and Creator hath not made them inferior to Europeans...Nature knows no difference between Europeans and Americans in blood, birth, bodies, &c. God having of one blood made all mankind, Acts 17....The same Sun shines on a Wilderness that doth on a garden. (Rider, 1904, 49, 53, 78)

Williams also wrote: "Boast not, proud English, of thy birth and blood; Thy brother Indian is by birth as good" (Brockunier, 1940, 141).

By implication, the Puritans had no right to take land and resources from Native Americans by "divine right." Williams's statement was the first expression in English, on American soil, of a belief that would power the American Revolution a century and a half later: "All men are created equal, and endowed by their Creator with certain inalienable rights."

In some ways, Williams found what Europeans called "Christian values" better embodied in Native American societies: "There are no beggars amongst them, nor fatherless children unprovided for" (Rider, 1904, 29). The *Key* not only was a grammar but also was a lesson in humility directed at the most pompous and ethnocentric of the English:

> When Indians heare the horrid filths,
>   Of Irish, English men
> The horrid Oaths and Murthurs late
>   Thus say these Indians then:
> We weare no Cloathes, have many Gods,
>   And yet our sinnes are lesse:
> You are Barbarians, Pagans wild,
>   Your land's the wildernesse.
>   —Rider, 1904, 9

The *Key* became a standard text for English-speaking people wishing to learn the languages of New England's Native peoples. The small book was printed in England and widely distributed there, but not in Boston. Despite diplomatic aid that might have saved the Massachusetts Bay Colony, Williams still was regarded as a dangerous radical by orthodox Puritans. Addressing Christian hypocrisy, using his image of the Indian as counterpoint, Williams minced no words:

How often have I heard both the English and the Dutch[,] not only the civil, but the most debauched and profane say: "These Heathen Doggs [sic], better kill a thousand of them than we Christians should be endangered or troubled with them; they have spilt our Christian blood, the best way to make riddance of them is to cut them all off and make way for Christians." (Ernst, 1932, 251)

To Williams, the Natives of America were just as godly, even if not as Christian, as Europeans:

He that questions whether God made the World, the Indians will teach him. I must acknowledge I have received in my converse with them many confirmations of these two great points, Heb. II.6, *viz*: 1. That God is[.] 2. That hee [*sic*] is a rewarder of all that diligently seek him. (Roger Williams, 1936, 123)

Roger Williams called Indian governmental organizations "monarchies" (as did many Europeans in the earliest colonial days), then contradicted himself by catching the scent of popular opinion in them. In his *Key*, Williams described the workings of Native American polities in ways similar to the structure he was erecting in the new colony: "The sachims ... will not conclude of ought that concerns all, either Lawes, or Subsidies, or warres, unto which people are averse, or by gentle perswasion cannot be brought" (1963, 1:224).

When some Puritans asked whether a society based on individual choice instead of coerced consent would degenerate into anarchy, Williams found the Indians' example instructive:

Although they have not so much to restraine them (both in respect of knowledge of God and lawes of Men) as the English have, yet a man shall never heare of such crimes amongst them [as] robberies, murthurs, adultries &c., as among the English. (Roger Williams, 1963, 1:225)

Among the colonists of Providence Plantations, as among the Indians he knew, Williams envisioned a society where "all men may walk as their consciences perswade them" (Kennedy, 1950, 42–44). Williams's ideal society also shared with the Indian societies he knew a relatively egalitarian distribution of property, with political rights based on natural law: "All civil liberty is founded in the consent of the People; ... Natural and civil Right and Privilege due ... as a Man, a Subject, a Citizen" (Ernst, 1932, 276–277).

Establishing such a utopian society was easier said than done. As Williams watched, some of the early settlers of Providence Plantations established land companies similar to those in other colonies as they tried to hoard land that could be sold at a higher price to future arrivals. The same land earlier had been set aside for newcomers to prevent growth of a landless underclass in the colony. In 1654, in a letter to the town of Providence, Williams showed how isolated he sometimes felt in his quest for a new way of life: "I have been charged with folly for that freedom and liberty that I always have stood for—I say, liberty and equality in both land and government" (Miller, 1953, 221–222).

Williams argued vehemently against assertions that only Christians possessed soul and conscience. If all peoples were religiously equal, Crusades made no sense; this Williams took to be God's word, and like many preachers, he often spoke for himself by invoking deity. To Williams, religion seemed to mean less a professed doctrine than possession of an innate sense of justice and morality, and he saw that capacity in all people, Christian and not. From observing the Indians, he learned that such morality was endowed in human-kind naturally, not by membership in a church or adherence to a doctrine: "It is granted, that nature's light discovers a God, some sins a judgement, as we see in the Indians" (Roger Williams, 1963, 4:441). In his extensive travels with the Narragansetts, Williams sensed "the conscience of good and evil that every savage Indian in the world hath" (ibid., 4:443).

Williams's efforts helped to maintain a shaky peace along the frontiers of New England for nearly two generations after the Pequot War. In 1645, Williams's efforts barely averted another Native uprising against encroaching European American settlements. By the 1660s, however, the aging Williams was watching his lifelong pursuit of peace unravel yet again. This time, he felt more impotent than before: His English ancestry drove him to protect English interests, as wave after wave of colonists provided Native peoples with powerful grievances by usurping their land without permission or compensation. In this matter, Williams had never changed his mind: Neither the Puritans nor any other Europeans had any right, divine or otherwise, to take Indian land. The final years of Williams's life were profoundly painful for a sensitive man who prized peace and harmony above all.

Entering his sixties, Williams's body grew old quickly. In 1663, he complained often of "old pains, lameness, so th't sometimes I have not been able to rise, nor goe, or stand" (Winslow, 1957, 267). Williams found himself using his pastoral staff as more than a ministerial ornament. Massasoit also was aging and becoming disillusioned with the colonists as increasing numbers of European immigrants drove his people from their lands.

On Massasoit's death in 1661, Alexander, one of Massasoit's sons, briefly served as grand sachem of the Wampanoags until his own death. Visiting Boston during 1662, Alexander fell gravely ill and died as Wampanoag warriors rushed him into the wilderness. When Alexander died, the warriors beached their canoes, buried his body in a knoll, and returned home with rumors that he had been a victim of the English. Alexander's death stirred memories of Mixanno, also Massasoit's son, who had been assassinated in 1643. His murder never had been avenged as rumors circulated that the English had plotted the murder and that they were harboring the assailant.

In this context, Metacom, whom the English called King Philip, became grand sachem after Alexander. About 25 years old in 1662, Metacom distrusted nearly all European Americans, with Williams one of the few exceptions. Metacom also was known as a man who did not forgive insults easily. It was once said that he chased a white man named John Gibbs from Mount Hope to Nantucket Island after Gibbs insulted his father. Throughout his childhood, Metacom had watched his people dwindle before the English advance. By 1671, about 40,000 people of European descent lived in New England. The Native population, double that of the Europeans before the Pequot war, was now about 20,000. European farms and pastures were crawling toward Mount Hope, driving away game and creating friction over land that the Indians had used without question for so many generations they had lost count of them. By 1675, the Wampanoags held only a small strip of land at Mount Hope, and settlers wanted it.

Metacom became more embittered by the day. He could see his nation being destroyed before his eyes. English cattle trampled Indian cornfields as encroaching farms forced game animals further into the wilderness. Metacom was summoned to Plymouth to answer questions, and other people in his nation were interrogated by Puritan officials. Traders fleeced Indians, exchanging furs for liquor. The devastation of alcohol and disease and the loss of land destroyed families and tradition. These were Metacom's thoughts as he prepared to go to war against the English.

As rumors of war reached Williams, he again tried to keep the Narragansetts out of it. This time, he failed. Nananawtunu, son of Mixanno, told his close friend Williams that although he opposed going to war, his people could not be restrained. They had decided the time had come to die fighting rather than to expire slowly as a people. Williams's letters of this time were pervaded with sadness as he watched the two groups he knew so well slide toward war.

Shortly after hostilities began in June 1675, Williams met with Metacom, riding with the sachem and his family in a canoe not far from Providence. Williams warned Metacom that he was leading his people to extermination. Williams compared the Wampanoags to a canoe on a stormy sea of English fury. "He answered me in a consenting, considering kind of way," Williams wrote, saying "My canoe is already overturned" (Giddings, 1957, 33).

When Indians painted for war appeared on the heights above Providence, Williams picked up his staff, climbed the bluffs, and told the war parties that if they attacked the town, England would send thousands of armed men to crush them. "Well," one of the sachems leading the attack told Williams, "Let them come. We are ready for them, but as for you, brother Williams, you are a good man. You have been kind to us for many years. Not a hair on your head shall be touched" (Straus, 1894, 220–224).

Williams was not injured, but his house was torched as he met with the Indians on the bluffs above Providence on March 29, 1676. Williams watched flames spread throughout the town. "This house of mine now burning before mine eyes hath lodged kindly some thousands of you these ten years," Williams told the attacking Indians (Swan, 1969, 14). If the colony was to survive, Williams, for the first time in his life, had to become a military commander. With a grave heart, Williams sent his neighbors out to do battle with the sons and daughters of native people who had sheltered him during his winter trek from Massachusetts forty years earlier. As Williams and others watched from inside a hastily erected fort, nearly all of Providence burned. Fields were laid waste and cattle slaughtered or driven into the woods.

Colonists, seething with anger, caught an Indian, and Williams was put in the agonizing position of ordering him killed rather than watching him tortured. The war was irrefutably brutal on both sides as the English fought

PHILLIP alias METACOMET of Pokanoket.

Metacom. (Courtesy of Smithsonian National Anthropological Archives.)

The Landing of Roger Williams

RHODE ISLAND.

The landing of Roger Williams, greeted by Indians, 1636. (Courtesy of the Library of Congress.)

with their backs literally to the sea for a year and a half before going on the offensive. At Northfield, Indians hung two Englishmen on chains, placing hooks under their jaws. At Springfield, colonists arrested an Indian woman, then offered her body to dogs, which tore her to pieces.

By August 1676, the war ended as the Mohawks and Mohegans opted out of their alliance with the Wampanoags, leaving after the English had exterminated the Narragansetts. Nearly all of Metacom's warriors, their families, and friends had been killed or driven into hiding. Metacom himself fled toward Mount Hope, then hid in a swamp. When English soldiers found him, they dragged Metacom out of the mire, then had him drawn and quartered. His head was sent to Plymouth on a giblet, where it was displayed much as criminals' severed heads were shown off on the railings of London Bridge. Metacom's hands were sent to Boston, where a local showman charged admission for a glimpse of one of them. The remainder of Metacom's body was hung from four separate trees.

In terms of deaths in proportion to total population, King Philip's War was among the deadliest in American history. About 1,000 colonists died in the war; many more died of starvation and war-related diseases. Every Native nation bordering the Puritan settlements was reduced to ruin—those whose members, in happier days, had offered the earliest colonists their first Thanksgiving dinner. Many of the survivors were sold into slavery in the West Indies, by

CAPTURE OF THE INDIAN FORTRESS.

Capture of an Indian fortress during King Philip's War, 1675. (Courtesy of the Library of Congress.)

which the colonists served two purposes: removing them from the area and raising money to help pay their enormous war debts. Metacom's son was auctioned off with about 500 other slaves following a brief, but intense, biblical debate over whether a son should be forced to atone for the sins of his father.

Williams died March 15, 1683, in Providence, with the pain of the world bowing his creaking shoulders, likely realizing just how out of step he was with the temper of his time. He was a peacemaker in time of war; a tolerant man in a world full of ideologues; a democrat in a time of ecclesiastical and secular sovereigns; a dissenter wherever self-interest masqueraded as divinity. Williams had planted seeds in American soil that would not fully flower for more than another century. He would have relished the company of Thomas Jefferson, for example, at a time when his ideas were the common currency of political revolution.

HARDER TIMES FOR NATIVE PEOPLES IN THE NORTHEAST

Harder times were to come for the Native peoples of New England. By 1703, Massachusetts was paying £12 sterling for an Indian scalp, an amount worth about $500 today. In 1722, the bounty rose to £100, about $4,000 today, adjusted for inflation. Although the folklore price of Manhattan Island was $24 worth of beads and trinkets, the actual price was 60 Dutch gulden, worth about $10,000 to $15,000 today. The Native peoples of Manhattan probably thought they were accepting a gift to share the land, not selling it, because they did not buy and sell real estate as Europeans did.

The human price of ceding the land was much higher for some Native people in the region. In 1643, the Dutch governor of Manhattan (who was drunk at the time) ordered the massacre of several Wappingers who had fled to the Dutch settlements for protection from the Mohawks. The Dutch lulled the Wappingers with kind treatment for a few days, then slaughtered eighty men, women, and children in their beds. Their heads were severed and taken to Fort Amsterdam on Manhattan Island, where a Dutch dowager stirred considerable attention by playing kickball with them in the street. A Hackensack Indian was tortured in front of a crowd, stripped of his skin piece by piece, then forced to eat it. The Native man tried to sing his death song as he was castrated and dragged through the streets, his raw flesh peeled from head to knees. Still alive, he was trussed to a millstone and beaten to death by Dutch soldiers. The Dutch governor, no bleeding heart, laughed heartily at the scene.

In 1752, General Jeffrey Amherst, commander-in-chief for North America, was reported to have advocated the use of smallpox as a military tactic against the Ottawas, Ojibways, and other Native peoples in the Great Lakes area. "You will be well advised," Amherst told his subordinates, "to infect the Indians with sheets upon which small pox patients have been lying or by any other means which may serve to exterminate this accursed race" (Johansen and Grinde, 1997, 10). Amherst also recommended hunting Indians with trained dogs. An oral history account of the Ottawas, related by Andrew J. Blackbird (1897), nineteenth century Ottawa historian, indicated that smallpox came to them in a box from a white man. They opened the box to find another, smaller one. Inside the second box was a third, even smaller. Inside the last box, the Ottawas found moldy particles, the smallpox "patients."

THE PIVOTAL ROLE OF THE IROQUOIS CONFEDERACY

The Iroquois Confederacy was well known to the British and French colonists of North America because of its pivotal position in diplomacy between the colonists, as well as among other native confederacies. Called the Iroquois by the French and the Five (later Six) Nations by the English, the Haudenosaunee (meaning People of the Longhouse) controlled the only relatively level land passage between the English colonies on the seaboard and the French settlements in the St. Lawrence Valley. The five original nations (Mohawk, Oneida, Onondaga, Cayuga, and Seneca) were joined by the Tuscaroras about 1700 C.E.

Each Iroquois nation has its own council, which sends delegates to a central council, much as each state in the United States has its own legislature, as well as senators and representatives who travel to the central seat of government in Washington, D.C. When representatives of the Iroquois nations meet in Onondaga, they form two groups: the Elder Brothers (Mohawks and Senecas) and the Younger Brothers (Cayugas and Oneidas). The Onondagas are the firekeepers. (In the U.S. Congress, this position is held by the Speaker of the House.) At Onondaga, the site of the struggle with Tadadaho, the Iroquois built a perpetual council fire, The Fire That Never Dies.

The Iroquois Confederacy was founded by the Huron prophet Deganawidah, who is called the Peacemaker in oral discourse among many traditional Haudenosaunee. Deganawidah enlisted the aid of a speaker, Aionwantha (also called Hiawatha) to spread his vision of a united Haundenosaunee Confederacy. Deganawidah needed a spokesman in the oral culture of the Iroquois because he stuttered so badly he could hardly speak, an impediment that Iroquois oral history attributes to a double row of teeth. The confederacy was founded before first European contact in the area, about 1100 C.E. Deganawidah sought to replace blood feuds that had devastated the Iroquois with peaceful modes of decision making. The result was the Great Law of Peace (sometimes called the Great Binding Law).

Peace among the formerly antagonistic nations was procured and maintained through the Haudenosaunee's Great Law of Peace (*Kaianerekowa*), which was passed from generation to generation using wampum, a form of written communication that outlined a complex system of checks and balances between nations and genders.

According to Iroquois oral history, the visionary Hiawatha tried to call councils to eliminate the blood feud, but was thwarted by the evil and twisted wizard Tadadaho, an Onondaga who used magic and spies to rule by fear and intimidation. Failing to defeat the wizard, Hiawatha traveled to Mohawk, Oneida, and Cayuga villages with his message of peace and brotherhood. Everywhere he went, his message was accepted with the proviso that he persuade the formidable Tadadaho and the Onondagas to embrace the covenant of peace.

Just as Hiawatha was despairing, the prophet Deganawidah entered his life. Together, the two men developed a powerful message of peace. Deganawidah's vision gave Hiawatha's oratory substance. Through Deganawidah's vision, the constitution of the Iroquois was formulated. In his vision, Deganawidah saw a giant white pine reaching to the sky and gaining strength from three counterbalancing principles of life. The first axiom was that a stable mind and healthy body should be in balance so that peace between individuals and groups could occur. Second, Deganawidah stated that humane conduct, thought, and speech were a requirement for equity and justice among peoples. He foresaw a society in which physical strength and civil authority would reinforce the power of the clan system.

With such a powerful vision, Deganawidah and Hiawatha were able to subdue the evil Tadadaho and transform his mind. Deganawidah removed evil feelings and thoughts from the head of Tadadaho as he pledged to make reason and the wisdom of peaceful minds prevail. The evil wizard became reborn into a humane person charged with implementing the message of Deganawidah. After Tadadaho had submitted to the redemption, Onondaga became the central fire of the Haudenosaunee, and the Onondagas became the firekeepers of the new confederacy. To this day, the Great Council Fire of the confederacy is maintained in the land of the Onondagas, south of Syracuse, New York.

Each of the five Iroquois nations in Deganawidah's confederacy maintains its own council, whose sachems are nominated by the clan mothers of families holding hereditary rights to office titles. The Grand Council at Onondaga was drawn from the individual national councils.

For each of the Iroquois nations' own councils, sachems are nominated by the clan mothers of families holding hereditary rights to office titles. The Grand Council at Onondaga is drawn from the individual national councils. The Grand Council also may nominate sachems outside the hereditary structure based on merit alone. These sachems, called *pine tree chiefs*, are said to spring from the body of the people as the symbolic Great White Pine springs from the earth.

Rights, duties, and qualifications of sachems are explicitly outlined. Clan mothers may remove (impeach) a sachem found guilty of any of a number of abuses of office, from missing meetings to murder. An erring chief is summoned to face charges by the war chiefs, who act in peacetime as the peoples' eyes and ears in the council, somewhat as the role of the press was envisaged by Jefferson and other founders of the United States. A sachem is given three warnings, then removed from the council if he does not mend his ways. A sachem found guilty of murder not only loses his title, but also deprives his entire family of its right to representation. The women relatives holding the rights to the office are "buried," and the title is transferred to a sister family.

For details on the Iroquois Confederacy's role in the founding of U.S. political institutions, see chapter 4.

GEORGE COPWAY: LONGFELLOW'S HIAWATHA

The name Hiawatha is best known in American popular history through the poetry of Henry Wadsworth Longfellow, who seems to have known little or nothing about the life of the Iroquois cultural hero of the same name. Instead, George Copway (Kahgegwagebow, Stands Fast Chippewa/Ojibway; 1818 to ca. 1863) may have been the model for Longfellow's Hiawatha. Copway was a close friend of Longfellow and was noted among the Ojibways for his physical strength and skill at hunting. Copway also was one of the first Native Americans to write books that were widely read by non-Indians.

Copway was born near the mouth of the Trent River, Ontario, Canada, in 1818. He was raised as a traditional Ojibway; his father was a noted leader and medicine man, but the family often went hungry during Copway's youth. His traditional training included stress on physical strength; Copway once carried 200 pounds of flour and other supplies on his back for a quarter mile without rest. In the spring of 1841, he is said to have run across much of Wisconsin to warn the Ojibways of a Sioux raiding party, traveling 240 miles in four days.

Copway was converted to Methodism in 1830 and attended Ebenezer Academy (Jacksonville, IL) for two years. Copway became a Methodist minister in 1834, after which he translated several religious texts from English into Algonquian and worked with several religious publishers. During 1851, in New York City, Copway started a newspaper about American Indian affairs, *Copway's American Indian*. Only one issue is known to have been published, on July 10, 1851.

Copway wrote *The Life, History and Travels of Kah-Ge-Ga-Gah-Bowh* (1847), which was revised in 1850 as *The Traditional History and Traditional Sketches of the Ojibway Nation*. The same book was reissued again in 1858 as *Indian Life and Indian History*. He also wrote *The Ojibway Conquest* (1850); *The Organization of a New Indian Territory East of the Missouri River* (1850); and *Running Sketches of Men and Places in England, Germany, Belgium, and Scotland* (1851). Copway also toured Europe; in England, he denounced European and American deals for Ojibway ancestral lands as frauds and robberies. Copway died near Pontiac, Michigan, at 45 years of age.

RETHINKING THE IROQUOIS CONFEDERACY'S FOUNDING DATE

The Haudenosaunee (Iroquois) Confederacy is one of the oldest continually operating consensual governments in the world, one that is at least three centuries older than most previous estimates according to research completed during the middle 1990s by Barbara Alice Mann and Jerry Fields of the

University of Toledo, Ohio. Using a combination of documentary sources, solar eclipse data, and Iroquois oral history, Mann and Fields make a case that the Iroquois Confederacy's body of fundamental law was adopted by the Senecas (the last of the five nations to ratify it) August 31, 1142. The ratification council convened at a site that is now a football field in Victor, New York. The site is called Gonandaga by the Seneca.

Mann and Fields concluded that the only eclipse that meets all requisite conditions—an afternoon occurrence over Gonandaga that darkened the sky—is the eclipse of 1142. The duration of darkness would have been a dramatic interval of three-and-a-half minutes, long enough to wait for the sun and long enough to impress everyone with Deganawidah's power to call forth a sign in the sky (B. A. Mann and Fields, 1997, 105). Heretofore, many experts have dated the formation of the confederacy to the year 1451, at the time of another solar eclipse. Mann and Fields contend that the 1451 eclipse was total, but that its shadow fell over Pennsylvania, well to the southwest of the ratifying council's location.

Mann was a doctoral student in English at Ohio's University of Toledo at the time (by 2003, she was a faculty member there); Fields was an astronomer and an expert in the history of solar eclipses. The Senecas' oral history mentions that the Senecas adopted the Iroquois Great Law of Peace shortly after a total eclipse of the sun. Mann and Fields are the first scholars to combine documentary history with oral accounts and precise solar data in an attempt to date the origin of the Iroquois League. Depending on how democracy is defined, their date of 1142 C.E. would rank the Iroquois Confederacy with the government of Iceland and the Swiss cantons as the oldest continuously functioning democracy on earth. All three precedents have been cited as forerunners of the U.S. system of representative democracy.

According to Mann, the Seneca nation was the last of the five Iroquois nations to accept the Great Law of Peace. In an article "A Sign in the Sky: Dating the League of the Haudenosaunee," Mann estimated that the journey of Deganawidah (the Peacemaker) and Hiawatha in support of the Great Law had begun with the Mohawks, at the "eastern door" of the confederacy, about 25 years earlier (B. A. Mann and Fields, 1997).

The argument that the Iroquois League was established substantially before contact with Europeans is supported by oral history accounts. Another traditional method to estimate the founding date is to count the number of people who have held the office of Tadadaho (speaker) of the confederacy. A graphic record is available in the form of a cane that the eighteenth century French observer Lafitau called the Stick of Enlistment and modern-day anthropologist William N. Fenton calls the Condolence Cane.

Mann and Fields used a figure of 145 Tadadahos (from Mohawk oral historian Jake Swamp) and then averaged the tenure of other lifetime appointments, such as popes, European kings and queens, and U.S. Supreme Court justices. Cautioning that different socio-historical institutions are being compared, they figure into their sample 333 monarchs from eight European countries, 95 Supreme Court justices, and 129 popes. Averaging the tenures of all three groups, Mann and Fields found an estimated date that compares roughly to the 1142 date indicated by the eclipse record and the 1090 date calculated from family lineages by Underwood.

Mann and Fields also make their case with archeological evidence. The rise in interpersonal violence that pre-dated the Iroquois League can be tied to a cannibal cult and the existence of villages with palisades, both of which can be dated to the middle of the twelfth century. The spread of the league can be linked to the adoption of corn as a dietary staple among the Haudenosaunee, which also dates between 900 and 1100 C.E., Mann and Fields contend.

Mann and Fields's case has been questioned by David Henige, who also ridiculed Henry Dobyns's population numbers (see chapter 1). In *Numbers from Nowhere* (1998) Henige accuses Dobyns of overemphasizing disease as a cause of death. His critique of Mann and Fields's work (Henige, 1999) contends that they overemphasize a solar eclipse as a method of dating the origin of the confederacy.

As with his critique of Dobyns, Henige develops no extant case of his own. He advances no alternative founding date for the confederacy and no explanation of what the Haudenosaunee account calls a "sign in the sky." Henige does not regard his lack of a case as a shortcoming, however. Henige justifies his vagueness with a quotation from William N. Fenton: "All of these dates I regard as spurious. The whole search for an exact date of the formation of the Iroquois seems to be nonsense" (Henige, 2004, 127). Henige thus is satisfied to perform an intellectual hit-and-run, sowing doubt about new work without advancing the state of knowledge. Henige seems to fall back on an amorphous belief that the Haudenosaunee origin story is a "myth" that cannot be dated. Thus, he renders the entire debate largely a figment of imagination as he reduces the most important events in Haudenosaunee political history to a sort of shimmering make-believe. Having criticized Mann and Fields for falling short of standard cannons for historical evidence, his own case dissolves into pure, unverified speculation.

So, when did the Haudenosaunee "invent" their myth? Henige gives no credit to oral history: "The Iroquois League was not founded on this day [August 31, 1142], or any other day before its first mention in contemporaneous sources" (Henige, 2004, 127). For history to matter, to Henige it must be written, usually by Europeans. Believing this, he can, for example, reduce Hiawatha to an imaginary figure who appears in the record about 1800 or afterward. He does so with an air of scholarly certainty.

Mann also offers another example of what she believes to be the European- and male-centered nature of existing history. Most accounts of the Iroquois League's origins stress the roles played by the Peacemaker Deganawidah and Aionwantha (or Hiawatha), who joined him in a quest to quell the blood feud and establish peace. Mann asserts that most histories largely ignore the role of a third person, a woman, Jingosaseh, who insisted on gender balance in the Iroquois constitution.

Under Haudenosaunee law, clan mothers choose candidates (wh⌐ chiefs. The women also maintain ownership of the land and home veto power over any council action that may result in war.

Although a high degree of gender equity existed in Iroquois law, ge⌐ roles often were (and remain) very carefully defined, down to the version ot history passed down by people of either gender. Men, the vast majority of anthropological informants, tended to play up the role of Deganawidah and Aionwantha, which was written into history. Women, who would have described the role of Jingosaseh, were usually not consulted. Mann points out that Jingosaseh, originally the name of an historical individual, subsequently a title, was a leader of clan mothers. The historic figure Tadadaho, originally Deganawidah's and Aionwantha's main antagonist, became the title of the league's speaker. Occasionally in Iroquois history, a title also may become a personal name; Handsome Lake (a reference to Lake Ontario) was the title to one of the fifty seats on the Iroquois Grand Council before it was the name of the nineteenth century Iroquois prophet. According to Mann, "It is only after the Peacemaker agrees to her terms that she throws her considerable political weight behind him. . . . She was, in short, invaluable as an ally, invincible as a foe. To succeed, the Peacemaker needed her" (Johansen, 1995, 63).

"Jingosaseh is recalled by the Keepers as a co-founder of the League, alongside of Deganawidah and Hiawatha," said Mann. "Her name has been obliterated from the white record because her story was a woman's story and nineteenth-century male ethnographers simply failed to ask women, whose story hers was, about the history of the League" (Johansen, 1995, 63).

The story of how Jingosaseh joined with Deganawidah and Hiawatha is one part of an indigenous American epic that has been compared to the Greeks' Homer, the Mayan *Popul Vu*, and the Tibetan *Book of the Dead*. Although encapsulated versions of the Great Law have been translated into English for more than 100 years, the Great Law of Peace is still being discovered by scholars. As recently as 1992, Syracuse University Press published the most complete available translation of the Iroquois Great Law (Woodbury, Henry, and Webster, 1992). Once every five years, until his death in 1998, the Cayuga Jake Thomas recited the entire epic at the confederacy's central council fire in Onondaga, New York. The recitation usually took him three or four 8-hour days, during which he spoke until his voice cracked. Although numerous other Native confederacies existed along the borders of the British colonies, many of the specific provisions of their governments have been lost.

THE IROQUOIS INFLUENCE ON TREATY DIPLOMACY

Between the mid-seventeenth century and the end of the nineteenth century, the Haudenosaunee negotiated more than a hundred treaties with English (and later United States) representatives. Until about 1800 C.E., most of these treaties were negotiated according to Haudenosaunee protocol. By the mid-eighteenth century, this protocol was well established as the "lingua franca" of diplomacy in eastern North America. According to this protocol, an alliance was adopted and maintained using certain rituals.

Initial contacts between negotiating parties usually were made "at the edge of the forest," on neutral ground, where an agenda and a meeting place and time could be agreed on. Following the "approach to the council fire," the place of negotiation, a Condolence Ceremony was recited to remember those who had died on both sides since the last meeting. A designated party kindled the council fire at the beginning of negotiations and covered it at the end. A council was called for a specific purpose (such as making of peace) and could not be changed once convened. Representatives from both sides spoke in a specified order. No important actions were taken until at least one night had elapsed since the matter's introduction before the council. The passage of time was said to allow the various members of the council to attain unanimity— "one mind"—necessary for consensual solution of a problem.

Wampum belts or strings were exchanged when an important point was made or an agreement reached. Acceptance of a belt was taken to mean agreement on an issue. A belt also might be refused, or thrown aside, to indicate rejection of a proposal. Another metaphor that was used throughout many of the councils was that of the Covenant Chain, a symbol of alliance. If proceedings were going well and consensus was being reached on major issues, the chain (which was often characterized as made of silver) was being "polished" or "shined." If agreement was not being reached, the chain was said to be "rusting."

During treaty negotiations, a speaker was generally allowed to complete a statement without interruption, according to Haudenosaunee protocol, which differs markedly with the cacophony of debate in European forums such as the British House of Commons. Often, European representatives expressed consternation when carefully planned schedules were cast aside so that everyone (warriors as well as their leaders) could express an opinion on an important issue. Many treaties were attended by large parties of Iroquois, each of whom could in theory claim a right to speak.

The host of a treaty council was expected to supply tobacco for the common pipe as well as refreshments (usually alcoholic in nature) to extinguish the sour taste of tobacco smoking. Gifts often were exchanged and great feasts held during the proceedings, which sometimes were attended by entire Haudenosaunee families. A treaty council could last several days even under the most agreeable circumstances. If major obstacles were encountered in negotiations, a council could extend two weeks or longer, sometimes as long as a month.

A main treaty council often was accompanied by several smaller ones during which delegates with common interests met to discuss problems that concerned them. Usually, historical accounts record only the proceedings of the main body, leaving out the many important side conferences, which, in the diplomatic language of the time, were often said to have been held "in the bushes."

Treaty councils were conducted in a ritualistic manner to provide common points of understanding between representatives who otherwise were separated by barriers of language and cultural interpretation. The abilities of a good interpreter who was trusted by both sides (an example was Conrad Weiser in the mid-eighteenth century) could greatly influence the course of negotiations. Whether they knew the Iroquois and Algonquian languages or not, Anglo-American negotiators had to be on speaking terms with the metaphors of Iroquois protocol, such as the council fire, condolence, the tree of peace, and many others.

Haudenosaunee treaty relations, including trading relationships, were characterized in terms of kinship, hospitality, and reciprocity over and above commercial or diplomatic interests. The Dutch in particular seemed to be easily annoyed when they were forced to deal with trade relationships based on anything other than commerce. They, among other Europeans, seemed not to understand that, to the Iroquois, trade was conceived as part of a broader social relationship. The Mohawks seemed to resent the attitude of the Dutch negotiators, who saw negotiations as a commercial transaction. During September 1659, a party of Mohawks complained as follows:

> The Dutch, indeed, say we are brothers and are joined together with chains, but that lasts only as long as we have beavers. After that, we are no longer thought of, but much will depend on it [alliance] when we shall need each other. (Dennis, 1993, 171)

From the first sustained contact with Europeans, shortly after 1600, until the end of the French and Indian War (1763), the Haudenosaunee Confederacy utilized diplomacy to maintain a balance of power in northeastern North America between the colonizing British and French. This use of diplomacy and alliances to play one side against the other reached its height shortly after 1700, during the period that Richard Aquila called the Iroquois Restoration (Aquila, 1983, 16–17).

This period was followed by alliance of most Haudenosaunee with the British and the eventual defeat of the French. By the 1740s, England's developing industrial base had become much better at supplying trade goods to the Haudenosaunee and other Native American peoples; the balance of alliance was shifting. According to Aquila, the Iroquois' power had declined dangerously by about 1700, requiring a concerted effort on the part of the Grand Council to minimize warfare and build peaceful relations with the Haudenosaunee's neighbors. By 1712, the Haudenosaunee's military resources amounted to about 1,800 men. Disease as well as incessant warfare also caused declines in Haudenosaunee populations at about this time; major outbreaks of smallpox swept through Iroquoia in 1696 and 1717. At the same time, sizable numbers of dissenting Haudenosaunee, especially Mohawks, moved to Canada and cast their lots with the French.

Alcohol also was devastating the Iroquois at this time, a fact emphasized by the many requests for restrictions on the liquor trade by Haudenosaunee leaders at treaty councils and other meetings. Aquila wrote as follows:

> Sachems complained that alcohol deprived the Iroquois people of their senses, was ruining their lives . . . and was used by traders to cheat them out of their furs and lands. The Iroquois were not exaggerating. The French priest Lafitau reported in 1718 that when the Iroquois and other Indians became intoxicated they went completely berserk, screaming like madmen and smashing everything in their homes. (1983, 115)

After 1763, the Haudenosaunee were no longer able to play the French and the English against each other. Instead, the Iroquois faced pressure to ally with native peoples to their west against the English. Many Senecas sided with Pontiac against the English in 1763 and 1764.

Today, some members of the Iroquois Grand Council travel the world on their own national passports. The passport states that it has been issued by the Grand Council of the League of the Haudenosaunee, and that "The Haudenosaunee continues as a sovereign people on the soil it has occupied on Turtle Island since time immemorial, and we extend friendship to all who recognize our constitutional government and who desire peaceful relations" (Hill, 1987, 12). The passports were first issued in 1977 to Haudenosaunee delegates who attended a meeting of the United Nations in Switzerland. Since then, the United States, Holland, Canada, Switzerland, France, Belgium, Germany, Denmark, Italy, Libya, Turkey, Australia, Great Britain, New Zealand, Iran, and Colombia have been among the nations that have recognized the Haudenosaunee documents. Even so, it takes a talented travel agent to get a visa on an Iroquois passport because formal diplomatic relations often do not exist between the country recognizing the document and the Haudenosaunee Grand Council.

THE FUR TRADE

Trade and diplomacy were linked as functions of friendly international relations. Many of the rituals were similar. Native American economic relationships often were carried on according to principles of reciprocity involving mutual gift giving. Trade among Native peoples often was conducted as an exchange of gifts. European traders later adopted some of the Native peoples gift-giving practices when they traded in North America.

Notions of reciprocity permeated the daily lives of many Native American peoples. Among the Tlinget, for example, the two major clans (Wolf and Raven) built houses for each other, a process accompanied by feasting and gift giving. Among the Wyandots (Hurons), relations of friendship and material reciprocity were extended beyond the Wyandot Confederacy in the form of trading arrangements. Foreign trade was not merely an economic activity. It was embedded in a network of social relations that were fundamental extensions of the kin relationships within the Huron Confederacy. Like the Iroquois, the Wyandots sometimes formally adopted traders with whom they had frequent and mutually beneficial relations. Traders so adopted often lodged with their friends while visiting; sometimes traders, who were male, took Native American wives.

Across much of North America, Native Americans initially became part of the European cash economy through the fur trade. The type of animal harvested varied (from beaver in the Northeast to deer in the Southeast, bear in the Rocky Mountains, and sea otters along the Alaskan coast, for example), but the economic system was largely the same. The fur trade flourished in most areas until the early to mid-nineteenth century, after which it was curtailed by near extinction of some species as well as changes in European fashions, especially in coats and headgear.

Historian John Fahey described ways in which the fur trade changed Native American societies:

> In little more than a generation, the traditional base of Indian life vanished. The fur traders equipped Indians with better weapons—guns, iron arrowheads, traps, and steel knives—that allowed hunters to deplete game faster; they goaded the Indians to trap fur-bearing animals well beyond their own needs. Some districts became barren because the cycle of reproduction was destroyed. (1986, 44)

During the fur trade, Native American men harvested most of the furs; Native women prepared the skins for market. Native people also provided many goods and services that supported the fur trade, such as corn, maple sugar, wild rice, canoes, and snowshoes. The fur trade brought social as well as economic change to Native American societies. The number of men with more than one wife increased in some Plains cultures, for example, because an individual male hunter could employ more than one woman tanner.

Historian Colin Calloway outlined the mixed blessings of the fur trade:

> [T]he new commercial situation was at best a mixed blessing. The fur trade proved to be a Trojan Horse in Indian North America, unleashing catastrophic forces at the same time as it delivered desired gifts. The trade tied its Indian patrons into the expanding world of European capitalism and threw neighboring customers into desperate competition. Access to hunting grounds and to European traders became major considerations governing the movement and location of Indian bands and the decisions of band chiefs. Tribes clashed in escalating conflicts for pelts, trade, and survival. (1990, 43)

The Haudenosaunee were pivotal in the regional fur trade, as well as in diplomacy. In exchange for furs, the Iroquois took trade goods such as iron needles, copper kettles, and knives. Traders with the Iroquois and other Native peoples soon learned to sell the Indians kettles of thinner metal, using an early form of planned obsolescence because they cost less to manufacture and wore out more quickly, increasing sales (Snow, 1994, 78).

Epidemics, first of measles, then smallpox, reached Haudenosaunee country with the fur trade, peaking in 1634 and 1635. Societies and economies were stressed severely. Mohawk population dropped from 7,740 to 2,830 within a matter of months (Snow, 1994, 99–100). Firearms reached the Haudenosaunee within a generation following the advent of the fur trade. In 1639, the Dutch tried, without success, to outlaw the sale of guns to Indians. By 1648, however, Dutch merchants in Albany were enthusiastic participants in the firearm trade, in part because the use of guns increased Native Americans' productivity as harvesters of beaver and other fur-bearing animals.

By 1640, the Wyandot and many other Native nations in eastern Canada and adjacent areas had become heavily dependent on export of furs, mainly beaver. At the same time, increasing demands for European trade goods were creating new conflicts between various Native peoples and deepening old enmities. According to Fahey:

> The fur trade, without intending it, largely destroyed the Indian way of life by depleting small game and speeding extermination of the buffalo; it mapped the West and estimated the locations and sizes of Native populations; it demonstrated the agricultural promise of large areas previously unknown or discounted as desert. The zenith of the fur trade immediately preceded a period in the United States when white men moved westward to escape crowding on older frontiers, to evade political or military obligations, to hunt gold, or simply to regain lost confidence in individual worth. (1974, 63)

According to David J. Wishart, a historian of the fur trade, "The traders also caused fragmentation by meddling in the power hierarchy of Indian communities. They enriched Indians who were accommodating to their demands and undermined the influence of chiefs who opposed them" (1994, 47). Finally, "and most disastrously," wrote Wishart, "Fur Traders co-opted Indians in the destruction of their own resource base" (ibid., 47). Native people became employees in a worldwide capitalistic enterprise that relaxed traditional inhibitions against overhunting. The beaver often was the first to disappear under intense hunting pressure because of its low reproduction rate.

In the late twentieth century, historians and anthropologists debated how the fur trade changed Native Americans' relationships with animals and the natural world. Calvin Martin, a professor of history at Rutgers University (New Brunswick, NJ), instigated debate with his publication of *Keepers of the Game* (1979), which argued that Native Americans abandoned their environmental ethics because they thought that animals were responsible for epidemic diseases ravishing human populations.

Martin's thesis virtually ignores the fact that Native Americans were being drawn into a capitalistic world economy. Martin also ignores diversity among native cultures, as well as the fact that in many cases epidemic diseases reached Native populations after (not before) the fur trade reached its height. The most important indicators that Martin's thesis lacks validity are Native American oral and written histories. These histories accurately attribute imported diseases to human beings (usually European immigrants) rather than animals that were native to North America. Historian William Cronon commented:

> The fur trade was thus far more complicated than a simple exchange of European metal goods for Indian beaver skins. It revolutionized Indian economies less by its new technology than by its new commercialism, at once utilizing and subverting Indian trade patterns to extend European commercial ones.... The essential lesson for the Indians was that certain things began to have prices that had not had them before.... Formerly, there had been little incentive for Indians to kill more than a fixed number of animals. (1983, 97)

The fur trade eroded native peoples' traditional inhibitions against killing of animals above and beyond their own needs. In New England, beaver populations ceased to be commercially exploitable after 1660, but animals continued to be harvested in areas that had been reached in later years. By the nineteenth century, however, beaver populations had fallen below sustainable levels in most of North America. Fortunately for the beaver, European hat styles changed, sparing surviving stocks in North America from extinction.

THE BEAVER WARS

Beaver Wars has become a historical shorthand reference for the Haudenosaunee campaign against the Wyandots that culminated in their defeat and assimilation by the Haudenosaunee about 1650. Like most wars, this one had more than one provocation. The most prominent reason for the antipathy leading to the war, however, was competition over diminishing stocks of beaver and other fur-bearing animals. The Haudenosaunee cause during this conflict was aided immeasurably by their relatively recent acquisition of European firearms, which the Wyandots for the most part lacked. The Mohawks, situated near trading centers at Albany and Montreal, were among the first to acquire a stock of firearms; one French source estimated that they had close to 300 guns by 1643 (Richter, 1992, 62).

At the beginning of the seventeenth century, the Wyandots, who lived near Georgian Bay on Lake Huron, were a prosperous confederacy of 25,000 to 30,000 people, comparable to the Haudenosaunee. By 1642, the Wyandots had allied with the French and had entered an alliance with the Susquehannocks, south of the Iroquois. In 1642, 1645, and 1647, the Haudenosaunee tried to secure peace with the French, to no avail. After the third try, they decided

to break the alliance. The Wyandots had built a confederacy similar in structure to the Haudenosaunee (although more geographically compact).

By 1640, the Wyandots' economy was nearly totally dependent on trade
with the French. At the same time, as they were weakened by disease, the
Wyandots found themselves facing waves of raids by the Iroquois (principally
Mohawks and Senecas), who were seeking to capture the Wyandots' share of
the fur trade. The Mohawks had been exposed to European trade goods
earlier than the Wyandots and may have been looking for furs to trade. The
Wyandots' location at the center of several trade routes also made them an
appealing point of attack at a time when demand was rising for beaver pelts,
and the available supply of the animals was declining.

For nearly a decade, the Mohawks and Senecas harassed the Wyandots.
Fearing Iroquois attacks, the Wyandots curtailed their trade with the French
during the 1640s. Between 1647 and 1650, a final Iroquois drive swept over the
Wyandots' homeland, provoking the dissolution of their confederacy as well as
usurpation of the Wyandots' share of the fur trade by the Senecas and Mohawks.

Iroquois pressure against the Wyandots continued for several years after the
conclusion of the Beaver Wars as Wyandot refugees sought new homes throughout the Great Lakes and St. Lawrence Valley. Many of the Wyandot refugees
experienced acute hunger, and a sizable number starved during this diaspora.
Some Wyandots became so hungry that they ate human excrement; others dug up
the bodies of the dead and ate them, a matter of desperation and great shame
because cannibalism is directly contrary to Wyandot belief and custom.

Scattered communities of Wyandot gradually revived traditional economies
after the hungry years of the 1650s. Many Wyandot settled in or near European
communities (including Jesuit missions). Even those who became Christianized and Europeanized continued to live in longhouses during these years.
They continued to hunt and trap as much as possible and to practice slash-and-
burn agriculture.

A number of Wyandot refugees were adopted after the Beaver Wars by their
former enemies, who, true to their own traditions, socialized Wyandot prisoners into the various Haudenosaunee families and clans. The Iroquois also
were replenishing their societies, which had been hard hit by European diseases and the casualties of continual war.

RELIGIOUS ADAPTATIONS TO EUROPEAN INVASION

One of the major ways in which the Haudenosaunee adapted to the European invasion was religious. The religion of Handsome Lake, which began
as a series of visions in 1799, combined Quaker forms of Christianity with
Native traditions. Its influence is still strongly felt among the traditional Iroquois, who often call the Code of Handsome Lake the "Longhouse Religion."

Handsome Lake's personal name was *Ganeodiyo*; Handsome Lake is one of
the fifty chieftainship lines of the Iroquois Confederacy, a title bestowed on

him by clan mothers. Handsome Lake was a half-brother of the Seneca Chief Cornplanter and an uncle of Red Jacket.

The Code of Handsome Lake is one of several Native American religions that evolved in reaction to European colonization by fusing traditional Native and Western European (usually Christian) elements. These religions combined Native American beliefs and rituals with the introduction of a Christian-style "savior" who was said to be able to recapture for Native Americans the better days they had known before colonization. One well-known example of this fusion was the Ghost Dance Religion, which was begun by the prophet Wovoka, who had been raised with both Native American and Christian influences. Neolin (also known as the Delaware Prophet) also formulated a religion that combined both traditions during the eighteenth century.

Handsome Lake was born at Conawagus, a Seneca village near contemporary Avon, New York, on the Genesee River. He and many other Senecas sided with the British in the French and Indian War and the American Revolution. George Washington and his subcommanders, principally General John Sullivan, were merciless with Native Americans who supported the British. During the late stages of the revolution, many Seneca communities were laid waste by scorched-earth marches that destroyed crops, livestock, and homes.

After that war, many Iroquois and other Native Americans who had supported the British were forced into Canada, principally to lands secured by Joseph Brant at Grand River. Others fled westward to join other Native Americans who were still free. Those who remained in their homelands were forced onto small, impoverished reservations as repeated attempts were made to force them out. By 1794, the Iroquois population bottomed out at about 4,000 people according to Ronald Wright in *Stolen Continents* (1992).

Handsome Lake's revival occurred in an atmosphere of dissension within a fractured Iroquois League. His life course reflected the devastation of his people. Born into a prominent family of the Turtle Clan, Handsome Lake distinguished himself as a leader as a young man before the American Revolution, when Iroquois society was still largely intact. Handsome Lake's decline began after his birthplace was taken by whites, and he was forced to move to the Allegheny Seneca reservation. The Seneca ethnologist Arthur Parker characterized Handsome Lake as "a middle-sized man, slim and unhealthy looking . . . [who became] a dissolute person and a miserable victim of the drink" (Johansen and Grinde, 1997, 160).

After four years lying ill in a small cabin under the care of a daughter, Handsome Lake began having a series of visions. Later, he used these visions to rally the Iroquois at a time when some of them were selling their entire winter harvest of furs for hard liquor, turning traditional ceremonies into drunken brawls, and, in winter, often dying of exposure in drunken stupors.

By the spring of 1799, Handsome Lake experienced considerable remorse over his alcoholism but did not stop drinking until he was nearly dead. Arthur Parker described him as little more than a shell of yellowed skin and dried bones. During 1799, Handsome Lake also experienced a number of visions in which he was taken on a great journey to the sky. He was shown a number of personages and events, past, present, and future. In one of his visions, Handsome Lake met George Washington, who had died in 1799, and heard him confirm the sovereignty of the Iroquois.

After the series of visions, Handsome Lake stopped drinking alcohol and later committed the Code of Handsome Lake to writing. He persuaded many other Iroquois to stop drinking and to reconstruct their lives. During his lifetime, Handsome Lake achieved some political influence among the Senecas, but his popularity slid because of his ideological rigidity. In 1801 and 1802, he traveled to Washington, D.C., with a delegation of Senecas to meet with President Thomas Jefferson and to resist the reduction of their peoples' landholdings.

The Code of Handsome Lake combines European religious influences with a traditional Iroquois emphasis on family, community, and the centrality of the land to the maintenance of culture. The largest following for Handsome Lake came after his death. Adherents to his code accepted his concepts of social relationships as well as concepts of good and evil that closely resemble Quakerism, which Handsome Lake had studied. The Quaker creed appealed to many Iroquois because they had been persecuted before coming to America and because they had no ornate temples and lived frugally and communally, doing their best to respect their Native American neighbors.

A nationalistic figure in a religious context, Handsome Lake also borrowed heavily from the Iroquois Great Law of Peace, popularizing concepts such as looking into the future for seven generations and regarding the earth as mother. These ideas have since become part of pan-Indian thought across North America and, from there, have been incorporated into late twentieth century popular environmental symbolism. With its combination of Old and New World theologies, the Code of Handsome Lake sought a middle path, a way to reconcile the faiths of Europe and America.

The Code of Handsome Lake is still widely followed in Iroquois country. By the early twenty-first century, roughly a third of the 30,000 Iroquois in New York State attended longhouse ceremonies. Although his code remains popular among many Iroquois, others have accused Handsome Lake of having "sold out" to the Quakers and white religious interests in general. Louis Hall, ideological founder of the Warrior movement in Iroquois Country, regarded the religion of Handsome Lake as a bastardized form of Christianity grafted onto Native traditions. Hall called Handsome Lake's visions "the hallucinations of a drunk" (Johansen, 1993, 160). Opposition to these teachings is one plank in an intellectual platform that allows the Warriors to claim that the Mohawk Nation Council at Akwesasne, and the Iroquois Confederacy Council as well, are enemies of the people, and that the Warriors are the true protectors of "Mohawk sovereignty." Hall, who died in 1993, regarded Handsome Lake's followers as traitors or "Tontos" (Johansen, 1993, 160).

Hall's Warriors split bitterly with followers of Handsome Lake over gambling and other issues, leading to violence at Akwesasne that peaked in 1990 with the deaths of two Mohawks.

FURTHER READING

Aquila, Richard. *The Iroquois Restoration: Iroquois Diplomacy on the Colonial Frontier, 1701–1754*. Detroit: Wayne State University Press, 1983.

Arden, Harvey. The Fire that Never Dies. *National Geographic*, September 1987, 374–403.

Beals, Ralph L., and Harry Hoijer. *An Introduction to Anthropology*. New York: Macmillan, 1965.

Benedict, Ruth. *Patterns of Culture*. Boston: Houghton Mifflin, 1934.

Blackbird, Andrew J. *Complete Both Early and Late History of the Ottawa and Cheppewa* [sic] *Indians of Michigan: A Grammar of Their Language, Personal and Family History of the Author*. Harbor Springs, MI: Babcock and Darling, 1897.

Bolton, Herbet Eugene, ed. *Spanish Exploration in the Southwest, 1542–1706*. New York: Scribner, 1916.

Bolton, Herbet Eugene. *Coronado on the Turquoise Trail*. Albuquerque: University of New Mexico Press, 1949.

Boyd, Julian P., ed. *Indian Treaties Printed by Benjamin Franklin, 1736–1762*. Philadelphia: Historical Society of Pennsylvania, 1938.

Bradford, William. *History of Plymouth Plantation*. Edited by Charles Deane. Boston: Private printing, 1856.

Bradford, William. *History of Plymouth Plantation*. Edited by Samuel Eliot Morison. New York: Modern Library, 1967.

Brandon, William. *The American Heritage Book of Indians*. New York: Dell, 1961.

Brockunier, Samuel H. *The Irrepressible Democrat: Roger Williams*. New York: Ronald Press, 1940.

Brown, Jennifer S. H. *Strangers in Blood: Fur Trade Families in Indian Country*. Vancouver, BC: University of British Columbia Press, 1981.

Caduto, Michael J., and Joseph Brudhac, *Keepers of the Earth: Native American Stories and Environmental Activities for Children*. Golden, CO: Fulcrum, 1988.

Calloway, Colin. *The Western Abenakis of Vermont, 1600–1800: War, Migration, and the Survival of an Indian People*. Norman: University of Oklahoma Press, 1990.

Canby, Thomas Y. The Anasazi: Riddles in the Ruins. *National Geographic*, November 1982, 554–592.

Champagne, Duane. *American Indian Societies: Strategies and Conditions of Political and Cultural Survival*. Cambridge, MA: Cultural Survival, 1989.

Chapin, Howard H. *Sachems of the Narragansetts*. Providence: Rhode Island Historical Society, 1931.

Chittenden, Hiram M. *The American Fur Trade of the Far West*. New York: Press of the Pioneers, 1935.

Chupack, Henry. *Roger Williams*. New York: Twayne, 1969.

Church, Thomas. *Diary of King Philip's War, 1676–77*. Edited by Alan and Mary Simpson. Chester, CT: Pequot Press, 1975.

Colden, Cadwallader. *The History of the Five Nations Depending on the Province of New York in America*. Ithaca, NY: Cornell University Press, [1727, 1747] 1958.

Cook, Sherburne F. Interracial Warfare and Population Decline among the New England Indians. *Ethnohistory* 20:1(Winter 1973):1–24.

Copway, George. *The Life, History, and Travels of Kah-Ge-Ga-Gah-Bowh*. New York: Weed & Parsons, 1847.

Copway, George. *The Ojibway Conquest*. New York: G. P. Putnam, 1850.

Copway, George. *The Organization of a New Indian Territory East of the Missouri River*. New York: S. W. Benedict, 1850.

Copway, George. *The Traditional History and Characteristic Sketches of the Ojibway Nation*. London: Charles Gilpin, 1850.

Copway, George. *Running Sketches of Men and Places in England, Germany, Belgium, and Scotland*. New York: Riker, 1851.

Copway, George. *Indian Life and Indian History*. Boston: Colby, 1858.

Covey, Cyclone. *The Gentle Radical: A Biography of Roger Williams*. New York: Macmillan, 1966.

Cronon, William. *Changes in the Land: Indians, Colonists, and the Ecology of New England*. New York: Hill and Wang, 1983.

Dennis, Matthew. *Cultivating a Landscape of Peace*. Ithaca, NY: Cornell University Press, 1993.

DeVoto, Bernard. *The Course of Empire*. Boston: Houghton-Mifflin, 1952.

Dittert, Alfred E., Jr. The Archaeology of Cebolleta Mesa and Acoma Pueblo: A Preliminary Report Based on Further Investigation. *El Palacio* 59(1952):191–217.

Driver, Harold E. *Indians of North America*. 2nd ed., rev. Chicago: University of Chicago Press, 1969.

Ellis, George W., and John E. Morris. *King Philip's War*. New York: The Grafton Press, 1906.

Gallegos, Hernan. Relacion [diary]. In George P. Hammond and Agapito Rey, *The Rediscovery of New Mexico, 1580–1594*. Albuquerque: University of New Mexcico Press, 1966, 47–144.

Ernst, James. *Roger Williams: New England Firebrand*. New York: Macmillan, 1932.

Fahey, John. *The Flathead Indians*. Norman: University of Oklahoma Press, 1974.

Fahey, John. *The Kalispel Indians*. Norman: University of Oklahoma Press, 1986.

Fenton, William N. *Roll Call of the Iroquois Chiefs*. Washington, DC: Smithsonian Institution, 1950.

Fenton, William N., ed. *Parker on the Iroquois*. Syracuse, NY: Syracuse University Press, 1968.

Giddings, James L. Roger Williams and the Indians [1957]. Typescript, Rhode Island Historical Society.

Green, Michael D. The Expansion of European Colonization to the Mississippi Valley, 1780–1880. In Bruce G. Trigger and Wilcomb E. Washburn, eds., *The Cambridge History of the Native Peoples of the Americas*. Cambridge: Cambridge University Press, 1996: 461–538.

Guild, Reuben Aldridge. *Footprints of Roger Williams*. Providence, RI: Tibbetts and Preston, 1886.

Hale, Horatio. *The Iroquois Book of Rites*. Philadelphia: D. G. Brinton, 1883.

Hamilton, Charles. *Cry of the Thunderbird*. Norman: University of Oklahoma Press, 1972.

Henige, David. *Numbers from Nowhere: The American Indian Contact Population Debate*. Norman: University of Oklahoma Press, 1998.

Henige, David. Can a Myth Be Astronomically Dated? *American Indian Culture and Research Journal* 23:4(1999):127–157.

Hewitt, J. N. B. *Legend of the Founding of the Iroquois League.* Washington, DC: Smithsonian Institution, 1892.

Hewitt, J. N. B. *Iroquois Cosmology.* Washington, DC: Smithsonian Institution, 1903.

Hewitt, J. N. B. *A Constitutional League of Peace in the Stone Age of America.* Washington, DC: Smithsonian Institution, 1918.

Hewitt, J. N. B. Notes on the Creek Indians. In J. R. Swanton, ed., *Bureau of American Ethnology Bulletin No. 123.* Washington, DC: U.S. Government Printing Office, 1939: 124–133.

Hill, Richard. Continuity of Haudenosaunee Government: Political Reality of the Grand Council. *Northeast Indian Quarterly* 4:3(Autumn 1987):10–14.

Hoover, Dwight W. *The Red and the Black.* Chicago: Rand-McNally, 1976: 15.

Jacobs, Wilbur. *Diplomacy and Indian Gifts: Anglo-French Rivalry Among the Ohio and Northwest Frontiers, 1748-1763.* Stanford, CA: Stanford University Press, 1950.

Johansen, Bruce E. *Life and Death in Mohawk Country.* Golden, CO: Fulcrum/North American Press, 1993.

Johansen, Bruce E. Dating the Iroquois Confederacy. *Akwesasne Notes* New Series 1(3/4) (Fall 1995):62–63.

Johansen, Bruce E., and Donald A. Grinde, Jr. *The Encyclopedia of Native American Biography.* New York: Henry Holt, 1997.

Josephy, Alvin, Jr. *The Patriot Chiefs.* New York: Viking, 1961.

Kennedy, John Hopkins. *Jesuit and Savage in New France.* New Haven, CT: Yale University Press, 1950.

Labaree, Benjamin L. *America's Nation-Time: 1607–1789.* Boston: Allyn and Bacon, 1972.

Las Casas, Bartholeme. *The Devastation of the Indies* [1542]. Translated by Herma Briffault. New York: Seabury Press, 1974.

Lopez de Gomara, Francisco. *Historia del Illvstriss[imo] et Valorosiss[ims] Capitano Don Ferdinando Cortes Marchese della Valle.* Trans. Agustino de Cravaliz. Rome: Valerio & Luigi Dorici Fratelli, 1556.

Mann, Barbara A., and Jerry L. Fields. A Sign in the Sky: Dating the League of the Haudenosaunee. *American Indian Culture and Research Journal* 21:2(1997): 105–163.

Mann, Charles C. 1491: America Before Columbus Was More Sophisticated and More Populous than We Have Ever Thought—and a More Livable Place than Europe. *The Atlantic Monthly* March 2002, 41–53.

Martin, Calvin. *Keepers of the Game.* Berkeley: University of California Press, 1979.

Mather, Increase. *A Brief History of the War with the Indians in New England.* London: Richard Chiswell, 1676.

Maxwell, James A., ed. *America's Fascinating Indian Heritage.* Pleasantville, NY: Reader's Digest, 1978.

McManus, John C. An Economic Analysis of Indian Behavior in the North American Fur Trade. *Journal of Economic History* 32(1972):36–53.

Miller, Perry. *Roger Williams: His Contribution to the American* Tradition. Indianapolis: Bobbs-Merill, 1953.

Minge, Ward Alan. *Acoma: Pueblo in the Sky.* Albuquerque: University of New Mexico Press, 1991.

Morgan, Lewis Henry. *League of the Ho-de-no-sau-nee, or Iroquois.* New York: Corinth Books, [1851] 1962.

Page, Jake. *In the Hands of the Great Spirit: The 20,000 Year History of the American Indian.* New York: Free Press, 2003.

Parrington, Vernon Louis. *Main Currents in American Thought.* New York: Harcourt, Brace, 1927.

Phillips, Paul C. *The Fur Trade.* 2 vols. Norman: University of Oklahoma Press, 1961.

Reaman, G. Elmore. *The Trail of the Iroquois Indians: How the Iroquois Nation Saved Canada for the British Empire.* London: Frederick Muller, 1967.

Richter, Daniel K. *The Ordeal of the Longhouse: The Peoples of the Iroquois League in the Era of European Colonization.* Chapel Hill, NC: University of North Carolina Press, 1992.

Rider, Sidney S. *The Lands of Rhode Island as They Were Known to Caunonicus and Miantunnomu When Roger Williams Came in 1636.* Providence, RI: private printing, 1904.

Saum, Lewis. *The Fur Trader and the Indian.* Seattle: University of Washington Press, 1965.

Segal, Charles M., and Stineback, David C. *Puritans, Indians, and Manifest Destiny.* New York: Putnam, 1977.

Siegel, Beatrice. *Fur Trappers and Traders.* New York: Walker, 1981.

Slotkin, Richard, and James K. Folsom, eds. *So Dreadful a Judgement: Puritan Responses to King Philip's War 1676–1677.* Middleton, CT: Wesleyan University Press, 1978.

Snow, Dean. *The Iroquois.* London: Blackwell, 1994.

Spicer, Edward H. *Cycles of Conquest.* Tucson: University of Arizona Press, 1962.

Stannard, David E. *American Holocaust: Columbus and the Conquest of the New World.* New York: Oxford University Press, 1992.

Stuart, George E. Etowah: A Southeast Village in 1491. *National Geographic,* October 1991, 54–67.

Straus, Oscar S. *Roger Williams: Pioneer of Religious Liberty.* New York: Century, 1894.

Swan, Bradford F. New Light on Roger Williams and the Indians. *Providence Sunday Journal Magazine,* November 23, 1969, 14.

Tehanetorens [Ray Fadden]. *Tales of the Iroquois.* Rooseveltown, NY: Akwesasne Notes, 1976.

Tehanetorens [Ray Fadden]. *Basic Call to Consciousness.* Rooseveltown, NY: Akwesasne Notes, 1986.

Tehanetorens [Ray Fadden]. *Wampum Belt.* Onchiota, NY: Six Nations Museum, n.d.

Trelease, Allen W. *Indian Affairs in Colonial New York: The Seventeenth Century.* Ithaca, NY: Cornell University Press, 1960.

Trigger, Bruce G. *Children of the Aataentsic: A History of the Huron People.* Montreal: McGill-Queen's University Press, 1976.

Van Kirk, Sylvia. *Many Tender Ties: Women in Fur Trade Society, 1670–1870.* Norman: University of Oklahoma Press, 1983.

Vaughan, Alden T. *New England Frontier: Puritans and Indians, 1620–1675.* Boston: Little, Brown, 1965.

Wallace, Anthony F. C. *The Death and Rebirth of the Seneca.* New York: Random House, 1969.

Wallace, Paul A. W. *The White Roots of Peace.* Santa Fe, NM: Clear Light Publishers, 1994.

White Roots of Peace. *The Great Law of Peace of the Longhouse People.* Rooseveltown, NY: White Roots of Peace, 1971.

Williams, Richard B. The True Story of Thanksgiving. November 19, 2002. Available at IndigenousNewsNetwork@topica.com.

Williams, Roger. *A Key Into the Languages of America.* London: Gregory Dexter, 1643; Providence, RI: Tercentenary Committee, 1936.

Williams, Roger. *The Complete Writings of Roger Williams.* Vol. 1. New York: Russell and Russell, 1963.

Wilson, Edmund. *Apologies to the Iroquois.* New York: Farrar, Strauss, and Cudahy, 1960.

Winslow, Elizabeth Ola. *Master Roger Williams.* New York: Macmillan, 1957.

Wishart, David J. *The Fur Trade and the American West, 1807–1840.* Lincoln: University of Nebraska Press, 1979.

Wishart, David J. *An Unspeakable Sadness: The Dispossession of the Nebraska Indians.* Lincoln: University of Nebraska Press, 1994.

Wood, William. *New England's Prospect.* Amherst: University of Massachusetts Press, 1977.

Woodbury, Hanni, Reg Henry, and Harry Webster, comps. *Concerning the League: The Iroquois League Tradition as Dictated in Onondaga by John Arthur Gibson.* Algonquian and Iroquoian Linguistics Memoir No. 9. Winnipeg, Manitoba: University of Manitoba Press, 1992.

Wright, Ronald. *Stolen Continents.* Boston: Houghton-Mifflin, 1992.

CHAPTER 4

The Transfer of Ideas

NATIVE CONFEDERACIES AND THE EVOLUTION OF DEMOCRACY

Europe did not discover America, but America was quite a discovery for Europe. For roughly three centuries before the American Revolution, the ideas that made the American Revolution possible were being discovered, nurtured, and embellished in the growing English and French colonies of North America. America provided a counterpoint for European convention and assumption. It became, for Europeans in America, at once a dream and a reality, a fact and a fantasy, the real and the ideal. To appreciate the way in which European eyes opened on the "New World," we must take the phrase literally, with the excitement evoked in our own time by travel to the moon and planets. There was one electrifying difference: the voyagers of that time knew that their New World was inhabited. They had only to look and learn, to drink in the bewildering newness and enchanting novelty of seeing it all for the first time.

THE TRANSATLANTIC IDEOLOGICAL INCUBUS

Coming from societies based on hierarchy, early European explorers and immigrants came to America seeking kings, queens, and princes. What they sought they believed they had found, for a time. Quickly, however, they began to sense a difference: The people they were calling kings had few trappings that distinguished them from the people they "ruled" in most native societies. They only rarely sat at the top of a class hierarchy with the pomp of European rulers. More important, Indian kings usually did not rule. Rather, they led by mechanisms of consensus and public opinion that Europeans often found admirable.

COLONISTS' PERCEPTIONS OF NATIVE POLITIES

European colonists' lives were pervaded by contact with Native American peoples to a degree that we today sometimes find difficult to comprehend. Especially in its early years, colonization was limited to a few isolated pockets of land, widely dispersed, on a thin ribbon along the eastern seaboard. In the mid-eighteenth century, the frontier ran from a few miles west of Boston, through Albany, to Lancaster, Pennsylvania, or roughly to the western edges of today's eastern seaboard urban areas. The new Americans looked inland across a continent they already knew to be many times the size of England, France, and Holland combined. They did not know with any certainty just how far their new homeland extended. Maps of the time did not comprehend accurately the distances between the Atlantic and Pacific Oceans. A few Spanish and French trappers and explorers had left their footprints in this vast expanse of land, but at that time at least 90 percent of North America was still the homeland of many hundreds of Native peoples.

The people of that time were conditioned by their perceptions of time and space, just as we are. In a time when the fastest method of communication and transportation was by wind-powered sail, it took six weeks for King George III to learn that the thirteen newly united colonies had posted the Declaration of Independence. Overland, on a fresh horse traveling the trails worn by Native peoples, a person could cover as much ground in a day as a late-twentieth century automobile covers in 20 minutes or a jet aircraft in three minutes. In our day, news travels around the world in a fraction of a second.

Although hostile encounters between European immigrants and Native peoples took uncounted lives during those early years, day-to-day life was usually peaceful. History, like the daily news, tends to accentuate conflict, so we are left with a record that overstates the role that war actually played in history. In fact, on a daily basis the immigrants and Native peoples traded, socialized, and concluded treaties more often than they went to war. Enlightened eyes looked westward with a degree of curiosity, respect, and even awe, drinking in the ways of peoples who knew America better than they did. In the written perceptions of the immigrants, there is a pervasive sense that the native peoples held the keys to ways of ordering society that Europeans were only beginning to understand.

Increasingly, Native societies in America came to serve the transplanted Europeans, including some of the United States' most influential founders, as a counterpoint to the European order. They found in the Native polities the values that the seminal documents of the time celebrated: life, liberty, happiness, a model of government by consensus, with citizens enjoying rights due them as human beings. The fact that native peoples in America were able to govern themselves in this way provided advocates of alternatives to monarchy with practical ammunition for a philosophy of government based on the rights of the individual, which they believed had worked, did work, and would work for them, in America.

This is not to say they sought to replicate Native polities among societies in America descended from Europeans. The new Americans were too practical to believe that a society steeped in European cultural traditions could be turned on its head so swiftly and easily. They chose instead to borrow, to shape what they had with what they saw before them, to create a new order that included aspects of both worlds. They may be faulted in our time for failing to borrow certain aspects of Native American societies, such as important political and social roles for women.

NATIVE AMERICAN CONFEDERACIES

All along the Atlantic Seaboard, Native American nations had formed confederacies by the time they encountered European immigrants, from the Creeks, which Hector St. John de Crevecoeur called a "federated republic" (Crevecoeur, [1801] 1964, 461), to the Cherokees and Choctaws, to the Iroquois and the Wyandots (Hurons) in the St. Lawrence Valley, as well as the Penacook federation of New England, among many others. The Illinois Confederacy; the "Three Fires" of the Chippewa, Ottawa, and Pottawatomi; the Wapenaki Confederacy, the Powhatan Confederacies; and the tripartite Miami also were members of confederations.

Each of these Native confederacies developed its own variation on a common theme of counselor democracy. Most were remarkably similar in broad outline. By the late eighteenth century, as resentment against England's taxation flared into open rebellion along the Atlantic seaboard, the colonists displayed widespread knowledge of Native governmental systems. Thomas Jefferson, Benjamin Franklin, and others the length of the coast observed governmental systems that shared many similarities.

Colonists arriving in eastern North America encountered variations of a confederacy model, usually operating by methods of consensus that were unfamiliar to people who had been living in societies usually governed by queens, princes, and kings. The best known of these consensual governments was the Haudenosaunee (Iroquois Confederacy), which occupied a prominent position in the diplomacy of the early colonies.

THE IMPORTANCE OF THE IROQUOIS CONFEDERACY

Observations of Indian governments showed a remarkable similarity all along the seaboard. Everywhere they looked, immigrant observers found confederacies of Native nations loosely governed by the kind of respect for individual liberty that European savants had established only in theory or as relics of a distant European golden age. Indian languages, customs, and material artifacts varied widely, but their form of government, perhaps best characterized as counselor democracy, seemed to be nearly everywhere.

The ideas and political systems of the Iroquois and other confederations were so appealing that 300 years ago while he was still in England, William Penn described the functioning of the Iroquois Confederacy in glowing terms:

> Every King hath his council, and that consists of all the old and wise men of his nation...nothing is undertaken, be it war, peace, the selling of land or traffick [sic], without advising with them; and which is more, with the youngmen also....The kings move by the breath of their people. It is the Indian custom to deliberate....I have never seen more natural sagacity. ("William Penn to the Society," 1982, 2:452–453)

Penn described the Native confederacies of eastern North America as political societies with sachemships inherited through the female side. Penn also was familiar with the Condolence Ceremony of the Iroquois, which was crucial for an understanding of their confederacy. He stated that when someone kills a "woman they pay double [the wampum]" because "...she breeds children which men cannot" ("William Penn to the Society," 1982, 454). In 1697, after lengthy personal exposure to American Indian forms of government, Penn proposed a Plan for a Union of the Colonies in America ("Mr. Penn's Plan," 1853, 4:296–297).

The Iroquois' system was the best known to the colonists in large part because of the Haudenosaunee's pivotal position in diplomacy not only between the English and French, but also among other Native confederacies. Called the Iroquois by the French and the Five (later Six) Nations by the English, the Haudenosaunee controlled the only relatively level land pass between the English colonies on the seaboard and the French settlements in the St. Lawrence Valley, later the route of the Erie Canal.

Without authority to command, Iroquois and other Native American political leaders honed their persuasive abilities, especially their speaking skills. In his *History of the Five Nations* ([1727] 1958), Cadwallader Colden attributed the Iroquois' skill at oratory to the republican nature of their government. Colden described the intense study that the Iroquois applied to the arts of oral persuasion, to acquisition of grace and manner before councils of their peers. Franklin compared the decorum of Native American councils to the rowdy nature of debate in British public forums, including the House of Commons. This difference in debating customs persists to our day.

Each Iroquois nation has its own council, which sends delegates to a central council, much as each state in the United States has its own legislature, as well as senators and representatives who travel to the central seat of government in Washington, D.C. When representatives of the Iroquois nations meet at Onondaga, they form two groups: the Elder Brothers (Mohawks and Senecas) and the Younger Brothers (Cayugas and Oneidas). The Onondagas are the firekeepers. (In the U.S. Congress, a similar position is held by the Speaker of the House.)

The Iroquois built certain ways of doing business into their Great Law to prevent anger and frayed tempers. For example, an important measure may not be decided the same day it is introduced to allow time for passions to cool. Important decisions must take at least two days to allow leaders to "sleep on it" and not to react too quickly. The Great Law may be amended just as one adds beams to the rafters of an Iroquois longhouse. The Great Tree of Peace is regarded as a living organization. Its roots and branches are said to grow in order to incorporate other peoples.

The Iroquois also are linked to each other by their clan system, which ties each person to family members in every other nation of the federation. If a Mohawk of the Turtle Clan has to travel, the Mohawk will be hosted by Turtles in each other Iroquois nation.

A leader is instructed to be a mentor for the people at all times. Political leaders must strive to maintain peace within the league. A chief may be *de-horned* (impeached) if he engages in violent behavior of any kind. Even the brandishing of a weapon may bring sanction. The traditional headdress of an Iroquois leader (an emblem of office) includes deer antlers, which are said to have been "knocked off" if the sachem has been impeached. Chiefs of the Iroquois League are instructed to take criticism honestly and that their skins should be seven spans thick to absorb the criticism of the people they represent in public councils. Political leaders also are instructed to think of the coming generations in all of their actions.

Sachems are not allowed to name their own successors or carry their titles to the grave. The Great Law provides a ceremony to remove the antlers of authority from a dying chief. The Great Law also provides for the removal from office of sachems who can no longer adequately function in office, a measure remarkably similar to a constitutional amendment adopted in the United States during the late 20th century providing for the removal of an incapacitated president. The Great Law of Peace also includes provisions guaranteeing freedom of religion and the right of redress before the Grand Council. It also forbids unauthorized entry of homes, one of several measures that sound familiar to U.S. citizens through the Bill of Rights.

In some ways, the Grand Council operates like the U.S. House of Representatives and Senate, with their conference committees. As it was designed by Deganawidah, the Peacemaker (founder of the confederacy with his spokesman Hiawatha), debating protocol begins with the Elder Brothers, the Mohawks and Senecas. After debate by the Keepers of the Eastern Door (Mohawks) and the Keepers of the Western Door (Senecas), the question is then thrown across the fire to the Oneida and Cayuga statesmen (the Younger Brothers) for discussion in much the same manner. Once consensus is achieved among the Oneidas and the Cayugas, the discussion is then given back to the Senecas and Mohawks for confirmation. Next, the question is laid before the Onondagas for their decision.

Peacemaker in Stone Canoe. (Courtesy of John Kahionhes Fadden.)

At this stage, the Onondagas have a power similar to judicial review; they may raise objections to the proposed measure if it is believed inconsistent with the Great Law. Essentially, the legislature can rewrite the proposed law on the spot so that it can be in accord with the constitution of the Iroquois. When the Onondagas reach consensus, Tadadaho asks Honowireton (an Onondaga sachem who presides over debates between the delegations) to confirm the decision. Finally, Honowireton or Tadadaho gives the decision of the Onondagas to the Mohawks and the Senecas so that the policy may be announced to the Grand Council as its will.

BENJAMIN FRANKLIN AND THE LANCASTER TREATY COUNCIL (1744)

If the U.S. government's structure closely resembles that of the Iroquois Confederacy in some respects, how did the founders observe the Native model? The historical trail begins in 1744, as Pennsylvania officials met with Iroquois sachems in council at Lancaster. Canassatego, an Onondaga sachem, advised the Pennsylvania officials on Iroquois concepts of unity. Canassatego and other Iroquois sachems were advocating unified British management of trade at the time. Although the Iroquois preferred English manufactured products to those produced in France, the fact that each colony maintained its own trading practices and policies created confusion and conflict:

> Our wise forefathers established Union and Amity between the Five Nations. This has made us formidable; this has given us great Weight and Authority with our neighboring Nations. We are a powerful Confederacy; and by your observing the same methods, our wise forefathers have taken, you will acquire such Strength and power. Therefore whatever befalls you, never fall out with one another. (Van Doren and Boyd, 1938, 75)

Richard Peters provided the following word portrait of Canassatego at Lancaster: "a tall, well-made man," with "a very full chest and brawny limbs, a manly countenance, with a good-natired [sic] smile. He was about 60 years of age, very active, strong, and had a surprising liveliness in his speech" (Boyd, [1942] 1981, 244–245). Dressed in a scarlet camblet coat and a fine, gold-laced hat, Canassatego is described by Peters as possessing a captivating presence that turned heads whenever he walked into a room.

Benjamin Franklin probably first learned of Canassatego's 1744 advice to the colonies as he set his words in type. Franklin's press issued Indian treaties in small booklets that enjoyed a lively sale throughout the colonies. Beginning in 1736, Franklin published Indian treaty accounts on a regular basis until the early 1760s, when his defense of Indians under assault by frontier settlers cost him his seat in the Pennsylvania Assembly. Franklin subsequently served the colonial government in England.

Using Iroquois examples of unity, Franklin sought to shame the reluctant colonists into some form of union in 1751:

> It would be a strange thing...if Six Nations of ignorant savages should be capable of forming such an union and be able to execute it in such a manner that it has subsisted for ages and appears indissoluble, and yet that a like union should be impractical for ten or a dozen English colonies, to whom it is more necessary and must be more advantageous, and who cannot be supposed to want an equal understanding of their interest." (Smyth, 1905–1907, 3:42)

Canassatego. (Courtesy of the Library of Congress.)

As he often did, Franklin put a backward spin on the phrase "ignorant savages." He showed that the original peoples of America had much to teach the immigrants. In October 1753, Franklin began a distinguished diplomatic career that would later make him the premier U.S. envoy in Europe by attending a treaty council at Carlisle, Pennsylvania. During the same year, Franklin also recognized the enormous appeal of American Indian ways to the American people. He wrote that American Indian children reared in Anglo-American society returned to their people when they took but "one ramble with them." Furthermore, Franklin asserted that when "White persons of either sex have been taken prisoners young by Indians, and lived a while among them, tho' ransomed by their friends... [they] take the first good opportunity of escaping again into the woods, from whence there is no reclaiming them" (Labaree, 1961, 4:481).

During the Carlisle treaty council with the Iroquois and the Ohio Indians, Franklin saw the rich imagery and ideas of the Iroquois at close hand. On October 1, 1753, he watched an Oneida chief, Scarrooyady, and a Mohawk, Cayanguileguoa, condole the Ohio Indians for their losses against the French. Franklin listened while Scarrooyady spoke of the origins of the Iroquois Great Law to the Ohio Indians:

> We must let you know, that there was friendship established by our and your Grandfathers, and a mutual Council fire was kindled. In this friendship all those then under the ground, who had not obtained eyes or faces (that is, those unborn) were included; and it was then mutually promised to tell the same to their children and children's children. (Van Doren, 1938, 197–198.)

The following day, Franklin and the other treaty commissioners echoed earlier admonitions of the Iroquois when they stated the following:

> We would therefore hereby place before you the necessity of preserving your faith entire to one another, as well as to this government. Do not separate; Do not part on any score. Let no differences nor jealousies subsist a moment between Nation and Nation, but join together as one man. (Van Doren, 1938, 131)

In replying to these remarks, Scarrooyady took for granted the treaty commissioners' knowledge of the Iroquois Confederacy's structure when he requested that "You will please to lay all our present transactions before the council at Onondago, that they may know we do nothing in the dark" (Van Doren, 1938, 131).

ANGLO-IROQUOIS SYNTHESIS IN THE ALBANY PLAN OF UNION

On the eve of the Albany Conference in 1754, Franklin already was persuaded that the words of Canassatego (who had died in 1750) were good counsel. He was not alone in these sentiments. James DeLancey, acting governor of New York, sent a special invitation to Tiyanoga (ca. 1680–1755), a Mohawk sachem the English called Hendrick, to attend the Albany Conference, where he provided insights into the structure of the League of the Iroquois for the assembled colonial delegates. The Albany Plan of Union proposed a federal union of the colonies but retained colony autonomy except for matters of mutual concern, such as diplomacy and defense; this structure was very similar to the Iroquois Confederacy that Canassatego had urged the colonists to emulate ten years earlier. Although the Albany Plan was not approved by the colonies or the Crown, it became a model on which the Articles of Confederation later was based.

Tiyanoga was a major figure in colonial affairs between 1710, when he was one of four Mohawks invited to England by Queen Anne, and 1755, when he

CHARLES WILLSON PEALE, P. A.

Benjamin Franklin. (Courtesy of the Library of Congress.)

died in battle with the French as an ally of the British. A member of the Wolf Clan, Tiyanoga knew both Iroquois and English cultures well. He converted to Christianity and became a preacher of its tenets sometime after 1700. In England, he was painted by John Verelst and called the Emperor of the Five Nations. Hendrick was perhaps the most important individual link in a chain of alliance that saved the New York frontier and probably New England from

Hendrick (Tiyanoga) ca. 1710. (Courtesy of Smithsonian
National Anthropological Archives.)

the French in the initial stages of the Seven Years' War, which was called the
French and Indian War (1754–1763) in North America. Tiyanoga died at the
Battle of Lake George in the late summer of 1755 as Sir William Johnson
defeated Baron Dieskau. The elderly Mohawk was shot from his horse and
bayoneted to death while on a scouting party September 8.

A lifelong friend of Sir William Johnson, Tiyanoga appeared often at Johnson Hall, near Albany, and had copious opportunities to rub elbows with visiting English. Sometimes, he arrived in war paint, fresh from battle. Thomas Pownall, a shrewd observer of colonial Indian affairs, described Hendrick as "a bold artful, intriguing Fellow and has learnt no small share of European Politics, [who] obstructs and opposes all [business] where he has not been talked to first" (Jacobs, 1966, 77).

Well known as a man of distinction in his manners and dress, Hendrick visited England again in 1740. At that time, King George presented him with an ornate green coat of satin, fringed in gold, which Hendrick was fond of wearing in combination with his traditional Mohawk ceremonial clothing. Crevecoeur, himself an adopted Iroquois who had sat in on sessions of the Grand Council at Onondaga, described Hendrick in late middle age, preparing for dinner at the Johnson estate, within a few years of the Albany Congress:

> [He] wished to appear at his very best. . . . His head was shaved, with the exception of a little tuft of hair in the back, who which he attached a piece of silver. To the cartilage of his ears . . . he attached a little brass wire twisted into very tight spirals. A girondole was hung from his nose. Wearing a wide silver neckpiece, a crimson vest and a blue cloak adorned with sparkling gold, Hendrick, as was his custom, shunned European breeches for a loincloth fringed with glass beads. On his feet, Hendrick wore moccasins of tanned elk, embroidered with porcupine quills, fringed with tiny silver bells. (1926, 170)

By the time Hendrick was invited to address colonial delegates at the Albany Congress, he was well known on both sides of the Atlantic among Iroquois and Europeans alike. At the Albany Congress, Hendrick repeated the advice Canassatego had given colonial delegates at Lancaster a decade earlier, this time at a conference devoted not only to diplomacy, but also to drawing up a plan for the type of colonial union that both the Iroquois and Franklin had advocated. The same day, the colonial delegates were in the early stages of debate over the plan of union.

At the Albany Congress, Hendrick admonished the Americans to use Iroquois-style unity and to bring "as many into this covenant chain as you possibly can" (O'Callaghan, 1855, 6:869). With this admonition and his knowledge of the imagery and concepts of the Iroquois Great Law at hand, Franklin met with colonial and Iroquois delegates to create a plan of unity that combined the Iroquois and English systems. Franklin said that the debates over the Albany Plan "went on daily with the Indian business" (Bigelow, 1868, 295). During these discussions, Hendrick openly criticized the colonists and hinted that the Iroquois would not ally with the English colonies unless a suitable form of unity was established among them. Hendrick asserted on July 9, 1754, that "we wish [that] this . . . [tree] of friendship may grow up to a great height and then we shall be a powerful people" (O'Callaghan, 1855, 6:869–884).

DeLancey replied to Hendrick's speech using Iroquois metaphors: "I hope that by this present Union, we shall grow up to a great height and then we shall be as powerful and famous as you were of old" (O'Callaghan, 1855, 6:884).

Hendrick followed that admonition with an analysis of Iroquois and colonial unity, when he said, "We the United Nations shall rejoice of our strength...and...we have now made so strong a Confederacy" (Colonial Records of Pennsylvania, 1851, 98). Benjamin Franklin was commissioned to compose the final draft of the Albany Plan the same day.

Franklin's Albany Plan of Union included a Grand Council and a Speaker and called for a "general government...under which...each colony may retain its present constitution" (Labaree, 1962, 5:387–392). The plan also included an English-style chief administrator. Although representation on the Iroquois Grand Council was determined by custom, the number of delegates that each colony would have had on Franklin's council was to be determined by each colony's proportional tax revenues. In 1943, after editing Franklin's Indian treaties, Julian P. Boyd stated that Benjamin Franklin in 1754 "proposed a plan for union of the colonies and he found his materials in the great confederacy of the Iroquois." Boyd also believed that the ability of the Iroquois to unite peoples over a large geographic expanse made their form of government "worthy of copying" (Boyd, 1942, 239, 246).

THE BOSTON TEA PARTY'S "MOHAWKS"

Few events of the revolutionary era have been engraved on America's popular memory like the Boston Tea Party. Nearly everyone, regardless of sophistication in matters American and revolutionary, knows that the patriots who dumped tea in Boston Harbor dressed as American Indians—Mohawks, specifically. Regarding why the tea dumpers chose this particular form of disguise, we are historiographically less fortunate. Judging by the dearth of commentary on the matter, one might conclude that it was chosen out of sheer convenience, as if Paul Revere and a gaggle of late-eighteenth century "party animals" had stopped by a costume shop on their way to the wharf and found the Mohawk model was the only one available in quantity on short notice.

Boston's patriots were hardly so indiscriminate. The Tea Party was a form of symbolic protest—one step beyond random violence, one step short of organized, armed rebellion. The tea dumpers chose their symbols with utmost care. As the imported tea symbolized British tyranny and taxation, so the image of the Indian, and the Mohawk disguise, represented its antithesis: a "trademark" of an emerging American identity and a voice for liberty in a new land. The image of the Indian was figured into the tea dumpers' disguises not only in Boston, but also in cities the length of the Atlantic seaboard. The tea parties were not spur-of-the-moment pranks, but the culmination of a decade of colonial frustration with

British authority. Likewise, the Mohawk symbol was not picked at random. It was used as a revolutionary symbol, counterpoised to the tea tax.

The image of the Indian (particularly the Mohawk) also appears at about the same time, in the same context, in revolutionary songs, slogans, and engravings. Paul Revere, whose "midnight rides" became legendary through the poems of Henry Wadsworth Longfellow, played a crucial role in forging this sense of identity, contributing to the revolutionary cause a set of remarkable engravings that cast an American Indian woman as America's first national symbol, long before Brother Jonathan or Uncle Sam.

The colonists used the American Indian as a national symbol in their earliest protests of war taxes. In an engraving titled "The Great Financier, or British Economy for the Years 1763, 1764 and 1765," George Grenville, first Lord of the Admiralty, held a balance, while a subordinate loaded it with rubbish. Lord William Pitt, the prime minister, leaned on a crutch at one side as an Indian, representing the colonies, and groaned, on one knee, under the burden of royal taxes. In this early engraving, America was shown enduring the load, but within a dozen years, the same symbol assumed a more aggressive stance, pointing arrows on taut bows at the hearts of their oppressors, a prelude to armed insurrection by the colonists themselves.

Before the tea parties, the Sons of Liberty, of which Paul Revere was one of the earliest members, advertised its intentions in handbills. One was titled "Mohawk Tea Proclamation," purportedly the work of "Abrant Kanakartophqua, chief sachem of the Mohawks, King of the Six Nations and Lord of all Their Castles." The broadside asserted that tea is "an Indian plant . . . and of right belongs to Indians of every land and tribe." It urged "Indians" to abstain from the "ruinous Liquor Rum, which they [the British] have poured down our throats, to steal away our Brains." The "Mohawk Tea Proclamation" concluded that British tea should be "poured into the Lakes," and that any true American should be able to break addictions to European beverages in favor of pure, cold American water (Goss, 1972, 123–124).

While they emptied British tea into Boston Harbor, those posing as Mohawks sang the following:

> Rally Mohawks, and bring your axes
> And tell King George we'll pay no taxes
>   on his foreign tea;
> His threats are vain, and vain to think
> To force our girls and wives to drink
>   his vile Bohea!
> Then rally, boys, and hasten on
> To meet our chiefs at the Green Dragon!
> Our Warren's here, and bold Revere
> With hands to do and words to cheer,
>   for liberty and laws;

Our country's "braves" and firm defenders
Shall ne'er be left by true North Enders
    fighting freedom's cause!
Then rally, boys, and hasten on
To meet our chiefs at the Green Dragon
    —Goss, 1972, 123–124

Between the Boston Tea Party and his most famous midnight ride on April 18, 1775, Paul Revere created a remarkable series of engravings akin to modern political cartoons. The engravings were meant to galvanize public opinion against the British. Many of them used the Indian (usually a woman) as a symbol of independent American identity, much as the Mohawk disguise had been used in the Tea Party, which Revere also helped to plan and execute.

Revere's engravings that used an Indian woman as a patriotic symbol often were sharply political. One of them, "The Able Doctor, or America Swallowing the Bitter Draught," portrayed an Indian woman (symbolic of America being held down by British officials) forced to drink "the vile Bohea." Lord Mansfield, in a wig and judicial robe, held America down as Lord North, with the Port Act in his pocket, poured tea down her throat. Lord Sandwich occupied his time peering under "America's" skirt as Lord Bute stood by with a sword inscribed "Military Law." The bystanders (Spain and France) considered aid for the colonies. In the background, Boston's skyline is labeled "cannonaded." A petition of grievances was shredded in the foreground, symbolic of the British government's failure to provide justice for America (Grinde and Johansen, 1991, 128).

Revere was not the only artist to use Native images as symbols of liberty during the revolutionary period. About the same time that Revere contributed political engravings to the *Royal American Magazine*, another artist was using the same ideas in Philadelphia. This engraving is believed to have been the work of Henry Dawkins. Again, patriots are represented as Indians. Instead of shouldering Britain's burdens as they had a dozen years earlier, these Indians, drawn on the eve of the Declaration of Independence, aimed their arrows across the Atlantic Ocean straight at Lord North's heart. British officials lined the English shore, discussing the tea crisis and related events. On the North American side, Tories did the same, dressed in European garb, unlike the newly aggressive "Indians" (Grinde and Johansen, 1991, 132).

An anonymous engraving created at the beginning of the Revolutionary War in 1776 pitted "The Female Combatants"—an Englishwoman under an enormous beehive hairdo—against America, an Indian woman. The English woman said: "I'll force you to Obedience, you Rebellious Slut," to which America replied: "Liberty, Liberty forever, Mother, while I exist" (Grinde and Johansen, 1991, 134).

THE IROQUOIS AND THE DEBATE OVER INDEPENDENCE

After the Albany Plan failed to receive colonial approval, British attempts to raise taxes following the war with France spurred talk of colonial union again. During the Stamp Act crisis, the New York City Sons of Liberty sent wampum belts to the Iroquois asking them to intercept British troops moving down the Hudson to occupy New York City. After this appeal, the Sons of Liberty put up a "pine post...called...the Tree of Liberty" where they conducted their daily exercises (*Journals*, 1868, 14:357, 367–368).

As symbolic protest turned to armed rebellion against England, delegates of the Continental Congress met with Iroquois leaders at several points along the frontier to procure their alliance in the coming war for independence. At Cartwright's Tavern in German Flats, near Albany, New York, on August 25, 1775, treaty commissioners met with the sachems and warriors of the Six Nations. The commissioners (acting on instructions from John Hancock and the Second Continental Congress) told the sachems that they were heeding the advice Iroquois forefathers had given to the colonial Americans at Lancaster, Pennsylvania, in 1744, as they quoted Canassatego's words:

Brethren, We the Six Nations heartily recommend Union and a good agreement between you our Brethren, never disagree but preserve a strict Friendship for one another and thereby you as well as we will become stronger. Our Wise Fore-fathers established Union and Amity between the Five Nations....We are a powerful Confederacy, and if you observe the same methods...you will acquire fresh strength and power. (*Proceedings*, 1775, no page).

After quoting Canassatego, the Americans said their forefathers had rejoiced to hear his words and that they had

sunken deep into their Hearts, the Advice was good, it was Kind. They said to one another, the Six Nations are a wise people, let us hearken to their Council and teach our children to follow it. Our old Men have done so. They have frequently taken a single Arrow and said, Children, see how easy it is broken, then they have tied twelve together with strong Cords—And our strongest Men could not break them—See said they—this is what the Six Nations mean. Divided a single Man may destroy you—United, you are a match for the whole World. (*Proceedings*, 1775, no page)

The delegates of the Continental Congress then thanked the "great God that we are all united, that we have a strong Confederacy composed of twelve Provinces." The delegates also pointed out that they have "lighted a Great Council Fire at Philadelphia and have sent Sixty five Counselors to speak and act in the name of the whole." The treaty commissioners also invited the Iroquois to visit and observe our "Great Council Fire at Philadelphia" (*Proceedings*, 1775, no page).

NATIVE AMERICAN POLITICAL SYSTEMS AND THE THOUGHTS OF FRANKLIN, JEFFERSON, AND PAINE

As Americans, and as revolutionaries who believed in the universal moral sense of all peoples, Benjamin Franklin, Thomas Jefferson, and Thomas Paine bristled at suggestions that nature had dealt the New World an inferior hand. Under the guise of science, so-called degeneracy theories had gained some currency in Europe during the late eighteenth century. This particular school of pseudoscience was pressed into service as a justification for colonialism in much the same way that craniology (which linked intelligence to the volume of a race's skulls) would be a century later.

Jefferson wrote *Notes on the State of Virginia* ([1784] 1955) partially to refute assertions of France's Comte de Buffon, among others, that the very soil, water, and air of the New World caused plants and animals (including human beings) to grow less robustly and enjoy less sexual ardor than their Old World counterparts. The ongoing debate over the innate intelligence of American Indians also was factored into this debate, with France's Count de Buffon and compatriots asserting inferiority. Franklin and Jefferson took the lead in countering the degeneracy theorists, maintaining that Native peoples of America enjoyed mental abilities equal to those of Europeans. In *Notes on Virginia*, Jefferson used the eloquent speech of Logan (delivered after whites had massacred his family) as evidence that American Indians were not lacking intelligence and compassion.

While serving as ambassador to France, Jefferson was fond of describing a dinner attended by Franklin, a few other Americans, and French degeneracy theory advocates while Franklin was representing the new United States there. Franklin listened to Abbe Raynal, a well-known proponent of American degeneracy, describe how even Europeans would be stunted by exposure to the New World. Franklin listened quietly, then simply asked the French to test their theory "by the fact before us. Let both parties rise," Franklin challenged, "and we shall see on which side nature has degenerated." The table became a metaphorical Atlantic Ocean. The Americans, on their feet, towered over the French. "[The] Abbe, himself particularly, was a mere shrimp," Jefferson smirked (Boorstin, 1948, 307).

In a letter to John Adams, Jefferson pointed out that, as a child and as a student, he was in frequent contact with Native Americans:

Concerning Indians, in the early part of my life, I was very familiar, and acquired impressions of attachment and commiseration for them which have never been obliterated. Before the Revolution, they were in the habit of coming often and in great numbers to the seat of government, *where I was very much with them*. I knew much the great Ontassete, the warrior and orator of the Cherokees; he was always the guest of my father, on his journey's to and from Williamsburg. (Bergh, 1903–1904, 11:160, emphasis added)

Thomas Jefferson. (Courtesy of the Library of Congress.)

A few months before the Constitutional Convention, Jefferson wrote John Madison about the virtues of American Indian government. "Societies...as among our Indians...[may be]...best. But I believe [them]...inconsistent with any great degree of population" (Boyd, 1950, 11:92–93).

While Jefferson, Franklin, and Paine were too pragmatic to believe they could copy the "natural state," ideas based on their observations of Native societies were woven into the fabric of the American Revolution early and prominently. Jefferson wrote: "The only condition on earth to be compared with ours, in my opinion, is that of the Indian, where they have still less law than we" (Commager, 1975, 119). When Paine wrote that "government, like dress, is the badge of lost innocence" (1892, 1) and Jefferson said that the best government governs least, they were recapitulating their observations of Native American societies either directly or through the eyes of European philosophers such as Locke and Rousseau. Franklin used his image of Indians and their societies to critique European society:

The Care and Labour of providing for Artificial and fashionable Wants, the sight of so many Rich wallowing in superfluous plenty, while so many are kept poor and distress'd for want; the Insolence of Office ... [and] restraints of Custom, all contrive to disgust them [Indians] with what we call civil Society. (Labaree, 1973, 17:381)

As primary author of the Declaration of Independence and Bill of Rights, Jefferson often wove his perceptions of Native American polities into his conceptions of life, liberty, and happiness. Conversely, Jefferson described the class structure of Europe as hammers pounding anvils, horses mounting riders, and wolves gouging sheep. As a student of government, Jefferson found little ground less fertile than the Europe of his day. The political landscape of England was, to Jefferson, full of things to change, not to emulate.

Jefferson characterized the Native societies he knew in his *Notes on Virginia*. This wording was inserted into the 1787 edition, as the Constitutional Convention was meeting. Native Americans, wrote Jefferson, had never

submitted themselves to any laws, any coercive power and shadow of government. Their only controls are their manners, and the moral sense of right and wrong.... An offence against these is punished by contempt, by exclusion from society, or, where the cause is serious, as that of murder, by the individuals whom it concerns. Imperfect as this species of control may seem, crimes are very rare among them. ([1784] 1955, 93)

The lesson here seemed clear to Jefferson:

Insomuch that it were made a question, whether no law, as among the savage Americans, or too much law, as among the civilized Europeans, submits man to the greater evil, one who has seen both conditions of existence would pronounce it to be the last. (Ford, 1892, 3:195n)

Writing to Edward Carrington during 1787, Jefferson associated freedom of expression with happiness, citing American Indian societies as an example:

The basis of our government being the opinion of the people, our very first object should be to keep that right; and were it left to me to decide whether we should have a government without newspapers or newspapers without a government, I should not hesitate for a moment to prefer the latter.... I am convinced that those societies [as the Indians] which live without government enjoy in their general mass an infinitely greater degree of happiness than those who live under European governments. (Boyd, 1950, 11:49)

To Jefferson, "without government" could not have meant without social order. He, Franklin, and Paine all knew Native American societies too well to argue that their members functioned without social cohesion, in the classic

Noble Savage image, as autonomous wild men of the woods. It was clear that the Iroquois, for example, did not organize a confederacy with alliances spreading over much of northeastern North America without government. They did it, however, with a non-European conception of government, one of which Jefferson, Paine, and Franklin were appreciative students who sought to factor "natural law" and "natural rights" into their designs for the United States during the revolutionary era.

Franklin's Articles of Confederation (1775) resembled the political structure of the Iroquois and other native nations that bordered the thirteen colonies. This resemblance included the language Franklin used when he called the proposed confederacy "a firm league of friendship." The new states retained powers similar to those of the individual tribes and nations within many native confederacies; local problems were to be solved by the local unit of government best suited to their nature, size, and scope; national problems, such as diplomacy and defense, were to be handled by the national government. This notion of "federalism" was very novel to European eyes at that time.

THE TAMMANY SOCIETY'S INFLUENCE

By 1786, the Tammany Society had become a major factor in American politics in its birthplace, Philadelphia, as well as in many other cities along the eastern seaboard. In April 1786, the Tammany Society welcomed Cornplanter and five other Seneca leaders to Philadelphia. In an impressive ceremony, Tammany Society leaders escorted the Senecas from their lodgings at the Indian Queen Tavern to Tammany's wigwam on the banks of the Schuylkill River for a conference on governmental unity.

A few days after his address to the Tammany Society, Cornplanter and the Senecas traveled to New York City to address the national government. Echoing his concern for the nature of American government and unity, Cornplanter stated the following:

> Brothers of the Thirteen Fires, I am glad to see you. It gives me pleasure to see you meet in council to consult about public affairs. May the Great Spirit above direct you in such measures as are good. I wish to put the chunks together to make the Thirteen Fires burn brighter. (*Virginia Gazette*, 1786, no page)

DISCUSSION OF NATIVE GOVERNANCE IN JOHN ADAMS'S DEFENCE OF THE CONSTITUTIONS

Sensing the need for an analysis of American and world governments, John Adams wrote his *Defence of the Constitutions . . . of the United States* in 1786 and published it in 1787 on the eve of the Constitutional Convention. The *Defence* has been called "the finest fruit of the American Enlightenment" (Wood, 1969, 568). Adams saw two conflicting views on the nature of government in America on that eve. He recognized in Franklin's admonitions of a unicameral legislature (as in the Pennsylvania Constitution of 1776) a sense of serenity of character because the Pennsylvania Constitution placed a great deal of faith in one house as the best way to express the will of the people. However, Adams believed in a kind of intellectual perpetual motion in which balancing the interests of the aristocracy and the common people through a divided or "complex" government seemed the best course to avoid anarchy and tyranny.

The *Defence*, which was used extensively at the Constitutional Convention, examined the strengths and weaknesses of ancient and modern forms of government, including an analysis of American Indian traditions. Rather than having faith, as Franklin did, in the voice of the people, Adams was more pessimistic about human nature and all orders of society in his *Defence*. He believed that separation of powers in government was crucial to maintain a republic. Adams remarked that in Native American governments, the "real sovereignty resided in the body of the people." Adams also observed that personal liberty was so important to the Mohawks that in their society they have "complete individual independence" (Charles F. Adams, 1851, 4:511).

Drawing on his knowledge and experience with American Indians, Adams's *Defence* urged the founders at the Constitutional Convention to investigate "the government of . . . modern Indians" because the separation of powers in their three branches of government is marked with a precision "that excludes all controversy" (Charles F. Adams, 1851, 4:296, 4:298, 511, 566–567). Adams wrote that a Native American sachem is elected for life and lesser "sachems are his ordinary council." In this ordinary council, all "national affairs are deliberated and resolved" except declaring war when the "sachems call a national assembly round a great council fire." At this council, the sachems "communicate to the people their resolution, and sacrifice an animal." No doubt, the animal sacrifice is a reference to the White Dog Ceremony of the Iroquois. Adams further described Iroquois custom when he stated that "The people who approve the war . . . throw the hatchet into a tree" and then "join in the subsequent war songs and dances." Adams also exhibited an understanding of the voluntary nature of Iroquois warfare when he asserted that those who do disapprove of the decision to go to war "take no part in the sacrifice, but retire" (ibid., 4:511, 566–567).

Adams' *Defence* was not an unabashed endorsement of Native American models for government. Instead, Adams was refuting the arguments of Franklin, who advocated a one-house legislature resembling the Iroquois Grand Council that had been used in the Albany Plan and Articles of Confederation. Adams did not trust the consensus model that seemed to work for the Iroquois. Adams believed that without the checks and balances built into two houses, the system would succumb to special interests and dissolve into anarchy or despotism. When Adams described the Mohawks' independence, he exercised criticism; Franklin wrote about Indian governments in a much more benign way.

Adams sought to erect checks on the caprice of the unthinking heart. Thus, he cited the Iroquois Grand Council (the fifty families) as a negative example, ignoring the fact (as Franklin had written to his printing partner James Parker in 1751) that it "has subsisted for ages" (Smyth, 1905–1907, 3:42). Franklin was more of a utopian: He still sought a government based on the best in human nature, calling its citizens to rise to it. He did not fear unrestrained freedom as did Adams. During the convention, Franklin, according to James Madison's notes, argued that "We shd. not depress the virtue & public spirit of our common people.... He did not think the elected had any right in any case to narrow the privileges of the electors" (Grinde and Johansen, 1991, 204). A consensus in the United States, having tasted revolution and near-anarchy under the Articles of Confederation, seemed ready in 1787 to agree with Adams, whose advocacy of two houses prevailed over Franklin's unicameral model. Still, the example of Native liberty exerted a telling pull on the national soul, and conceptions of Native America played an important role in these debates. The fact that Adams repeatedly called on Native imagery even in opposition to its use is evidence of how widely these ideas were discussed.

FURTHER READING

Adams, Charles F. *Works of John Adams*. Boston: Little-Brown, 1851.

Adams, John. *Defence of the Constitutions ... of the United States*. Philadelphia: Hall and Sellers, 1787.

Bergh, Albert E., ed. *The Writings of Thomas Jefferson*. Vol. 11. Washington, DC: Jefferson Memorial Association, 1904.

Bigelow, John, ed. *Autobiography of Benjamin Franklin*. Philadelphia: J. B. Lippincott, 1868.

Boorstin, Daniel J. *The Lost World of Thomas Jefferson*. New York: Henry Holt, 1948.

Boyd, Julian P., ed. *The Papers of Thomas Jefferson*. Vol. 11. Princeton, NJ: Princeton University Press, 1955.

Boyd, Julian. Dr. Franklin, Friend of the Indian. In Ray Lokken Jr., ed. *Meet Dr. Franklin*. Philadelphia: Franklin Institute, 1981.

Butterfield, Lyman H., ed. *The Diary and Autobiography of John Adams*. Cambridge, MA: Harvard University Press, 1961.

Colden, Cadwallader. *The History of the Five Nations Depending on the Province of New York in America*. Ithaca, NY: Cornell University Press, [1727, 1747] 1958.

Colonial Records of Pennsylvania. Vol. 6. Harrisburg, PA: Theo. Penn & Co., 1851.

Commager, Henry Steele. *Jefferson, Nationalism and the Enlightenment*. New York: Braziller, 1975.

Crevecoeur, Hector St. Jean de. *Letters from an American Farmer*. New York: Dutton, 1926.

Crevecoeur, Hector St. John de. *Journey into Northern Pennsylvania and the State of New York* [in French]. Ann Arbor: University of Michigan Press, [1801] 1964.

Ford, Paul L., ed. *The Writings of Thomas Jefferson*. Vol. 3. New York: Putnam, 1892–1899.

Goss, Eldridge Henry. *The Life of Colonel Paul Revere*. Boston: Hall/Gregg Press, 1972.

Grinde, Donald A., Jr., and Bruce E. Johansen. *Exemplar of Liberty: Native America and the Evolution of Democracy*. Los Angeles: UCLA American Indian Studies Center, 1991.

Howard, Helen A. Hiawatha: Co-founder of an Indian United Nations. *Journal of the West* 10:3(1971):428–438.

Jacobs, Wilbur R. *Wilderness Politics and Indian Gifts*. Lincoln: University of Nebraska Press, 1966.

Jefferson, Thomas. *Notes on the State of Virginia*. Edited by Willam Peden. Chapel Hill: University of North Carolina Press, [1784] 1955.

Johansen, Bruce E. *Forgotten Founders: How the Iroquois Helped Shape Democracy*. Boston: Harvard Common Press, [1982] 1987.

Journals of Captain John Montresor, 1757–1778, 2nd set, Vol. 14. April 4, 1766, Collections of the New York Historical Society. New York: Printed for the Society, 1868–1949.

Labaree, Leonard W., ed. *The Papers of Benjamin Franklin*. Vol. 4. New Haven, CT: Yale University Press, 1961.

Mr. Penn's Plan for a Union of the Colonies in America, February 8, 1697. In E. B. O'Callaghan, ed., *Documents Relative to the Colonial History of New York*. Vol. 4. Albany: Weed, Parsons, 1853–1887.

O'Callagahan, E. B., ed. *Documentary History of the State of New York*. Vol. 1. Albany: Weed, Parsons, 1849.

O'Callaghan, E. B., ed. *Documents Relative to the Colonial History of New York*. Vols. 4, 6. Albany: Weed, Parsons, 1853–1887.

Paine, Thomas. *The Political Writings of Thomas Paine*. New York: Peter Eckler, 1892.

Proceedings of the Commissioners Appointed by the Continental Congress to Negotiate a Treaty with the Six Nations, 1775. Papers of the Continental Congress, 1774–89, National Archives (M247, Roll 144, Item No. 134). See "Treaty Council at German Flats, New York, August 15, 1775," unpaginated.

Smyth, Albert H., ed. *The Writings of Benjamin Franklin*. Vol. 3. New York: Macmillan, 1905–1907.

Van Doren, Carl, and Julian P. Boyd, eds. *Indian Treaties Printed by Benjamin Franklin 1736–1762*. Philadelphia: Historical Society of Pennsylvania, 1938.

Virginia Gazette, May 24, 1786, no page. Cited in Grinde and Johansen, 1991, 184.

Wallace, Paul A. W. *The White Roots of Peace*. Philadelphia: University of Pennsylvania Press, 1946.

William Penn to the Society of Free Traders, August 16, 1683. In Richard S. and Mary M. Dunn, eds., *The Papers of William Penn*. Vol. 2. Philadelphia: University of Pennsylvania Press, 1982.

Wood, Gordon S. *The Creation of the American Republic*. Chapel Hill: University of North Carolina, 1969.

CHAPTER 5

The Explosion Westward

THE ACCELERATING SPEED OF FRONTIER MOVEMENT

By 300 years after Columbus' first voyage, most of America north of the Rio Grande in 1792 was under claim by the new United States, Britain, France, and Spain. Most of the same area was still primarily occupied by Native American peoples. The edicts of European treaty making said that the United States extended westward to the east bank of the Mississippi River. In another decade, its European-issued title would extend, via the Louisiana Purchase, to the Rocky Mountains.

In reality, however, only the eastern seaboard was thickly settled by descendants of Europeans in 1792. The territory to the west was home to sparse settlements, a few mountain men, some traders, and a few soldiers in a few small forts. The main day-to-day U.S. diplomatic activity in 1792 was maintaining relationships with the many Native nations that still lived on lands they knew as theirs. At the same time, a thin ribbon of French trading and military activity followed the St. Lawrence River to the Great Lakes, then followed the Mississippi to New Orleans. Most of the present-day western United States south of the Oregon and Wyoming borders was claimed by a disintegrating Spanish Empire, which was no longer able to sustain its far-flung mission, military, and mining outposts.

Three centuries into America's discovery by Europe, many Native American peoples had yet to be touched significantly by European American migration. Others had adopted European animals (such as the horse), guns, and other trade goods. A majority still swore no allegiance to any European power or the United States of America. Within the space of one century, however, the frontier would leap from the East Coast to the West Coast, meanwhile also occupying the inland west and Great Plains. By 1892, very few of North America's surviving Native peoples would be able to say that they lived independently as their great-grandfathers and great-grandmothers had barely two or three generations earlier.

In one century, sped by a massive increase in immigration from Europe and technological change (most notably the arrival of transcontinental railroads) as well as the ravages of imported diseases, Native American free space in the contemporary United States (south of Alaska) shrank to nearly nothing. By the time of the massacre at Wounded Knee at the end of 1890, North Americas' Native peoples would be living mainly on reservations controlled by the U.S. government or in its rapidly growing cities. North America was about to witness the most rapid surge of humanity in the history of the human race. By the turn of the century, the non-Indian population of the U.S. portions of the Mississippi Valley had risen to 377,000. By 1830, the non-Indian population of the same area was roughly 900,000.

During the first two centuries of English-dominated settlement along the Atlantic seaboard, the settlement frontier barely reached the foothills of the Appalachian Mountains. Following the turn of the century, however, a tide of humanity spilled across the mountains into the rich bottomlands of the Mississippi, the fertile valley of the Ohio, northward, and westward. From 1830 to 1890, three human generations, the Anglo-American frontier advanced from the woods of Georgia with passage of the Removal Act, to California with the gold rush of 1849, and inland again to the prairies of South Dakota. In 1890, the U.S. census declared the frontier closed. Benjamin Franklin once conjectured that North America would not fill with the offspring of Europe for at least a thousand years, a risky prediction because he did not even exactly know the size of the continent. He missed the date the continent would fill with the progeny of Europe by roughly 900 years.

The nineteenth century is usually justly and correctly characterized as a time of exploding westward movement by European Americans. The same century, however, also provided many examples of shaping of the immigrants by Native American peoples and their culture. American feminism's founding mothers drew from the Iroquois matrilineal society as Frederick Engels's esteemed American Native peoples as examples of a possible future society without economic classes (see chapter 10). The poet Walt Whitman, writing to the Santa Fe City Council during 1883, advised:

> As to our aboriginal or Indian population . . . I know it seems to be agreed that they must gradually dwindle as time rolls on, and in a few generations more leave only a reminiscence, a blank. But I am not at all clear about that. As America . . . develops, adapts, entwines, faithfully identifies its own—are we to see it cheerfully accepting using all the contributions of foreign lands from the whole outside globe—and then rejecting the only ones distinctively its own? (Moquin, 1973, 5–6)

SACAJAWEA GUIDES LEWIS AND CLARK

The nineteenth century opened with the U.S. purchase of the Louisiana Territory from France, which quickly nearly doubled the country's size, at least on paper. A few months later, President Jefferson sent Meriwether Lewis and William Clark to survey that area and to reach the Pacific Ocean. They were led much of the way by Sacajawea (Bird Woman, Shoshoni, born ca. 1784; death dates vary widely). For nineteen months, Sacajawea guided Lewis and Clark over the Rocky Mountains toward the Pacific Coast near present-day Astoria, Oregon. Without her, the expedition probably would have halted for lack of direction. She also guaranteed friendly relations with Native peoples along the way.

Little was known of Sacajawea by whites other than Lewis and Clark until 1811, when she and her French-Canadian husband Toussaint Charbonneau traveled to St. Louis, site of Clark's office as a regional superintendent of Indian affairs. Sacajawea and her husband were visiting St. Louis to accept an offer by Clark to educate their son "Pomp," of whom Clark had become fond during the expedition. Clark's papers noted that Sacajawea died shortly after that visit, but some argue that Sacajawea returned to the Shoshonis and lived to be almost 100 years old. The source of the confusion seems to be the fact that Charbonneau (unknown to Clark) had two Shoshoni wives. An argument has been made that the wife who died was not Sacajawea, but Otter Woman, his other wife. Various historians cite accounts of Sacajawea into old age; others assert that Clark knew Sacajawea well enough not to mistake her for another woman.

ATTEMPTS AT NATIVE CONFEDERATION IN THE "OLD NORTHWEST"

As Euro-American immigration began to explode across the Appalachians into the Ohio Valley and Great Lakes shortly after 1790, Native resistance expressed itself in attempts at confederation along lines of mutual interest. Movements of this kind occupied the better part of a century, from Pontiac (during the eighteenth century), to Black Hawk during the 1830s, with the legendary Little Turtle and Tecumseh in between.

Frank Waters characterized Pontiac (Ponteach, Ottawa, ca. 1720–1769) as "a man of steel pounded between a British hammer and a French anvil" (Waters, 1993, 35). Pontiac, after whom General Motors named a long-lived automobile model, tried to erect a Native confederacy that would block Euro-American immigration into the "Old Northwest." Pontiac was a man of medium build and dark complexion who highly valued personal fidelity. If Pontiac owed a debt, he would scratch a promissory note on birch bark with his sign, the otter. The notes always were redeemed. He was an early ally of the French in 1755, at Fort Duquesne, now the site of Pittsburgh, along with an allied force of Ottawas, Ojibwas, Hurons, and Delawares. Pontiac also played a major role in the French defeat of English General Braddock in 1755 during the opening battles of what came to be known as the French and Indian War.

Pontiac was probably born along the Maumee River in northern Ohio of an Ottawa father and a Chippewa mother. He married Kantuckeegan and had two sons, Otussa and Shegenaba. Pontiac held no hereditary chieftainship among the Ottawas, but by about 1760 his oratorical skills and courage as a warrior had raised him to leadership. By 1763, Pontiac also had formed military alliances with eighteen other Native peoples from the Mississippi River to Lake Ontario.

After the British defeat of the French in 1763, Pontiac found himself faced on the southern shore of Lake Erie with an English force that included Robert Rogers's legendary Rangers, who were self-trained as forest warriors. Rogers told Pontiac that the land his people occupied was now under British ownership, having been ceded by France, and that Rogers's Rangers were taking possession of French forts. Pontiac said that although the French might have surrendered, his people had not. After four days of negotiations, Rogers agreed with Pontiac's point of view. Rogers was allowed to continue to the former French fort on the present-day site of Detroit. Power was transferred as hundreds of Indians watched. Rogers and Pontiac became friends.

Pontiac now looked forward to peaceful trade with the British, but Rogers left the area, and fur traders began swindling the Indians, getting many of them addicted to cheap liquor. Pontiac sent a belt of red wampum, signifying the taking up of arms as far eastward as the Iroquois Confederacy, then southward along the Mississippi. He appealed for alliance, telling assembled chiefs of each nation he visited that if they did not unify and resist colonization, English immigrants would flood their lands, like waves of an endless sea.

By the spring of 1763, a general uprising was being planned by the combined forces of the Ottawa, Wyandot (Huron), Delaware, Seneca, and Shawnee. According to plans, on May 9 each constituent of the alliance was to attack the closest English fort. Pontiac's plan was betrayed to the commander of the British fort at Detroit by an Ojibwa woman named Catherine, to whom the officer had made love. Pontiac laid siege to the fort at Detroit as other members of the alliance carried out their respective roles, but an appeal to the French for assistance was ignored. After a siege that lasted through the winter and into the spring of 1764, the fort received outside reinforcements, tipping the balance against Pontiac after fifteen months.

After the rebellion, European American immigrants swarmed into the Ohio Valley in increasing numbers. Pontiac now counseled peace. The younger warriors were said to have "shamed" him and possibly beat him in their frustration. With a small band of family and friends, Pontiac was forced to leave his home village and move to Illinois. On April 20, 1769, Pontiac was murdered in Cahokia. According to one account, he was stabbed by a Peoria Indian who may have been bribed with a barrel of whiskey by an English trader named Williamson.

~

The Goschochking (Ohio) Genocide, March 8, 1782

Barbara A. Mann

Goschochking (Gnadenhütten) was the site of the most brutal of the many genocides against Native American peoples in Ohio during the eighteenth and nineteenth centuries. It was conducted in 1782 by the Pennsylvania militia, 160 strong, commanded by Colonel David Williamson, who was acting under the authority of General George Washington.

The militia murdered 96 League Delaware-Mahicans in Gnadenhütten, a Moravian "praying town" within the territory of Goschochking, the Delaware capitol in Ohio. Another 30 Delaware-Mahicans taken prisoner during Williamson's hasty retreat to Fort Pitt were murdered along the way to silence everyone with any knowledge of the war crime. Despite the militia's attempt to eliminate all witnesses, some escaped: a young man who witnessed the opening fire and two adolescent boys who fled Gnadenhütten in the midst of the murders.

The Revolutionary War was fought on two fronts, along the Atlantic seacoast and on the league lands. To break the back of the league, General George Washington devised a plan to starve it out, ordering the destruction of New York's rich farmlands in 1779, following that up in 1781 (as soon as he could penetrate Ohio) by ordering his commander at Fort Pitt, Colonel Daniel Brodhead, to destroy Goschochking, a task he finally accomplished in 1782. Goschochking was actually a trio of League-Delaware towns (one for each Delaware clan). It lay along the Muskingum River, which had bottomlands that were quite fertile. For two years after the ravaging of the league's breadbaskets in New York, Goschochking had been sharing its harvests with the hungry leaguers of New York.

As part of his campaign, Brodhead was ordered to kill the league Delaware-Mahicans entirely. Learning of this plan, the league ordered the hasty removal of the Delaware-Mahicans from the Muskingum valley to the league Wyandot capitol at Upper Sandusky, in well-defended territory. Accordingly, from September 2–4, 1781, the Wyandots under Katepakomen (Simon Girty) and the Delaware under Hopocan (Captain Pipe) secretly escorted the entire Delaware-Mahican nation to safety, thwarting the planned genocide for the time being.

The removal to Upper Sandusky was accomplished over the objections of the tiny faction of Delaware-Mahicans who had converted to the Moravian sect of Christianity. They believed themselves to be safe from the Americans because they were Christians and because the Moravian missionary John Heckewelder was an important spy against the league for General Washington. The league had better information, however, and knew that the Moravian Delaware-Mahicans were meant to have been killed along with all the rest.

The winter in Upper Sandusky was hungry, although safe from attack, because the Wyandot also had been dependent on the Muskingum harvest. Unable to transport their harvest—a rich one in 1781—during their hasty withdrawal from Goschochking, the Delaware-Mahicans had buried it to prevent the American forces from looting. Thus, when Brodhead finally attacked Goschochking, he found both the people and the harvest gone. Burning the deserted towns, he returned to Fort Pitt empty-handed.

By midwinter, the league peoples had been reduced to walking skeletons, many dying during 1781 and 1782 from starvation. Dangerous though it was for league peoples to venture back to Goschochking, now easily struck by forces out of Fort Pitt, the league had no choice. The famine had reached crisis proportions, so the buried food had to be recovered. Still believing themselves safe as neutrals, the Christianized Delaware-Mahicans elected to return to the Muskingum fields as the bulk of the workers recovering the buried harvest. To reinforce the fact that they were a work crew and not a war party, the majority of those going were women and children. Accordingly, 140 Delaware-Mahicans left Upper Sandusky on March 3, 1781, heading back to Goschochking. Heckewelder promptly sent intelligence to Fort Pitt of their movements.

The Revolutionary Army's members, who also were starving (an unintended result of destroying the league fields), had every intention of resupplying themselves by finding and plundering the Muskingum harvest. In a March 8, 1782, memorandum to General William Irvine, the new commander at Fort Pitt, Washington said that he had taken care of the provisioning problem, indicating that Williamson and the Pennsylvania militia had been dispatched to Goschochking anew under his orders (Mann, 1997, 166).

Arriving at Goschochking on March 8, the militia first murdered Shebosh, a leader, an act witnessed by a youth Heckewelder called Jacob. Seeing what was afoot, Jacob instantly fled, his personal terror preventing him from warning anyone else. Next seeking out the bulk of the harvesters at Goschochking, Williamson and his men pretended that they had been piously sent to aid fellow Christians to retrieve their harvest. The militia had also brought along children to play with the Native children, to help lull the harvesters into a sense of well-being. Seeing both the piety of the militia and the presence of settler children as proof that they were indeed safe as Christians, the Delaware-Mahicans even helped Williamson locate all but one of the work crews.

Once the harvest was unearthed, however, the militia dropped its pretense, brutally taking the Delaware-Mahicans prisoner, shooting two young children. The militia then confined its prisoners in two huts at Gnadenhütten, the men and boys in one, the women and small children in the other. Williamson charged them with being a party of "Warriors" sent to attack the militia. They also charged the Delaware-Mahicans with horse theft. Both were capital crimes of which they were promptly convicted by Williamson's kangaroo court. The harvesters were sentenced to death.

The militia voted to club and scalp the Natives and then set the huts on fire to cover up the evidence of its crimes. Because of the heroics of the women, two children were hidden in a root cellar below the floorboards of the women's prison, but only one boy thereafter avoided death by smoke inhalation, escaping through a narrow vent to the outside. Unnamed by Heckewelder (because he was not a Christian convert), the boy later recalled that, as he lay on his back in the crawl space, the blood from the murdered women fell so profusely through the floorboards that he feared being drowned in it.

In the men's hut, an adolescent boy (called Thomas by the missionaries) escaped by lying among the stacked bodies, playing dead, and then stealing out inches behind the armed guards, just before the hut was set afire. These two eyewitnesses to the crimes made it back to Upper Sandusky, their stories recorded by a remorseful Heckewelder in "Captivity and Murder" (1971) and again in his *Narrative* ([1818] 1971). On the way back to Fort Pitt, the militia took thirty more league Delawares captive, murdering them all along the way. No one escaped this second massacre (P. A. W. Wallace, 1958, 197; Butterfield, 1890, 30).

When Katepakomen unmasked Heckewelder's treachery in a fraught public scene at Upper Sandusky, Weshkahattees, a young Delaware, raced to Goschochking to rescue his relatives, arriving March 8. At Welhik-Tuppeek (a field), he found a small group of harvesters not discovered by Williamson. As the militia celebrated its kill into the evening, Weshkahattees stole into Gnadenhütten, floating away a canoe from under the eyes of the armed guards, and in several trips silently ferried the survivors across the Muskingum, "west of death." With children and old folks on their backs, the party ran all the way back to Upper Sandusky, a night-long journey. On unloading the morning of March 9, they discovered that during their desperate flight, one child had died of hunger on its mother's back (Mann, 1997, 180–181).

The militia stole not only the harvest, but also 80 pack animals, furs, equipment, and the personal possessions of their victims (Marsh, 1967, 10; Mann, 1997, 222). Plundered items later sold by militiamen for personal profit at Pittsburgh also included "souvenir" shaving strops made from the skins of Delaware-Mahicans (Heckewelder [1820, 1876] 1971, 342), indicating the fate of the thirty who had been murdered on the way back to Fort Pitt.

In a deceitful report printed in the *Philadelphia Gazette*, Williamson boasted of the genocide as a great victory in battle, presenting the harvesters as warriors and their goods, as "provisions to supply their war parties" ("Notice," 1782). Aware of the truth, Heckewelder spent the rest of his life atoning for what he had done. He went on a campaign to set the record straight, later recording that he was "ashamed of being a *white man*" (italics in the original; Heckewelder, [1820, 1876] 1971, 76). Heckewelder's most faithful reader, James Fenimore Cooper, later immortalized the phrase "the last of the Mohicans," coined by settlers after the genocide. Though dramatic, it wrongly leaves the impression that all Delaware-Mahicans had perished on March 8, 1782.

After the details of the crime became clear to them, John Bull, the Euro-father of Shebosh, and the Moravians David Zeisberger and John Heckewelder raised a mighty ruckus, calling for justice. A half-hearted inquiry into the matter by Revolutionary officials allowed the Pennsylvania militia to stonewall the investigation (Mann, 1997, 227). No one was ever indicted. In fact, Williamson became a public figure and mayor of Catfish, Pennsylvania (ibid., 220). Washington was pleased enough with him to send him back into Ohio two months later under Colonel William

Little Turtle (Michikinikwa). (Courtesy of Smithsonian National Anthropological Archives.)

Crawford for an unsuccessful follow-up attack on the Delawares during May 1782.

~

LITTLE TURTLE'S WAR: A NEW ATTEMPT AT NATIVE CONFEDERATION IN THE OHIO VALLEY

A confederation comprising elements of the Shawnees, Delawares, Wyandots, Miamis, and Ottawas told the United States in 1790 that settlers were not to transgress beyond the Ohio River. Thousands of settlers were surging into the area, ignoring governmental edicts from both sides. The settlers, who were squatters in the Indians' eyes, sought military help after members of the Native confederacy began attacking their settlements. Military expeditions were sent into the Ohio country during 1790 and 1792, but the Native confederacy remained unbowed and unmoved. This resistance stiffened after allied Native American forces led by Little Turtle, whose Native name was Michikinikwa (1752–1812), during 1791 inflicted on the U.S. Army, under General Arthur St. Clair, its worst defeat of the Indian wars, measured by the number of troops killed in one battle. The victory was short-lived, however; in 1794, "Mad Anthony" Wayne's forces defeated Little Turtle and his allies at the Battle of Fallen Timbers. On August 3, 1795, by signing the Treaty of Greenville the Indians gave up most of their hunting grounds west of the Ohio River following the defeat.

Little Turtle was known as a master of battlefield strategy. Born as the son of a Miami chief and a Mohican mother, Little Turtle became a war chief of the Miamis because of his extraordinary personal abilities; under ordinary circumstances, the matriarchal nature of the culture would have prohibited a leadership role for him. In 1787, the hunting grounds of the Miamis and their allies had been guaranteed "in perpetuity" by the U.S. Congress. The act did not stop an invasion of immigrants from the east. By the early 1790s, Little Turtle had cemented an alliance that foreshadowed later efforts by Tecumseh, who assembled an alliance of several Native nations a generation later.

Little Turtle's principal allies in this effort were the Shawnee Blue Jacket (Weyapiersenwah) and the Delaware Buckongahelos. This alliance first defeated a 1,000-man force under Josiah Harmar during October 1790. Harmar dispatched an advance force of 180 men, who were drawn into a trap and annihilated. Harmar then dispatched 360 more men to "punish the Indians." They also were drawn into a similar trap, in which about a hundred of them were killed. The remainder of Harmar's force then retreated to Fort Washington, on the present-day site of Cincinnati.

Harmer's defeat stunned the Army, whose commanders knew that the Old Northwest would remain closed to immigrants as long as Little Turtle's alliance held. General Arthur St. Clair, who had served as president of the Continental Congress during the mid-1780s, gathered an army of 2,000 men during the summer of 1791, then marched into the Ohio country. About a quarter of the men deserted en route. To keep the others happy, St. Clair permitted about 200 soldiers' wives to travel with the army. Despite Harmar's defeat, they seemed to have little inkling of what lay in waiting for them.

On November 4, 1791, the Miami/Mohican Little Turtle was one of the principal chiefs among a coalition of Shawnees, Miamis, Delawares, Potawatomis, Ottawas, Chippewas, and Wyandots in the Old Northwest (Ohio country) who defeated St. Clair's army of 1,400 soldiers. Near St. Mary's Creek, a tributary of the Wabash River, about 1,200 warriors rallied by Little Turtle and aided by an element of surprise lured St. Clair's forces into the same sort of trap that had defeated Harmar's smaller force. Thirty-eight officers and 598 enlisted men died in the battle; 242 others were wounded, many of whom later died. Fifty-six wives also lost their lives, bringing the total death toll to about 950, a death toll higher than any inflicted on the United States by the British in any single battle of the American Revolution. The death toll was four times the number sustained by General George Armstrong Custer at the Little Big Horn in 1876. After the battle, St. Clair resigned his commission in disgrace.

Dealing from strength, Little Turtle's alliance refused to surrender land to the United States. In 1794, however, Mad Anthony Wayne was dispatched with a fresh army that revisited the scene of St. Clair's debacle. According to Wayne, "Five hundred skull bones lay in the space of 350 yards. From thence, five miles on, the woods were strewn with skeletons, knapsacks, and other debris" (Johansen and Grinde, 1997, 216). Little Turtle had more respect for Wayne than for Harmar or St. Clair, calling him "the chief who never sleeps" (ibid., 216). Aware that Wayne was unlikely to be defeated by his surprise tactics, Little Turtle proposed that the Indian alliance talk peace. A majority of the warriors rebuffed Little Turtle, so he relinquished his command to Blue Jacket, a Shawnee. The Native coalition under Blue Jacket's leadership was defeated by Wayne at the Battle of Fallen Timbers. Afterward, Blue Jacket signed the Treaty of Greenville (1795) and the Treaty of Fort Industry (1805), ceding millions of acres of Native land.

Little Turtle in 1802 addressed the legislatures of Ohio and Kentucky, urging members to pass laws forbidding the ingress of traders who supplied Indians with whiskey. He said that whiskey traders had "stripped the poor Indian of skins, guns, blankets, everything—while his squaw and the children dependent on him lay starving and shivering in his wigwam" (Johansen and Grinde, 1997, 217). Neither state did anything to stop the flow of whiskey, some of which was adulterated with other substances, from chili peppers to arsenic.

Little Turtle died July 14, 1812, at his lodge near the junction of the St. Joseph River and St. Mary Creek. He was buried with full military honors by Army officers who knew his genius. William Henry Harrison, who had been an aide to Wayne and who later defeated Tecumseh in the same general area, paid Little Turtle this tribute: "'A safe leader is better than a bold one.' This maxim was a great favorite of [the Roman] Caesar Augustus . . . who . . . was, I believe, inferior to the warrior Little Turtle" (Johansen and Grinde, 1997, 217).

For almost two centuries, local historians placed the site of the battle of Fallen Timbers along the Maumee River floodplain near U.S. Highway 24, near present-day Toledo, Ohio. A monument was erected at the site, even as Native Americans contended that the battle had really occurred a mile away in what is today a soybean field. In 1995, to settle the issue, G. Michael Pratt, an anthropology professor at Heidelberg College, Tiffin, Ohio, organized an archeological dig in the soybean field. He organized teams that included as many as 150 people who excavated the site, which yielded large numbers of battlefield artifacts, indicating conclusively that the Native American account of the site was correct.

TECUMSEH'S ALLIANCE

Native resistance surged again shortly after the turn of the century under the aegis of the Shawnee Tecumseh (ca. 1768–1813), which translates as Crouching Tiger. Tecumseh, a major military leader and alliance builder, sought to stop Euro-American expansion into the Ohio valley area early in the nineteenth century, after alliances led by Pontiac and Little Turtle had failed. Tecumseh assembled an alliance that posed the last major obstacle to Anglo-American expansion across the Ohio valley westward.

Tecumseh was born about 1768 near present-day Oldtown, Ohio. He fought, as a young warrior, the battle of Fallen Timbers. Tecumseh's influence grew rapidly as he came of age not only because of his acumen as a statesman and a warrior, but also because he forbade torture of prisoners. Immigrants and Tecumseh's Native American allies trusted Tecumseh implicitly.

Tecumseh was raised from birth to make war on the encroaching European Americans by his mother, Methoataske, whose husband, the Shawnee Puck-eshinwa, had been killed in cold blood by immigrants when Tecumseh was a boy. Tecumseh and his mother found him dying. As he watched his father die, Tecumseh vowed to become like "a fire spreading over the hill and valley, consuming the race of dark souls" (Johansen and Grinde, 1997, 383). A few years later, Tecumseh's hatred for the immigrants was compounded by the murder of Cornstalk, a Shawnee chief who had been his mentor.

By the turn of the century, as the number of non-Indian immigrants grew, Tecumseh began to assemble the Shawnees, Delawares, Ottawas, Ojibwas, Kickapoos, and Wyandots into a confederation with the aim of establishing a permanent Native American confederation that would act as a buffer zone between the United States to the east and English Canada to the north. One observer recalled Tecumseh as a commanding speaker. His voice was said to have "resounded over the multitude...his words like a succession of thunderbolts" (Johansen and Grinde, 1997, 384).

Rallying Native allies with an appeal for alliance about 1805, Tecumseh urged all Indians in the area to unite as brothers, as sons of one Mother Earth. He scoffed at the idea of selling the land. Why not sell the air? he asked. Sale of land, to Tecumseh, was contrary to the ways of nature. He tried to unite the southern tribes by appealing to history:

> Where today are the Pequot? Where are the Narraganset, the Mohican, the Pocanet, and other powerful tribes of our people? They have vanished before the avarice and oppression of the white man, as snow before the summer sun.... Will

Tecumseh. (Courtesy of Smithsonian National Anthropological Archives.)

we let ourselves be destroyed in our turn, without an effort worthy of our race? Shall we, without a struggle, give up our homes, our lands, bequeathed to us by the Great Spirit? The graves of our dead and everything that is dear and sacred to us? . . . I know you will say with me, never! Never! (Armstrong, 1984, 45)

Tecumseh told representatives of southern Native nations that they faced extinction:

> Our broad domains are fast escaping from our grasp. Every year our white intruders become more greedy, exacting, oppressive, and overbearing. . . . Before the palefaces came among us, we enjoyed the happiness of unbounded freedom, and were acquainted with neither riches, wants, nor oppression. How is it now? Wants and oppression are our lot. . . . Dare we move without asking, by your leave. Are we not being stripped, day by day, of the little that remains of our ancient liberty? Do they not even kick and strike us as they do their black-faces? How long will it be before they will tie us to a post and whip us, and make us work for them. . . . Shall we wait for that moment or shall we die fighting before submitting to such ignominy? (Johansen and Grinde, 1997, 384)

Territorial Governor (and Army general) William Henry Harrison (who later popularized his battle with Tecumseh at Tippecanoe in his successful campaign for the presidency with the campaign slogan "Tippecanoe and Tyler Too") tried to undermine the growing strength of Tecumseh's Native alliance by negotiating treaties with individual Native nations. Because only a portion of each tribe or nation's warriors elected to follow Tecumseh, Harrison found it easy enough to find "treaty Indians" among those who did not elect to fight. By 1811, Harrison had negotiated at least fifteen treaties, all of which Tecumseh repudiated.

Harrison's wariness of Tecumseh's power sprung from a deep respect for him:

> The implicit obedience and respect which the followers of Tecumseh pay to him is really astonishing and more than any other circumstance bespeaks him [as] one of those uncommon geniuses, which spring up occasionally to produce revolutions and to overturn the established order of things. . . . If it were not for the vicinity of the United States, he would, perhaps, be the founder of an Empire that would rival in glory Mexico or Peru. No difficulties deter him. (Hamilton, 1972, 159)

Tecumseh was particularly galled by Harrison's choice as his territorial capital the village of Chillicothe, the same site (with the same name) as the Shawnees' former principal settlement. The name itself is anglicized Shawnee for principal town. At one treaty council, Tecumseh found himself seated next to Harrison on a bench. Tecumseh slowly but aggressively pushed Harrison off the edge of the bench, then told him that this was what the immigrants were doing to his people. They were being slowly squeezed off their lands. During his last conference with Tecumseh, Harrison bid the chief to take a chair. "Your father requests you take a chair," an interpreter told Tecumseh, to which he replied, defiantly: "My father! The sun is my father and the Earth

William Henry Harrison. (Courtesy of the Nebraska State
Historical Society.)

is my mother. I will repose upon her bosom" (Gill, 1987, 14). Tecumseh then
sat, cross-legged, on the ground.

Tecumseh also was angry over Harrison's treaty of September 30, 1809,
with the Delawares, Potawatomies, Miamis, Kickapoos, Wea, and Eel River
peoples. For $8,200 in cash and $2,350 in annuities, Harrison had laid claim
for the United States to roughly 3 million acres of rich hunting land along the
Wabash River in the heart of the area in which Tecumseh wished to build his
Native confederacy. When Tecumseh and his brother, also a Shawnee war
chief, complained to Harrison that the treaty terms were unfair, Harrison at

first rebuked Tecumseh by saying that the Shawnees had not even been part of the treaty. The implicit refusal to recognize Tecumseh's alliance angered the Indians even more. Realizing that Tecumseh's influence made it politic, Harrison agreed to meet with him. At an August 12, 1810, meeting, each side drew up several hundred battle-ready warriors and soldiers. Harrison agreed to relay Tecumseh's complaints to the president, and Tecumseh said that his warriors would join the Americans against the British if Harrison would annul the treaty.

Nothing came of Harrison's promises, and during 1811, bands of warriors allied with Tecumseh began ranging out of the settlement of Tippecanoe to terrorize nearby farmsteads and small backwoods settlements. Harrison said he would wipe out Tippecanoe if the raids did not stop; Tecumseh said they would stop when the land signed away under the 1810 treaty was returned. Tecumseh then journeyed southward to bring the Creeks, Chickasaws, and Choctaws into his alliance. Tecumseh carried the message that he had used to recruit other allies:

> Brothers—When the white men first set foot on our grounds, they were hungry. They had no place on which to spread their blankets, or to kindle their fires. They were feeble; they could do nothing for themselves. Our fathers commiserated with their distress, and shared freely with them whatever the Great Spirit had given his red children. They gave them food when hungry, medicine when sick, spread skins for them to sleep on, and gave them ground so that they might hunt and raise corn. Brothers—the white people are like poisonous serpents: when chilled, they are feeble, and harmless, but invigorate them with warmth, and they sting their benefactors to death. (Johansen and Grinde, 1997, 385–386)

Tecumseh failed, for the most part, to acquire new allies. While Tecumseh was traveling, the command of the existing alliance fell to Tecumseh's brother Tenskwatawa, who was called the Prophet. On September 26, 1811, Harrison decamped at Vincennes with more than 900 men, two-thirds of them Indian allies. He built a fort and named it after himself on the present-day site of Terre Haute, Indiana. Harrison then sent two Miamis to the Prophet to demand the return of property Harrison alleged had been stolen in the raids, along with the surrender of Indians he accused of murder. The Miamis did not return to Harrison's camp. The governor's army marched to within sight of Tippecanoe and met with Tenskwatawa, who invited them to make camp, relax, and negotiate. Harrison's forces did stop, but set up in battle configurations as the Prophet's warriors readied an attack.

Within two hours of pitched battle, Harrison's forces routed the Indians, then burned the village of Tippecanoe as Tenskwatawa's forces scattered into the woods. Returning to the devastation from his travels, Tecumseh fled to British Canada, where, during the War of 1812, he was put in command of a force of whites and Indians as a British brigadier general. Harrison's forces met Tecumseh at the Battle of the Thames in Kentucky. Tecumseh was killed during that battle on October 5, 1813. After it, some of the Kentucky militia who had taken part found a body they thought was Tecumseh's and cut strips from it for souvenirs. His warriors, who had dispersed in panic when Tecumseh died, said later that they had taken his body with them. Having committed 20,000 men and $5 million to the cause, the United States had effectively terminated armed Indian resistance in the Ohio Valley and surrounding areas.

BLACK HAWK'S ALLIANCE

A member of the Thunder Clan of the Sauk Nation, Black Hawk (Makataimeshekiakiak, Sauk, ca. 1770–1838) won renown as a warrior from the time he carried home his first scalp at the age of 15 to his leadership of a Native rebellion that bears his name in the early 1830s.

Black Hawk was capable of murderous hatred as well as the most intense personal compassion. In one battle with the Osages, he personally killed nine people, but on another raid, against the Cherokees, he found only four people, three men and a woman. He took the woman captive and then freed the three men, figuring it was dishonorable to kill so few. During the siege of an American fort during the War of 1812, when he was allied with the British, Black Hawk found two white boys hiding in a bush. "I thought of my own children," he said later, "and passed on without noticing them" (Johansen and Grinde, 1997, 38). During the same war, Black Hawk learned that some of his Indian allies, who were aiding the British, were torturing white American prisoners. He halted the practice and poured his scorn on Colonel Henry Procter, the British commander, for permitting it. "Go and put on petticoats," Black Hawk stormed. "I conquer to save, and you to murder!" (ibid., 38).

About 1820, the Fox and Sauk divided over whether to resist European American expansion into their country in what is now southern Illinois. Keokuk and a number of his supporters decided to accommodate the expansion as they moved into Iowa. Black Hawk and his supporters remained at their principal village, Saukenuk, at the confluence of the Rock and Mississippi Rivers, the site of present-day Rock Island. The land provided abundant crops, and the river was a rich source of fish. Black Hawk consulted with the spiritual leaders White Cloud and Neapope, who advised him to seek allies in defense of the land.

In the meantime, George Davenport, Indian agent in the area, had purchased the site on which Saukenuk was built, including Black Hawk's own lodge and his people's graveyard. Anglo-American immigrants began to take land around the village. Illinois Governor John Reynolds ordered the state militia to march on Saukenuk. Black Hawk and his band moved west across the Mississippi but pledged to return.

Black Hawk recalled the following:

> Upon our return to Saukenuk from our winter hunting grounds last spring, we found the palefaces in our lodges, and that they had torn down our fences and were plowing our corn lands and getting ready to plant their corn upon the lands which the Sauks have . . . cultivated for so many winters that our memory cannot go back to them. . . . They are now running their plows through our graveyards, turning up the bones and ashes of our sacred dead, whose spirits are calling on us from the land of dreams for vengeance on the despoilers. (Johansen and Grinde, 1997, 39)

In 1832, Black Hawk's band recrossed the Mississippi and sought Winnebago support. Contrary to the promises of Neapope and White Cloud, only a few Winnebagos joined. Black Hawk, his warriors, and their homeless families then attacked frontier settlements in the area. In response, Governor Reynolds called out the militia again, assembling freshly recruited companies in the area. One of the new recruits was Abraham Lincoln, a young man at the time. Lincoln's unit was later disbanded after its members took a vote over whether to fight Black Hawk. The vote was a tie. Lincoln later reenlisted but saw no fighting.

Regular Army troops were brought in to pursue Black Hawk's band, whose members had been forced to subsist on roots in the swamplands near the Mississippi. Several Army and militia units caught Black Hawk and his people, their backs to the river, where the Indians hoisted a flag of truce. General Winfield Scott and other officers ignored the appeal for a truce and engaged in a one-sided slaughter that became known as the Battle of Black Ax. General Scott later apologized for the large number of women and children killed by his men. He complained that they could not be distinguished from warriors in the heat of battle.

Black Hawk, Neapope, and other survivors of the battle fled north to a Winnebago village, where they were betrayed for a bribe of twenty horses and $100. Black Hawk was defiant in surrender:

> You know the cause of our making war. It is known to all white men. The white men despise the Indians, and drive them from their homes. They smile in the face of the poor Indian, to cheat him; they shake him by the hand, to gain his confidence; they make him drunk, to deceive him. [Black Hawk continued, saying that he had] Done nothing for which an Indian ought to be ashamed. He has fought for his countrymen . . . against white men who came, year after year, to cheat them and take away their lands. You know the cause of our making war. It is known to all white men. They ought to be ashamed of it. (Rosenstiel, 1983, 118)

After his arrest, Black Hawk was led away in chains by Jefferson Davis, who later would become president of the Confederate States of America. After several months in prison, Black Hawk was taken on a tour of several eastern cities. As part of this tour, he met with President Andrew Jackson at the White

House. Jackson gave Black Hawk a military uniform and a sword, but the aging chief was not mollified. He told Jackson that he had made war to avenge injustice against his people. Behind Black Hawk's back, Jackson recognized Keokuk as principal chief of the Sauks and Foxes. The news came to Black Hawk and Keokuk as they stood together with Army officers. Angry and frustrated, Black Hawk removed a breechclout from his loins and slapped Keokuk across the face with it.

Black Hawk's body was still lean and firm at the age of 60, his "hawk-like face with its long nose, luminous dark eyes, and firm mouth. . . . All the hair above his high forehead had been shaved off except for a scalp lock, and by this one knew he was a warrior" (Waters, 1993, 69). Eventually, Black Hawk settled on land governed by Keokuk, near Iowaville on the Des Moines River. Shortly before his death in 1838, Black Hawk acknowledged his defeat without lingering bitterness, telling a Fourth of July gathering near Fort Madison the following:

> A few winters ago, I was fighting against you. I did wrong, perhaps, but that is past; it is buried; let it be forgotten. Rock River is a beautiful country. I liked my towns, my cornfields, and the home of my people. I fought for it. It is now yours. Keep it as we did; it will produce you good crops. (Johansen and Grinde, 1997, 40)

GENERAL JACKSON SUBDUES WILLIAM WEATHERFORD AND THE CREEKS

While Tecumseh was losing the Battle of Tippecanoe in absentia, he was building his alliance of Indian nations in the South among the Creeks and other Native nations. His eloquence inspired one man among the Creeks, William Weatherford (who was only one-eighth Indian). Weatherford raised a 1,000-man army whose members expressed the Creeks' frustration at the continuing usurpation of their land by Anglo-American immigrants by attacking roughly 500 whites, mixed bloods, and black slaves. This group had taken refuge at the fortified home of Samuel Mims, a Creek of mixed blood, along the Alabama River near the Florida border. On August 30, 1813, at noon, Weatherford's men sprang from the tall grass around the Mims stockade, rising like waves of heat on an exceptionally hot and humid day. Using arrows against the defenders' guns, the Creeks rampaged into the stockade, killing more than 400 people by sundown. When the Creek warriors began to withdraw after an initial assault on Mims's fortified house, Weatherford spurred them on by setting buildings on fire with flame-tipped arrows. Many of the victims were hacked to death.

The brutality of Weatherford's massacre brought calls for extermination of the Creeks from swelling numbers of Anglo-American immigrants across the South. The U.S. Army officer assigned to march against them was Andrew Jackson, whose name would scorch the memories of Native peoples in the South for years to come. First, Jackson made his name as an Indian fighter, and then, after he was elected president of the United States, as the premier architect of the "removal" of Native peoples to Indian Territory (now Oklahoma). Every bit as brash as Weatherford (who announced that he would kill any Indians who did not cooperate with him), Jackson blazed a trail of fire and blood through the South, refusing to retreat even when his superiors ordered him to relent. In a battlefield confrontation with Weatherford's Creeks, Jackson imprisoned assistants who advised retreat.

During December 1813, Weatherford narrowly escaped capture by Jackson's troops. On March 27, 1814, Jackson, leading 2,000 men, attacked Weatherford's force of 900, which was holed up in a stronghold at Horseshoe Bend in an area isolated by rivers on three sides and a high log rampart on the fourth. Jackson sent men to seize a fleet of canoes that Weatherford had been keeping for escape. Jackson sent his men into the Creek encampment by announcing that any officer or soldier who fled the enemy without being compelled to do so by superior force would be put to death.

The Creeks under Weatherford fought bitterly, but their clubs and tomahawks could not match the Army's bayonets. One of the first soldiers to invade the Creek camp was Ensign Sam Houston, who later would become a hero among Anglo-Americans in Texas. As Jackson's troops swarmed over the Creek camp, many of the Native people ran for their lives. Those who leaped into the river were picked off by Army sharpshooters. Jackson had restrained his initial attack while women and children were ferried across the river to a place that was supposed to spare them the worst of the battle. Several of them died anyway as the frenzy of battle spilled across the landscape. When the battle was over, Jackson's forces had sustained 49 killed and 157 wounded; Cherokees who had fought at his side sustained 18 killed and 36 wounded. Of the Creeks' 900-man force, about 750 were killed. Weatherford himself was not among the dead. Not expecting Jackson to attack so quickly, he had been elsewhere that day. A few days after the battle, Weatherford surrendered to Jackson personally, at the general's tent. By that time, word of Jackson's victory had spread eastward. The general was beginning to build the popular reputation that later would elect him president of the United States.

During July 1814, General Jackson returned to Horseshoe Bend for what was officially being called a treaty conference with the defeated Creeks. The location was symbolic; Jackson relished rubbing in defeat on his enemies. The general, who never made a point of studying the cultures of the Indians he subjugated, probably did not know he was compounding the Creeks' humiliation by holding the "treaty" on ground they regarded as sacred. This meeting contained none of the diplomatic equity that characterized eighteenth century frontier diplomacy. The Creeks were summoned to this parley on pain of death by Jackson, who demanded 23 million acres—60 percent of the area that would later become Alabama as well as nearly a quarter of Georgia. This was half the land previously under Creek control. When the Creek chiefs asked for time to seek concessions and to think the matter over,

Andrew Jackson. (Courtesy of the Nebraska State Historical Society.)

Jackson demanded an answer and hinted strongly that a negative reaction would be construed as a hostile act inviting retaliation by the U.S. Army. As he refused all concessions, Jackson watched the Creeks starve as they picked at grains of corn that the soldiers had fed their horses.

STALEMATE WITH THE SEMINOLES

Having subdued the Creeks, General Jackson next received orders to quell a disturbance that the War Department politely called "troubles" in Georgia, principally among the Seminoles. During 1818, Jackson's troops chased them into Florida, which was still under Spanish jurisdiction (the area was ceded to the United States in 1821). Having seized several Spanish forts along the way, Jackson then withdrew and endured a debate over his extranational expedition in Congress. Jackson also reaped popular acclaim from expansion-minded Americans, in the meantime building his reputation for a future presidential campaign.

The Seminoles, many of whom were descended from Creeks, had elected to ally themselves with the Spanish rather than the United States, an act of virtual treason in General Jackson's eyes. In addition, the Seminoles were giving shelter to escaped slaves. The pretext of Jackson's raid thus was recovery of stolen human property. After Florida was purchased from Spain by the United States, slave-hunting vigilantes invaded the area en masse, killing Seminoles as well as blacks.

Later, during the 1830s, when President Jackson proposed to remove the Seminoles to Indian Territory, they refused. Moving deep into the swamps of southern Florida (an area that ironically was being used as a removal destination for other Native peoples), the Seminoles fought U.S. Army troops to a bloody stalemate during seven years of warfare. They were never defeated and never moved from their new homeland.

Osceola (ca. 1803–1838), whose name was derived from *asi-yahola*, meaning Black Drink Crier, was the best-known leader of the Seminoles during their pursuit by the U.S. Army. He was born on the Talapoosa River near the border of Alabama and Georgia. His mother was Polly Copinger, a Creek woman, and she married William Powell, a white man. As a result of his mother's marriage to Powell, Osceola was sometimes called Bill Powell, but he considered Powell his stepfather and asserted that he was a full-blood. During his boyhood, Osceola moved with his mother to Florida and took up residence along the Apalachicola River about 1814. As a young man, he is believed to be a veteran of the First Seminole War of 1817–1918. Some reports during the war asserted that he was captured along the Enconfino River by troops under General Andrew Jackson in 1818 and then released because of his age.

In 1823, Seminole leaders agreed to the Treaty of Mounltrie Creek, which ceded land and created reservations for the Seminoles. Later, as a result of

U.S. removal policies, the Treaty of Payne's Landing of 1832 required all Seminoles to leave Florida for Indian Territory within three years. According to the treaty, Seminoles with African American blood were to be sold into slavery. In 1833, seven Seminole chiefs, including Charley Emathla and Foke Luste Hajo, endorsed the Treaty of Fort Gibson, which created a homeland in Oklahoma near the Creeks. However, most Seminoles did not comply with the requirements of the treaty. At this time, Osceola became a noted leader because he urged Seminoles to remain in Florida.

At Fort King during April 1835, Wiley Thompson, an Indian agent, dictated a new treaty with the Seminoles requiring their removal to Oklahoma. Several chiefs declined to endorse the treaty or to deal with white officials. Seminole oral history maintains that Osceola angrily slashed the treaty with his knife. Subsequently, Osceola was seized and jailed. Although Osceola continued to protest, in the end he agreed to the terms of the treaty. But after his release, he slipped into the marshes, and many Seminole people followed him into the swamps.

During preparations for removal, Osceola's forces ambushed Emathla. Osceola allegedly threw money that the whites had given Emathla onto his dead body. Osceola then attacked and killed Wiley Thompson on December 28, 1835. On the same day, Alligator, Micanopy, and Jumper led about 300 men in an attack on Major Francis Langthorne Dade's detachment of 108 soldiers. All except 3 soldiers were killed. On New Year's Eve 1835, Osceola's men won a battle against General Duncan Lamont Clinch's force of 800 men on the Withlacoochee River. There were 4 infantrymen killed, and only 3 Indians died. Osceola was injured but eluded capture.

While waging a guerilla war for two years, Osceola devastated the countryside. So that they could fight alongside the men, some Seminole women killed their own children. The war degenerated into a deadly search-and-destroy mission in the Everglades.

Finally, Micanopy and other rebel chiefs stopped fighting in the spring of 1837. Osceola forced Micanopy to flee with him into the swamps; however, Micanopy stopped fighting again later in the year.

Attempts to remove the Seminoles by force cost the lives of 1,500 U.S. soldiers. During October 1837, General Thomas S. Jesup summoned the Seminole chief Osceola to parlay under a flag of truce at Fort Augustine. Jesup surrounded the conference site with troops and took Osceola prisoner. Betraying the flag of truce, Jesup bound Osceola and incarcerated him at Fort Moultrie outside Charleston, South Carolina.

Once they were captured, many of the Seminoles eventually moved west to Indian Territory, but a few bands remained in the Everglades. The removal of the Seminoles was one of the most expensive Indian campaigns that the U.S. Army ever has waged. In addition to the 1,500 soldiers killed (1 for every 2 Seminoles eventually removed to Indian Territory), the government spent an average of $6,500 for each Native person transferred to Indian territory. At a time when the average job paid less than $1,000 a year, this amount represented a small fortune.

Varying accounts exist of Osceola's demise: Poisoning, malaria, or abuse in prison may have been the causes, but the whites were excoriated for their treachery and his tragic death. On January 30, 1838, Osceola died at Fort Moultrie in full battle regalia. Even in death, Osceola did not escape white exploitation. Dr. Frederick Weedon, the military surgeon, kept his head in a medical museum until it was destroyed by a fire in 1866. In spite of the death of their renowned leader, many Seminoles continued to resist removal to Oklahoma for many years, using the Florida swamps as a base for their operations.

THE ROAD TO THE TRAILS OF TEARS

With nearly a million U.S. citizens in the Mississippi valley by 1828, the area was acquiring political leverage, which expressed itself in widespread support for Andrew Jackson's election to the presidency. Eli Whitney's invention of the cotton gin in 1793 had opened the technological door to a whole new age of agriculture in the lands that the Cherokee, Choctaw, Chickasaw, Creek, and Seminole (the Five Civilized Tribes), among others, occupied. Lands that had been occupied by Native peoples in 1800 were planted in cotton, harvested by African slaves two generations later. As a politician, luck smiled on President Jackson, who arrived just in time to ride a wave of economic development across the South built on the economy of slavery, which demanded removal of the Native peoples. At times, Native Americans were exported as slaves; one author estimated that 30,000 to 50,000 Indians were shipped out of Charleston, South Carolina, in this fashion, and smaller numbers were sold through Boston and Salem, Massachusetts, as well as New Orleans (Gallay, 2003, 3-B).

Before 1800, Euro-American immigration in the South had been limited mainly to the pine barrens of coastal Georgia, on land that was practically useless for farming before the advent of modern commercial fertilizers. The immigrants, seeing the value of the developing cotton culture, cast a covetous eye on the fertile inland valleys that were occupied by the Five Civilized Tribes, who had utilized them for hundreds of years. As waves of land speculators and other immigrants moved in to evict them, the Creeks, Cherokees, Choctaws, Chickasaws, and others were doing exactly what the Jeffersonians thought they should: building farms and towns in the European manner. The civilized tribes were well on their way to becoming some of the most prosperous farmers in the South.

Whether in purposeful contravention of the treaties or because he thought he had the right to annul them personally, Jackson within a decade cooperated with the land-industry business to move tens of thousands of Native peoples from their homelands. Jackson, who as a general told his troops to root out Indians from their "dens" and kill Indian women and their "whelps," struck only a slightly more erudite tone as president in his second annual message to Congress. He reflected on the fact that some European Americans were growing "melancholy" over the fact that the Indians were being driven to their "tomb." These critics must understand, Jackson said, that "true philanthropy reconciles the mind to these vicissitudes as it does to the extinction of one generation to make way for another" (Stannard, 1992, 240).

Jackson's policy—to move the Indians out of territory that could be used by immigrating Anglo-Americans—became the national standard during his eight years as president. Alabama already had been created in 1819 from Creek and Cherokee territory; Mississippi was created in 1817 from Choctaw and Chickasaw country. These two states, along with Georgia, passed laws outlawing indigenous governments, subjecting their peoples to state jurisdiction, after which open season was declared on remaining Native lands. All of this violated treaties negotiated earlier. President Jackson told the Indians that he was unable to stand by the treaties, very likely because of the pressures caused by states' rights, an emerging issue in the decades before the Civil War. Instead, Jackson proposed that the Indians be moved westward. At first, the moving of whole tribes was proposed as a voluntary act. In the meantime, land speculators and squatters closed a deadly vise of lands that had been home to the newly civilized tribes for thousands of years.

In 1829, small amounts of gold were discovered on Cherokee land in the mountains of northern Georgia. The state legislature quickly passed a law forbidding the Cherokee to prospect or mine gold on their own land as more than 3,000 invaders surged onto Cherokee territory, wrecking the farmsteads and villages that they had so carefully built. When the Cherokee Nation indicted whites for destruction of Native life and property, Georgia courts, having asserted their jurisdiction over Cherokee lands and lives, dismissed all Cherokee testimony as incompetent.

Because Native peoples no longer enjoyed federal protection from predatory state interests promised in treaties, Indian lands were thrown open to anyone, including dealers in alcohol, who had a heyday exchanging land and anything else they could get their hands on for strong whiskey and rum. Actions could be brought against Indians in state courts, so their lands and other belongings often were taken for debt. State laws were enacted barring courts from accepting an Indian's testimony against white men in court. Thus, no legal claim by a white man, no matter how baseless, could be contested by any Native person.

By about 1830, white squatters were swarming onto the lands of the civilized tribes. Many Native people were dispossessed by force even before the removals began. They had the choice of two untenable options: move, usually to Indian Territory (later Oklahoma) or be pushed off their lands anyway. When a well-known Chickasaw leader, Emubby, was killed by a European American named Jones, the incident made the papers only because Emubby had served several campaigns with General Jackson. Before their removal westward, the Creeks were driven into the forests and swamps by non-Indian squatters. Their homes were taken, and many starved.

A newspaper of the time described their destitution:

> To see a whole people destitute of food—the incessant cry of the emaciated creatures being bread! bread! is beyond description distressing. The existence of many of the Indians is prolonged by eating roots and the bark of trees.... [N]othing that can afford nourishment is rejected, however offensive it may be.... They beg their food from door to door.... It is really painful to see the wretched creatures wandering about the streets, haggard and naked." (Brandon, 1964, 227)

Removals began with 4,000 Choctaws in 1831, bound for western Arkansas. The winter was harsh, but during the next few years it often was even worse. The cruelty of the removals was compounded by governmental mismanagement and by Indian agents, who kept for themselves much of the money that the government had appropriated to feed native people while they were being moved. In the summer of 1831, cholera spread through areas of the South, returning each summer until 1836. Only the Chickasaws managed to transport much of what they owned westward (agents complained about the bulk of their livestock and baggage). The rest of the people suffered cruelly, complaining that they had been driven off their own lands like wild wolves, with their women and children's shoeless feet bleeding from the long marches over rough terrain. Indian agents infamous for their penny pinching sometimes hired rotten boats to transport Indians across rivers. Many of the boats sank, with the loss of uncounted lives. Dead Indians did not cost anything to feed.

Alexis de Tocqueville, author of *Democracy in America*, witnessed portions of the early removals and wrote:

> At the end of the year 1831, whilst I was on the left bank of the Mississippi, at a place named by the Europeans Memphis, there arrived a numerous band of Choctaws. These savages had left their country, and were endeavoring to gain the right bank of the Mississippi, where they hoped to find an asylum that had been promised them by the American government. It was in the middle of the winter, and the cold was unusually severe; the snow had frozen hard upon the ground, and the river was drifting huge masses of ice. The Indians had their families with them; and they brought in their train the wounded and the sick, with children newly born, and old men upon the verge of death. They possessed neither tents nor wagons, but only their arms and some provisions. I saw them embark to pass the mighty river, and never will that solemn spectacle fade from my remembrance. No cry, no sob was heard amongst the assembled crowd; all were silent.... The Indians had all stepped into the bark which was to carry them across, but their dogs remained upon the bank. As soon as these animals perceived that their masters were finally leaving the shore, they set up a dismal howl and, plunging all together into the icy waters of the Mississippi, swam after the boat. (Tocqueville, 1898, 435–436, 448)

THE ORIGINS OF REMOVAL LEGISLATION

Provisions for "removal"—the relocation of entire Native nations from areas about to be annexed by non-Indians—were first laid down in a 1817 treaty between the United States and the Cherokee Nation (7 Stat. 156). By 1830, the federal government had passed general removal legislation aimed at the Five Civilized Tribes because of the intensive efforts they had made in adopting ways of life and political institutions resembling those of European Americans. Many other Native American nations (such as the Osage and Poncas) also were removed to Indian Territory during the nineteenth century. By 1883, twenty-five Indian reservations occupied by a total of thirty-seven nations had been established in Indian Country.

As president, Andrew Jackson thought that Indian treaties were anachronisms. "An absurdity," he called them, "Not to be reconciled with the principles of our government" (Johansen, 2000, 88). As Jackson elaborated, before his election to the presidency, in a letter to President James Monroe (another advocate of Indian removal) in 1817:

> The Indians are the subjects of the United States, inhabiting its territory and acknowledging its sovereignty. Then is it not absurd for the sovereign to negotiate by treaty with the subject? I have always thought, that Congress had as much right to regulate by acts of legislation, all Indian concerns as they had of territories, are citizens of the United States and entitled to all the rights thereof, the Indians are subjects and entitled to their protection and fostering care. (McNickle, 1949, 193)

The confusions of convoluted grammar aside, it is not easy to decipher what General Jackson is saying. Is he declaring the Indians to be citizens? Legally, that was not the case until a century later. Is he personally annulling the treaties, which had been signed by parties who regarded each other as diplomatic peers barely two generations earlier? Whatever the nature of his rhetoric, the ensuing decades made clear, especially for the Native peoples of the South, just what Jackson meant by "protection and fostering care."

The private rationale for removal was expressed by Henry Clay (like Jackson, a political product of the trans-Appalachian west). Clay's recitation, preserved in the *Memoirs* of John Quincy Adams, came at the end of a meeting of Adams's cabinet on December 22, 1825, during which the entire agenda was taken up by the conflict between the Creeks and Georgia. Clay was responding to a suggestion that the United States stop making treaties with the Indians and treat them as citizens. According to Adams, Clay said the following:

> It is impossible to civilize Indians.... There never was a full-blooded Indian who took to civilization. It was not in their nature. He said they are destined to extinction and, although he would never use or countenance inhumanity towards

them, he did not think them, as a race, worth preserving. He considered them as essentially inferior to the Anglo-Saxon race, which were now taking their place on this continent. They were not an improvable breed, and their disappearance from the human family will be no great harm to the world. (Drinnon, 1990, 179–180)

Clay's point of view was popular among Anglo-Americans in need of a rationale for relieving Native Americans of their land. The fact that the civilized tribes had become, in some respects, as Europeanized as the immigrants seemed not to matter. Removal was less an ideological statement than a convenient method to transfer land from one group of people to another. During the 1820s, before their forceful removal from their homelands, the Cherokees developed prosperous villages and a system of government modeled after that of the United States. The Cherokees owned 22,0000 cattle, 2,000 spinning wheels, 700 looms, 31 grist mills, 10 saw mills, 8 cotton gins, and 1,300 slaves. The Cherokees also had a written constitution that emulated that of the United States; a written language, developed by Sequoyah; and a bilingual newspaper, the *Cherokee Phoenix.*

Passage of the Removal Act of 1830 climaxed a years-long struggle. The Creeks, for example, had become concerned about non-Indian usurpation of their lands as early as 1818, when the Muscogee (Creek) Nation passed a law against the sale of any Native American land without council approval and under penalty of death for the transgressing party. The edict was enforced. In 1825, federal treaty commissioners bribed William McIntosh, leader of the Creek Lower Towns, to sign a land-cession agreement, the Treaty of Indian Springs, with a few of his close associates. The National Council declared McIntosh to be a traitor and on May 1, 1825, sent a delegation to torch his house. When McIntosh appeared at the door of his burning home, his body was riddled with bullets.

Removals for specific Native nations usually were negotiated by treaties (frequently under duress) in which specific nations surrendered what remained to them of their aboriginal homelands in exchange for lands west of the Mississippi River. Although some small bands (and a few members of larger nations) had been moving westward since the War of 1812, the Removal Act forced the wholesale removal of entire Native nations, notably the Five Civilized Tribes on the several trails of tears.

As the federal government prepared to remove entire nations of Native people west of the Mississippi River, little thought was given to the fact that Indians, European Americans, and Afro-Americans had been intermarrying among Native peoples for nearly a century. Many of the families forced to abandon their homes were nearly as European American genetically as their nonreservation neighbors. John Ross, the Cherokee best known as an opponent of removal, was only one-eighth Cherokee, for example. He lived in a plantation house and owned slaves.

Sequoyah. (Courtesy of the Library of Congress.)

These complications meant little to President Andrew Jackson, who had earned his national reputation as a general in the U.S. Army, which had the primary business of subjugating Indians. When he ran for president, Jackson sought frontier votes by favoring removal. Once in office, Jackson considered the Removal Act of 1830 to be the fulfillment of a campaign promise. Others felt less sanguine; even with extensive lobbying from the White House, the House of Representatives passed the Removal Act by only six votes (103 to 97). Representative William Ellsworth of Connecticut opposed the Removal Act in a passionate speech delivered on the House floor, when he said, in part:

> We must be just and faithful to our treaties. There is no occasion for collision. We shall not stand justified before the world in taking any step which shall lead to oppression. The eyes of the world, as well as of this nation, are upon us. I conjure this House not to stain the page of our history with national shame, cruelty, and perfidy. (Johansen, 1998, 275)

John Ross. (Courtesy of the Nebraska State Historical Society.)

John Ross (1790–1866; called Coowescoowe, meaning the Egret, among the Cherokee) was more than an opponent of the Removal Act. He also was the founder of a constitutional government among the Cherokees. Ross was the third of nine children. His father was Daniel Ross, a Scot, and his mother, Mary (Molly) McDonald, was a Scot-Cherokee. As a youth, he was called Tsan-usdi or Little John. Ross was educated at home by white tutors and then sent to Kingston Academy in Tennessee. In 1813, he married Quatie, Elizabeth Brown Henley, a full-blooded Cherokee. They had five children.

By 1811, at age 21, Ross was a member of the Standing Committee of the Cherokee Council. During 1813 and 1814, he served as an adjutant in a Cherokee regiment under the command of General Andrew Jackson and saw action with other Cherokees at Horseshoe Bend in 1813 against the Red Sticks commanded by William Weatherford. Ross led a contingent of Cherokee warriors in a diversionary tactic and thus was an important factor in Jackson's success in that battle.

In 1814, Ross established a ferry service and trading post at Ross's Landing. In 1817, he became a member of the Cherokee National Council and served as its president from 1819 to 1826. In 1820, a republican form of government was instituted by the Cherokee, similar in structure to the United States. As an advocate of education and mission work, Ross proposed that the Cherokee Nation become a state in the union with its own constitution.

When New Echota became the Cherokee national capital in 1826, Ross moved there with his family. In 1827, he became president of the Cherokee constitutional convention. From 1828 to 1839, Ross served as principal chief of the Cherokee Nation under the new constitution he had helped to draft.

Although Ross continued to resist removal policies as principal chief of the Cherokees, a dispirited minority of Cherokee leaders called the Treaty Party, including Major Ridge, John Ridge, Elias Boudinot, and Stand Watie, in 1835 consented to removal by signing the Treaty of New Echota. Ross and a majority of Cherokees sought to have the treaty reversed and sent a letter to Congress in 1836 asking for an investigation into its legality.

SEQUOYAH: THE ONLY PERSON TO SINGLY INVENT A WRITTEN LANGUAGE

One spectacular example of the Cherokee penchant for European-style civilization was Sequoyah (1776–1843), who invented the Cherokee alphabet in 1821 after twelve years of work. Sequoyah, a warrior who had been crippled in a hunting accident, became known in the history of letters as the only person in human history to single-handedly invent an entire written language.

Sequoyah was born in Taskigi near Fort Loudon, Tennessee, of a Cherokee mother named Wurtee and (some say) the Revolutionary War soldier and trader Nathaniel Gist. Sequoyah's name was anglicized from *sikwaji* or *sogwili*, meaning sparrow or principal bird in Cherokee; he also was known variously as George Gist, George Guess, and George Guest. As a boy of 12 living with his mother near Willstown, Alabama, Sequoyah learned to tend dairy cattle and make cheese. He also broke horses, planted corn, and gained skills in hunting and trading furs.

With a quick mind and an active imagination, Sequoyah was intrigued by the "talking leaves," the written language of the immigrants. Perhaps out of frustration with his disability and its effects on his hunting, Sequoyah developed a drinking habit as a young man. Realizing what alcohol was doing to him, he turned away from the habit and sought a new way of life. As a result, Sequoyah became an excellent silversmith. In 1815, he married Sarah (Sally), a Cherokee woman. They subsequently had several children.

By 1809, Sequoyah had started to work on a written version of the Cherokee language using pictorial symbols, but he abandoned this method as untenable after he had created more than 1,000 symbols. Next, Sequoyah reduced the Cherokee language initially to 200, then finally to 86 characters that represented all the syllables or sounds in the language. He derived the resulting syllabary in part from English, Greek, and Hebrew characters in mission school books. Some Cherokee were mystified by Sequoyah's work and accused him of witchcraft. At one point, his home was burned down and his notes lost.

Undaunted by allegations of witchcraft, Sequoyah in 1821 completed his writing system. The same year, before an assembly of Cherokee leaders, he proved the viability of his system by writing messages to his six-year-old daughter that she understood and answered independently. The Cherokee tribal council formally adopted Sequoyah's syllabary soon after this demonstration. Within a few months, several thousand Cherokees had learned Sequoyah's writing system. By 1824, white missionaries had translated parts of the Bible into Cherokee. In 1828, the Cherokee Tribal Council started a weekly newspaper called the *Cherokee Phoenix and Indian Advocate*, which was bilingual in English and Cherokee. The newspaper was published until it was suppressed in 1835 by the state of Georgia for advocating Cherokee rights to their lands in Georgia.

In 1829, Sequoyah moved with his wife and children to Indian Territory in what would become Sequoya County, Oklahoma. He also helped to unite uneasy eastern and western Cherokee factions in 1839. In 1841, the Cherokee National Council granted him a pension; Sequoyah became the first member of any Indian tribe to be rewarded in this manner.

In 1842, Sequoyah launched an expedition to find a group of Cherokees who had gone west during the American Revolution. The trip through Texas took a toll on Sequoyah's failing health. Suffering from dysentery, he died in August 1843 near San Fernando, Tamaulipas, Mexico, and he was buried there along with his treasured papers in an as-yet-undiscovered grave. Later, Oklahoma memorialized Sequoyah by placing his statue in the U.S. capitol's Statuary Hall. His homestead also was designated as an Oklahoma State historical site. As a testimony to his remarkable genius, Stephen Endilicher, the Hungarian botanist, named a species of giant California coastal redwood trees after him.

CHIEF JUSTICE JOHN MARSHALL'S CHEROKEE RULINGS

The assertion of states' rights vis-à-vis Native American territorial sovereignty provided the legal grist for a 1832 Supreme Court decision written by Chief Justice John Marshall (1755–1835); it has defined the relationship of Native American and states' rights for more than a century and a half.

Marshall's opinions outlining Native Americans' status in the U.S. legal system occurred as he defined the Supreme Court's place within U.S. politics.

When Marshall became chief justice during 1801, the Supreme Court was little more than a clause in the Constitution. For 35 years as chief justice, Marshall played a major role in defining the Court as an institution. According to author Jean Edward Smith (1996), if George Washington founded the United States, John Marshall legally defined it.

Chief Justice Marshall had long-running political differences with President Jackson, and he agonized over the conflicts between states' rights and Native sovereignty. In 1831, in *Cherokee Nation v. United States* [5 Peters 1 (1831)], Marshall held that the Cherokees had no standing at court to appeal the state of Georgia's seizure of their lands. This situation troubled Marshall so deeply that he said at one point that he thought of resigning from the Supreme Court because of it. A year later, in *Worcester v. Georgia* [31 U.S. (6 Pet.) 515 (1832)], Marshall held unconstitutional the imprisonment by Georgia of a missionary (Samuel Worcester) who had worked with the Cherokees. The specific issue was the refusal of Worcester, while resident on Cherokee land, to swear loyalty to the state of Georgia in conformance with a state law.

The case began when three white missionaries living on Cherokee territory refused to swear an oath of allegiance to the state of Georgia. They were arrested, chained to a wagon, and forced to walk more than 20 miles to jail. Two Methodist preachers who objected to the cruelty that accompanied the arrests also were chained and taken to jail. The three missionaries were tried, convicted, and sentenced to four years of hard labor at the Georgia state penitentiary. Two of them later swore allegiance and were released; one (Worcester) did not. When the case reached the Supreme Court (as *Worcester v. Georgia*), Justice Marshall wrote that Native nations had a degree of sovereignty that denied Georgia the right to compel an oath of loyalty.

Historians disagree over whether President Jackson actually said, "John Marshall has made his decision, now let him enforce it." Whether Jackson expressed himself in those words may be moot; his implementation of removal flew in the face of the law as interpreted by Marshall in *Worcester v. Georgia*. Marshall wrote that the Cherokees had

> always been considered as distinct, independent political communities, retaining their original natural rights . . . and the settled doctrine of the law of nations, that a weaker power does not surrender its independence—its right to self-government—by associating with a stronger, and taking its protection. . . . The Cherokee nation, then, is a distinct community, occupying its own territory, with boundaries accurately described, in which the laws of Georgia can have no force, and which the citizens of Georgia have no right to enter, but with the assent of the Cherokees, or in conformity with treaties, and with the acts of Congress. (*Worcester v. Georgia*, 1832)

Marshall reasoned in *Worcester v. Georgia* that the Constitution, by declaring treaties to be the supreme law of the land, had adopted and sanctified

On the Trail of Tears. (Courtesy of John Kahionhes Fadden.)

previous treaties with the Indian nations. The words *treaty* and *nation* are "words of our own language," wrote Marshall, "selected in our diplomatic and legislative proceedings, by ourselves, having each a definite and well-understood meaning. We have applied them to Indians, as we have applied them to the other nations of the earth; they are applied to all in the same sense" (*Worcester v. Georgia*, 1832). Marshall defined Indian nations not as totally sovereign or as colonies but as "domestic dependent nations."

Marshall's opinion was ignored by Jackson, an action that comprised contempt of the Supreme Court, an impeachable offense under the U.S. Constitution. The Congress, fearing that a confrontation over states' rights could provoke civil war, took no action against Jackson. After almost six years of delays, the Trail of Tears was initiated in 1838.

Although Marshall's opinion was ignored by President Jackson, it has shaped the relationship of the United States to Native American nations within its borders to the present day. The 1934 Indian Reorganization Act and legislative efforts promoting self-determination after the 1960s were based on Marshall's opinion that the rights of discovery did not extinguish the original inhabitants' claims to possession and use of their lands.

Although Ross continued to protest removal for several more years, the state of Georgia coerced Cherokees to sell lands for a fraction of their value. Marauding immigrants plundered Cherokee homes and possessions as they destroyed the *Cherokee Phoenix*'s printing press because it had opposed removal. The U.S. Army forced Cherokee families into internment camps to prepare for the arduous trek westward. As a result of unhealthy and crowded conditions in these hastily constructed stockades, many Cherokees died even before their Trail of Tears began. Although failing in his efforts to stop removal, Ross managed to gain additional federal funds for his people.

Before they were exiled from their homelands by force of arms, the Cherokee released a "memorial" expressing their feelings:

> The title of the Cherokee people to their lands is the most ancient, pure, and absolute known to man; its date is beyond the reach of human record; its validity confirmed by possession and enjoyment antecedent to all pretense of claim by any portion of the human race.
>
> The free consent of the Cherokee people is indispensable to a valid transfer of the Cherokee title. The Cherokee people have neither by themselves nor their representatives given such consent. It follows that the original title and ownership of lands still rests with the Cherokee Nation, unimpaired and absolute. The Cherokee people have existed as a distinct national community for a period extending into antiquity beyond the dates and records and memory of man. These attributes have never been relinquished by the Cherokee people, and cannot be dissolved by the expulsion of the Nation from its territory by the power of the United States Government. (O'Brien, 1989, 57)

In preparation for the Cherokees' removal, John Ross was evicted from his mansion and was living in a dirt-floored cabin. When John Howard Payne, author of the song "Home Sweet Home," came to visit him at the cabin, just across the Georgia State line in Tennessee, the Georgia State Guard crossed the state line and kidnapped both men. Realizing that the federal government did not intend to protect the Cherokees, Ross and others reluctantly signed the Treaty of New Echota in 1835 and prepared, with heavy hearts, to leave their homes.

The Cherokees displacement involved the most human suffering, and their phrase for the long, brutal march (*nuna-daa-ut-sun'y*, the trail where they cried) gave the march its enduring name. At least one-fourth of the Cherokees who were removed died along the way. According to one scholar who studied Cherokee mortality on the Trail of Tears, the conventional estimate of 4,000 dead is too low. The losses among the Cherokee alone may have reached 8,000 people. In 1838 and 1839, the U.S. Army removed the Cherokees by force, except for a few hundred who escaped to the mountains.

The many trails of tears during the 1830s and early 1840s resulted in immense suffering among the estimated 50,000 to 100,000 Native people who were forced to move. Between one-third and one-fourth of those who were removed died on the marches or shortly thereafter of exposure, disease, and starvation. Ross' wife, Quatie, was among the victims of this forced emigration.

Many Cherokees died after they arrived in Indian Territory as epidemics and food shortages plagued the new settlements.

James Mooney described how the Cherokees were forced from their homes:

> Squads of troops were sent to search out with rifle and bayonet every small cabin hidden away in the coves or by the sides of mountain streams.... Families at dinner were startled by the sudden gleam of bayonets in the doorway and rose up to be driven with blows and oaths along the trail that led to the stockade. Men were seized in their fields or going along the road, women were taken from their wheels, and children from their play. (Van Every, 1966, 242)

A U.S. Army private who witnessed the Cherokee removal wrote as follows:

> I saw the helpless Cherokee arrested and dragged from their homes, and driven by bayonet into the stockades. And in the chill of a drizzling rain on an October morning I saw them loaded like cattle or sheep into wagons and started toward the west.... Chief Ross led in prayer, and when the bugle sounded and wagons started rolling many of the children...waved their little hands goodbye to their mountain homes. (Worcester, 1975, 67)

Despite the cruelty of the marches they were forced to undertake and the death and disease that dogged their every step, the surviving members of the peoples who were removed to Indian Territory quickly set about rebuilding their communities. Much as they had in the southeast, the Creeks, Cherokees, and others built prosperous farms and towns, passed laws, and set about organizing themselves once again. Within three generations, however, this land that in the 1830s had been set aside as Indian Territory was being sought by non-Indians for its oil and because the frontier had closed everywhere else. At the turn of the century, as a rush for "black gold" inundated Oklahoma, the Allotment Act (1887) was breaking up the Native estate much as Georgia's state laws had done a little more than a half century earlier. There would be no trail of tears this time, however; there was no empty land left to occupy.

FURTHER READING

Armstrong, Virginia Irving. *I Have Spoken: American History Through the Voices of the Indians*. Athens, OH: Swallow Press, 1984.

Baker, Leonard. *John Marshall: A Life in Law*. New York: Macmillan, 1974.

Beckhard, Arthur J. *Black Hawk*. New York: Julian Messner, 1957.

Brandon, William. *The American Heritage Book of Indians*. New York: Dell, 1964.

Bryant, Martha F. *Sacajawea: A Native American Heroine*. New York: Council for Indian Education, 1989.

Butterfield, Consul Wilshire. *History of the Girtys, Being a Concise Account of the Girty Brothers—Thomas, Simon, James and George, and of Their Half-Brother, John Turner— Also of the Part Taken by Them in Lord Dunmore's War, in the Western Border War of the Revolution, and in the Indian War of 1790-1795.* Cincinnati: Robert Clark, 1890.

Carter, Harvey Lewis. *The Life and Times of Little Turtle: First Sagamore of the Wabash.* Urbana: University of Illinois Press, 1987.

Cherokee Nation v. Georgia 5 Peters 1 (1831).

Cole, Donald B. *Presidency of Andrew Jackson.* Lawrence: University Press of Kansas, 1993.

Collier, John. *Indians of the Americas.* New York: New American Library, 1947.

Deardorff, Merle H. *The Religion of Handsome Lake: Its Origins and Development.* American Bureau of Ethnology Bulletin No. 149. Washington, DC: BAE, 1951.

Deloria, Vine, ed. *American Indian Policy in the Twentieth Century.* Norman: University of Oklahoma Press, 1985.

Drinnon, Richard. *Facing West: Indian Hating and Empire Building.* New York: Schoken Books, 1990.

Eckert, Allan W. *A Sorrow in Our Heart: The Life of Tecumseh.* New York: Bantam, 1992.

Edmonds, Della, and Margot Edmonds. *Sacajawea of the Lewis and Clark Expedition.* Berkeley: University of California Press, 1979.

Eggleston, Edward, and Lillie Eggleston-Seelye. *Tecumseh and the Shawnee Prophet.* New York: Dodd, Mead & Co., 1878.

Edmunds, R. David. *The Shawnee Prophet.* Lincoln: University of Nebraska Press, 1983.

Edmunds, R. David. *Tecumseh and the Quest for Indian Leadership.* Boston: Little-Brown, 1984.

Frazier, Neta L. *Sacajawea: The Girl Nobody Knows.* New York: McKay, 1967.

Gallay, Alan. Indian Slave Trade Thrived in Early America. *Daytona Beach News-Journal,* August 3, 2003, 3-B.

Gill, Sam. *Mother Earth: An American Story.* Chicago: University of Chicago Press, 1987.

Griffith, Benjamin W., Jr. *McIntosh and Weatherford: Creek Indian Leaders.* Tuscaloosa: University of Alabama Press, 1988.

Hagan, William T. *The Sac and Fox Indians.* Norman: University of Oklahoma Press, 1958.

Hamilton, Charles, ed. *Cry of the Thunderbird.* Norman: University of Oklahoma Press, 1972.

Harold, Howard. *Sacajawea.* Norman: University of Oklahoma Press, 1971.

Hays, Wilma P. *Pontiac: Lion in the Forest.* Boston: Houghton-Mifflin, 1965.

Heckewelder, John. *History, Manners, and Customs of the Indian Nations Who Once Inhabited Pennsylvania and the Neighboring States.* The First American Frontier Series. New York: Arno Press and *The New York Times,* [1820] 1971.

Heckewelder, John. *Narrative of the Mission of the United Brethren among the Delaware and Mohegan Indians from Its Commencement, in the Year 1740, to the Close of the Year 1808.* New York: Arno Press, [1818] 1971.

Hobson, Charles F. *The Great Chief Justice: John Marshall and the Rule of Law.* Lawrence: University Press of Kansas, 1996.

Howells, William D. Gnadenhütten. In *Three Villages.* Boston: James R. Osgood and Company, 1884.

Jackson, Donald, ed. *Black Hawk: An Autobiography.* Urbana: University of Illinois Press, 1964.

Johansen, Bruce E., ed. *Encyclopedia of Native American Legal Tradition.* Westport, CT: Greenwood Press, 1998.

Johansen, Bruce E. *Shapers of the Great Debate on Native Americans: Land, Spirit, and Power.* Westport, CT: Greenwood Press, 2000.

Johansen, Bruce E., and Donald A. Grinde, Jr. *The Encyclopedia of Native American Biography.* New York: Holt, 1997.

Johnson v. MacIntosh 8 Wheaton 543 (1823).

Jones, Louis Thomas. *Aboriginal American Oratory.* Los Angeles: Southwest Museum, 1965.

Josephy, Alvin, Jr. *The Patriot Chiefs.* New York: Viking, 1961.

Mann, Barbara A. "The Last of the Mohicans" and "'The Indian-haters.'" Forbidden Ground: Racial Politics and Hidden Identity in James Fenimore Cooper's Leather-Stocking Tales. Ph.D. dissertation, University of Toledo, 1997: 168–182, 219–229.

Marsh, Thelma R. *Lest We Forget: A Brief Sketch of Wyandot County's History.* Upper Sandusky, OH: Wyandot County Historical Society, 1967.

McNickle, D'Arcy. *They Came Here First: The Epic of the American Indian.* Philadelphia: Lippincott, 1949.

McNickle, D'Arcy. *Native American Tribalism.* New York: Oxford University Press, 1973.

Moquin, Wayne. *Great Documents in American Indian History.* New York: Praeger, 1973.

Moulton, Gary. *John Ross: Cherokee Chief.* Athens: University of Georgia Press, 1978.

Moulton, Gary, ed. *The Journals of the Lewis and Clark Expedition.* 11 vols. Lincoln: University of Nebraska Press, 2001.

Nabokov, Peter. *Native Testimony.* New York: Viking, 1991.

Nebard, Grace R. *Sacajawea.* Glendale, CA: Arthur H. Clark, 1932.

Notice. Philadelphia Gazette, 2705, April 1782, 2.

O'Brien, Sharon. *American Indian Tribal Governments.* Norman: University of Oklahoma Press, 1989.

Oskinson, John M. *Tecumseh and His Times.* New York: J. P. Putnam, 1938.

Parker, Arthur. *The Code of Handsome Lake, the Seneca Prophet.* New York State Museum Bulletin No. 163. Albany, 1913.

Parker, Arthur. *Parker on the Iroquois.* Edited by William Fenton. Syracuse, NY: Syracuse University Press, 1968.

Parkman, Francis. *History of the Conspiracy of Pontiac.* Boston: Little, Brown, 1868.

Peckham, Howard H. *Pontiac and the Indian Uprising.* Chicago: University of Chicago Press, 1947.

Porter, C. Fayne. *Our Indian Heritage: Profiles of Twelve Great Leaders.* Philadelphia: Chilton, 1964.

Rogers, Robert. *A Concise Account of North America.* London: J. Millan, 1765.

Rogin, Michael Paul. *Fathers and Children: Andrew Jackson and the Subjugation of the American Indian.* New York: Knopf, 1975.

Rosenstiel, Annette. *Red and White: Indian Views of the White Man, 1492–1982.* New York: Universe Books, 1983.

Satz, Ronald N. *American Indian Policy in the Jacksonian Era.* Lincoln: University of Nebraska Press, 1975.

Seymour, Flora W. *Sacajawea: American Pathfinder.* New York: Macmillan, 1991.

Smith, Jean Edward. *John Marshall: Definer of a Nation.* New York: Holt, 1996.

Stannard, David. *American Holocaust: Columbus and the Conquest of the New World.* New York: Oxford University Press, 1992.

Tebbel, John, and Keith Jennison. *The American Indian Wars.* New York: Bonanza Books, 1960.

Thwaites, Reuben Gold. *The Original Journals of Lewis and Clark.* New York: Dodd, Mead & Co., 1904–1905.

Tocqueville, Alexis de. *Democracy in America.* Translated by Henry Reeve. New York: Century, 1898.

Tucker, Glenn. *Tecumseh: Vision of Glory.* Indianapolis: Bobbs-Merrill, 1956.

Vanderworth, W. C. *Indian Oratory.* Norman: University of Oklahoma Press, 1971.

Van Every, Dale. *Disinherited: The Lost Birthright of the American Indian.* New York: Morrow, 1966.

Wallace, Anthony F. C. *The Death and Rebirth of the Seneca.* New York: Knopf, 1970.

Wallace, Paul A. W., ed. Captivity and Murder. In *Thirty Thousand Miles with John Heckewelder.* Pittsburgh: University of Pittsburgh Press, 1958: 170–207.

Washburn, Wilcomb E., ed. *The American Indian and the United States: A Documentary History.* New York: Random House, 1973.

Waters, Frank. *Brave Are My People: Indian Heroes Not Forgotten.* Santa Fe: Clear Light, 1993.

Wheaton, Henry. *Elements of International Law.* Boston: Dana, 1866.

Wilkinson, Charles F. *American Indians, Time, and the Law: Native Societies in a Modern Constitutional Democracy.* New Haven, CT: Yale University Press, 1987.

Worcester, Donald, ed. *Forked Tongues and Broken Treaties.* Caldwell, ID: Caxton, 1975.

Worcester v. Georgia 31 U.S. (6 Pet.) 515 (1832).

Wright, Ronald. *Stolen Continents: The Americas through Indian Eyes Since 1492.* Boston: Houghton-Mifflin, 1992.

Young, Calvin. M. *Little Turtle.* Fort Wayne, IN: Public Library of Fort Wayne and Allen County, 1956.

Cumulative Index